BRITAIN'S NATIONAL PARKS

BRITAIN'S NATIONAL PARKS

· A VISITOR'S GUIDE ·

ROLAND SMITH

PHOTOGRAPHY BY MIKE WILLIAMS

DOLPHIN
PUBLICATIONS

*A National Park compromise: Hope Valley Cement
Works from Pin Dale, Peak District*

Title Spread: Picard's Tower, Tretower Castle, Brecon
Beacons

Contents

PREFACE 7

INTRODUCTION 9

DARTMOOR NATIONAL PARK 15

EXMOOR NATIONAL PARK 35

BRECON BEACONS NATIONAL PARK 55

PEMBROKESHIRE COAST NATIONAL PARK 75

SNOWDONIA NATIONAL PARK 95

PEAK DISTRICT NATIONAL PARK 115

YORKSHIRE DALES NATIONAL PARK 135

LAKE DISTRICT NATIONAL PARK 155

NORTH YORK MOORS NATIONAL PARK 179

NORTHUMBERLAND NATIONAL PARK 199

CONCLUSION 215

GENERAL READING LIST 221

USEFUL ADDRESSES 221

INDEX 222

Preface

A day out in the country, usually involving a short walk, is by far the most popular of Britain's outdoor recreations. According to Government statistics, more than 20 per cent of the population regularly go for country walks of at least two miles, and this pastime, already more popular than football, golf or darts, is enjoying something of a boom.

Increased leisure time – enforced or otherwise, through redundancy, early retirement or the shorter working week – has given us more opportunity than ever before to enjoy the magnificent heritage of our countryside. And our ten National Parks constitute the cream of this marvellous and increasingly valuable resource. All are situated in the upland parts of England or Wales, there are none in Scotland.

This book sets out, in words and pictures, to give the reader a taste of what our National Parks have to offer the visitor. It can only be a taste, because the variety of scenic, historic and wildlife interest in Britain's National Parks is unrivalled anywhere in the world.

Each chapter deals with a particular National Park and looks at its natural landscape (the first reason for its existence), its natural history, Man's influence on the area through prehistory to the present day, and its modern centres of population and tourism.

The concluding *What to do* section explains how to get to the Park and where to stay, and describes the attractions of each Park, with hints on where to obtain more information.

Ultimately your enjoyment of the National Parks will depend on your personal level of involvement. A celebrated survey in Dartmoor a few years ago discovered that the majority of visitors never ventured more than half a mile from their car.

These visitors may have thought they had seen the National Park, but they had only scratched the surface. You must be prepared to get your boots dirty if you really want to know Wildest Britain.

Finally, I must pay tribute to the forbearance of my long-suffering wife, Val, who has been bringing up our three children during the course of this book's preparation; to Mike Williams whose magnificent photographs say so much more than my words about our wild country, and to Irene Miller for an immaculately typed manuscript.

Roland Smith

Lyke Wake Walk, Urra Moor, North York Moors.

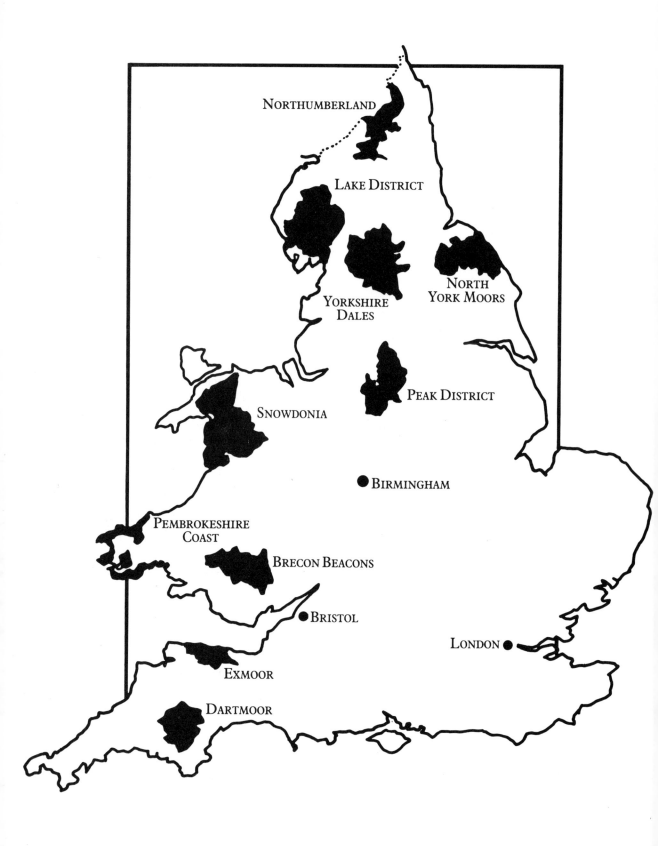

NORTHUMBERLAND

LAKE DISTRICT

YORKSHIRE
DALES

NORTH
YORK MOORS

PEAK DISTRICT

SNOWDONIA

● BIRMINGHAM

PEMBROKESHIRE
COAST

BRECON BEACONS

● BRISTOL

LONDON ●

EXMOOR

DARTMOOR

Introduction

In a small and crowded island such as ours, it may seem strange to talk about Britain's wild country.

Yet nearly ten per cent of England and Wales carries just that official designation, and forms the basis of our ten National Parks.

These range from the granite fastnesses of Dartmoor in Devon, to the boggy plateaux of Northumberland on the Scottish border.

In between are the gentle, heather-clad combes of Exmoor, the dramatic escarpments of the Brecon Beacons, and the towering cliffs of the Pembrokeshire Coast.

The rugged grandeur of Snowdonia's mountains foretell the sterner landscapes of the north and west. The Pennines start with the Peak District, an enchanting country of sharp contrasts which shares a subtle mix of limestone and gritstone with the Yorkshire Dales further north.

The biggest, and probably the best-known National Park is the Lake District; while that of the North York Moors on the east coast is an ever-popular playground for the industrial cities of Teeside.

However, none of Britain's National Parks are the uninhabited wildernesses that other, larger countries can afford. They are all living and working landscapes for the people who make their homes there. This is a fact often forgotten by the millions who flock to them every weekend.

To these teeming visitors, our National Parks offer an escape from the restrictions and monotonies of everyday life. Four out of five Britons live in towns or cities and, as leisure increases, the beautiful, unspoilt landscapes of our National Parks become increasingly precious and important. For they provide a breathing space in the hectic hustle of our urban life – a chance to relax, and appreciate the astonishing richness and variety of our scenic heritage.

Unfortunately there are still many misconceptions about our National Parks, so it might be useful to start by explaining what they are not.

Although called 'national parks', none in fact are nationalised – most of the land is still in private hands, just like anywhere else in Britain.

They are not living museums either. All are farmed, mostly by those traditional methods that to a large extent have shaped the individual landscapes we have come to admire.

They are not run by the National Trust, an independent charity with similar aims, which does, however, own large areas of some Parks, particularly in the Lake District and Peak District.

Although all our National Parks are important reservoirs of natural beauty, they are not merely vast nature reserves. The Nature Conservancy Council, however, has several large nature reserves in them, where botanists and birdwatchers can observe species brought to the edge of extinction elsewhere.

There is no more a right of access to open countryside in the Parks than there is to anywhere else in the countryside. Rights of way must be followed, especially through farmland, except in certain signposted areas of open moorland where the park authorities have negotiated special access-agreements with landowners.

So, our National Parks are not 'national' and nor are they 'parks' in the urban or playground sense. For example, you won't find swings and roundabouts on the brooding peat hags of Bleaklow, although the moorland plateau is less than 20 miles/32 km from the city centres of Manchester or Sheffield on either side of the Pennines.

National Parks were not specially set aside by Parliament for *that* sort of pursuit. After all, that can be obtained at the nearest town or country park.

Our National Parks are special places, offering the opportunity of a quieter, more serene communion with nature, and showing us the face of Britain before Man laid his destructive hand upon it.

The world's first National Park was set up in 1872 at Yellowstone in the USA, by far-sighted, gun-toting pioneers of the Old West. An extensive area of Montana and Wyoming was 'dedicated and set apart as a public park or pleasuring ground for the benefit of the people.'

The first recorded suggestion that Britain's unique scenic beauty should receive some sort of national protection had been made 60 years before this by the great Lakeland poet, William Wordsworth, in his *Guide through the District of the Lakes*.

No stranger to the wild beauty of the high fells round his Grasmere home, he foresaw the great leisure explosion which would follow the coming of the railways. He wrote 'persons of pure taste throughout the whole island' would 'deem the district a sort of national property, in which every man has an interest who has an eye to perceive and a heart to enjoy.'

But Wordsworth was also the first of the upper middle-class preservationists, who were later to be instrumental in founding the National Park movement. Wordsworth, in fact, believed the landscape would be destroyed if 'artisans, labourers and the humbler class of shopkeepers' were able to invade his precious fells.

A century and a half was to pass before Wordsworth's dream became a reality and the Lake District became Britain's second National Park.

In the years between, a protracted and sometimes bitter battle was fought to obtain the right of public access to open countryside, which had, for centuries before, been the common privilege of all.

The basis for this long-overdue legislation was the John Dower report of 1945, in which this enlightened Yorkshire architect and planner made what is still regarded as the definitive description of a British-style National Park:

A National Park may be defined, in application to Great Britain, as an extensive area of beautiful and relatively wild country in which, for the nation's benefit and by appropriate national decision and action:
a) the characteristic landscape beauty is strictly preserved
b) access and facilities for public open-air enjoyment are amply provided
c) wildlife and buildings and places of architectural and historic interest are suitably protected, while
d) established farming use is effectively maintained.

The 1949 National Parks and Access to the Countryside Act proposed 12 National Parks. But two, the South Downs of Sussex and the Norfolk Broads, were later rejected.

It was fitting that the first National Park to be designated in April, 1951, was the Peak District, scene of so many of the access battles in the 1930s when ramblers were actually sent to prison for exercising their 'right to roam'. The Lake District National Park – not quite the 'national property' Wordsworth had envisaged – came a month later, and the rest followed in regular succession until the

Peat bog, Kinder Scout, Peak District.

last – the Brecon Beacons – was set up in April 1957.

A further Welsh National Park, the Cambrian Mountains, covering the wild and empty hills of mid-Wales, was proposed in 1965 by the Countryside Commission, which had succeeded the National Parks Commission. But local opposition from farmers and landowners was so vociferous that the proposal was finally turned down by the Government in 1973.

The local interest has become an important consideration for National Park authorities, a fact recognised by the increased representation of district councillors on National Park authorities under the provisions of the Wildlife and Countryside Act.

Only two National Parks are run by independent, autonomous planning boards as recommended by the Dower and Hobhouse reports. It is perhaps significant that those two, the Peak District and the Lake District, are recognised as the most dynamic and efficient of the ten.

The others are run by special committees of the county councils in whose areas they lie, with a representation of two-thirds local councillors and one-third members appointed by the Secretary of State, theoretically to look after the national interest. About 75 per cent of the parks' income comes from Government grants, the rest from local rates.

All our National Parks are situated in upland Britain, to the south west, west and north of the country. This fact illustrates how much of our natural lowland landscape has been changed by ever-more intensive agriculture in the blind, headlong pursuit of productivity.

This has been one of the major criticisms of the British National Park system. The most threatened of our landscapes, those of intensively-farmed lowland Britain, remain unprotected from the large-scale changes wrought by modern agriculture and the continuing sprawl of urban development.

Hardline conservationists have suggested that, even taking into account the depredations of urban planning, the real enemy of our traditional landscape is the farmer – the man who has long been regarded as its custodian. Funded by blanket grants from the Ministry of Agriculture, farming 'improvements' have already destroyed most of the heaths of lowland Britain, and eaten into the supposedly 'protected' moorlands of most notably the Exmoor and North York Moors National Parks.

Marion Shoard, in *The Theft of the Countryside*, proposed the urgent designation of six new lowland National Parks; the Lower Wye Valley and Vale of

Herefordshire, the Somerset Levels, the Dorset Downs, the Chiltern Hills, the Norfolk Broads and the Western Downs of West Sussex and East Hampshire.

Hopes were high that the Wildlife and Countryside Act of 1981 would, at last, call a halt to the widespread destruction. That optimism was to be proved groundless when the Bill, after no fewer than 2,000 amendments, eventually emerged as a weak and watered-down document which did little to encourage hope for the future.

For example, section 39 of the Act creates the ludicrous situation of a farmer who, refused permission to improve (with grant aid) an important natural site, now has to be compensated by a National

Skiddaw from the Castlerigg Stone Circle, Lake District.

Park authority for *not* carrying out the work!

Meanwhile, the Ministry of Agriculture's budget for what amounts to the large-scale destruction of much of our National Park scenery continues to outstrip the funding of the National Park authorities by an amount which would be laughable were it not so serious.

Our National Parks are, of necessity, a compromise. With our severely limited national resources we must decide their best use not just for ourselves, but for those who will follow us. That, after all, is the essence of conservation.

As already mentioned, the majority of today's National Park visitors never stray more than half a mile from their cars; but if you are prepared, and equipped, to walk just that little bit further, you can still discover yourself surprisingly, sometimes even frighteningly, alone.

Then the adrenalin starts to pump, and you can find yourself overwhelmed by the fierce, elemental splendour of a landscape in which Man is suddenly put firmly in his place.

It is vitally important in our cosy, increasingly-cosseted and centrally-heated environment that such places exist. Even if we are not able to reach them ourselves, it is still heartening to know that they are there. Somewhere, at least, is still as it was.

Wildest Britain thankfully is still there, waiting for those who really want to find it. And in finding it, with luck they may also find themselves.

Dartmoor National Park

THE LAST WILDERNESS

Often described as the last wilderness in southern Britain, Dartmoor means different things to different people.

For many, it is synonymous with the bleak granite walls of Her Majesty's Prison at Princetown, in the very heart of the moor. Although this grim institution was built in 1809 to house Napoleonic French and American prisoners of war, it has been the most notorious of our criminal jails since 1850.

For others, Dartmoor is the setting of one of Sherlock Holmes's most famous and chilling cases, *The Hound of the Baskervilles*, first serialised in *The Strand Magazine* from August 1901 to April 1902, the same year that both its author, Arthur Conan Doyle, and his detective hero were offered knighthoods.

Perhaps it is Conan Doyle's description of Dartmoor, 'so vast, and so barren, and so mysterious' which colours most people's picture of it. Certainly, his description of the Great Grimpen Mire, where Jack Stapleton met his gruesome death, gave rise to the largely unfounded reputation of Dartmoor's quaking bogs.

Conan Doyle first heard the legend of the moor's spectral hound from a golfing partner, and within a month he was tramping the moor himself to taste its 'grim charms'. There is little doubt that Conan Doyle's hell-hound was based on the legends of Dartmoor's wisht hounds (wisht is a West Country term for 'sad' or 'uncanny'). These demonic dogs, said to herald a human death whenever seen or heard, are led by Dewer the Black Huntsman (Satan) and echo a familiar folk myth from several parts of Britain.

It is easy to scoff at these beliefs in these enlightened times, but when the clammy, all-enveloping mist is down on the moor, wreathing the tors and playing tricks with the imagination, then more than one experienced moorsman has sworn he's seen the black dog of death.

A well-known tale tells of a local farmer riding

Wheal Betsy lead and silver mine.

home one night who met Dewer and foolishly asked him what sport the huntsman had enjoyed. 'Good sport,' answered the huntsman, throwing him a warm bundle. When the farmer reached home and unwrapped it, there was the dead body of his newborn baby.

It is the loneliness and isolation of these weird, tortopped moors which gives Dartmoor its special quality. It is a place where legends can thrive and multiply, for Dartmoor has always been sparsely populated. Indeed, no road crossed the moor until a mere two centuries ago and, even then, a crossing was not to be considered lightly. Often, even today, the only living things in this stern and forbidding landscape are the wild-maned Dartmoor ponies.

Early travellers regarded the moor as a remote and inhospitable tract of country, supporting only peat cutters and tinners, a group of people described by Sir Walter Raleigh, a Lord Warden of the Stannaries (tin mines) as 'the roughest and most mutinous men in England'. One of Devon's first historian-topographers, John Hooker, dismissed Dartmoor with '. . . this one thinge is to be observed that all yere through out commonly it rayneth or it is fowle wether in that more or desert' in his *Synopsis Chronographical of Devonshire* in c1599.

But while the rest of southern Britain was gradually tamed, cultivated and enclosed, Dartmoor remained largely inviolate – a reminder of how the land lay when the earliest settlers came across the land bridge from Europe. Indeed, Dartmoor is one of few places left in Britain where the most obvious signs of Man are still the hut circles, cairns, stone circles and stone rows erected in the Bronze Age perhaps 4,000 years ago. The apparently barren moor has some of the richest concentrations of prehistoric remains anywhere in Britain, an indication that the climate of the moor was once much kinder than when Hooker described it, or than it is today, when the average annual rainfall is still 60 in/1.5 m – double that of the coastal holiday resorts of Torbay.

It was Dartmoor's largely untouched wilderness and 95,000 acres (38,000 ha) of common land which made it an obvious choice as one of the first British National Parks to be designated, in October, 1951. A total of 365 square miles (746 sq km) was protected in an area centred on the central granite-based moor itself but also including the more gentle, wooded and cultivated country to the east around the villages of Buckfastleigh, Ashburton, Moretonhampstead and Drewsteignton.

Lovers of Dartmoor's austere beauty heaved a sigh of relief when the designation was confirmed. For Dartmoor, despite its unique situation and importance, had already suffered more than a fair share of desecration of its natural beauty.

Apart from the eyesore of the prison, piecemeal enclosures had gone on over the years – although never on the scale of its north-coast neighbour, Exmoor – and the weird, lunar landscape of the china clay mines around Lee Moor in the south-west of the area was threatening to eat up even more of the southern wilderness.

The greatest scandal of Dartmoor, however, was the ever-increasing military use of those highest and wildest parts of the northern moor, including some of the most dramatic scenery and the highest points of

High Willhays (2,038 ft/621 m), Yes Tor (2,030 ft/ 619 m) and Hangingstone Hill (1,983 ft/604 m).

Military use of the moor has a long history, but the first serious incursion was the autumn manoeuvres of 1873, when 12,000 men and 2,100 horses marched across the southern moor from Hameldown to Roborough Downs in atrocious weather. The climate failed to put off the authorities, however, and two years later, the first permanent camp was established in Okehampton Park in the north, covering 3,000 acres (1,215 ha) between the East Okement and Taw rivers. World War 2 saw most of the moor to the north and west of the Tavistock/Two Bridges/ Moretonhampstead road being commandeered by the Army for use as a firing range and, in all, a total of 72,000 acres (29,140 ha) was eventually in military use, with the public excluded from 52,000 acres (21,040 ha) of this.

A public inquiry held in July, 1947 questioned the need for and the desirability of such widespread use, which effectively barred all public access to this unique heritage and prevented the use of a large area of Dartmoor's common land for the grazing of livestock. The inquiry resulted in a significant reduction in the total acreage under fire, but the Ministry of Defence still occupies 33,021 acres (13,369 ha) or more than 25 per cent of Dartmoor's high moorlands. Live firing ranges occupy an astonishing 78 per cent of the area the Dartmoor National Park authority has designated a 'wilderness area'.

Unfortunately, National Park designation has done little to curb desecration of this 'protected' area, which was supposedly set aside by Parliament for enjoyment by the public. A network of military-built roads now penetrates some of the most remote areas of the Park, coming as close as half a mile to that one-time greatest challenge to the Dartmoor wanderer, desolate Cranmere Pool. Helicopters and low-flying jets buzz overhead, and on the ground, tanks regularly churn the moor while shells pit its surface with craters of up to 20 ft (6.1 m) across.

Commercial afforestation has spread up on to the moor, particularly around the Fernworthy and Burrator reservoirs and around Bellever Tor near Postbridge, while another reservoir has been constructed, despite strong local opposition, in the moorland valley of the West Okemeet at Meldon.

All of which entitles the visitor to ask whether National Park designation has made *any* difference.

The Devon County Council committee which runs the Dartmoor National Park has stated that military

Arboreal graffiti, Becky Falls.

training on Dartmoor is 'inappropriate', and has stated that its objective is the ultimate withdrawal of military use – but while the Government holds the purse strings and while much of the northern training area is owned by the Government-bound Duchy of Cornwall, it seems that little can be done to improve the situation.

Perhaps the unfortunate paradox of Dartmoor was best summed-up by Malcolm MacEwen, that persistent agitator for more effective planning control in National Parks, when he wrote, 'The supreme irony of Dartmoor is to go there in search of freedom and to find its centre dominated by a jail, or to go there in search of peace and natural beauty and to find them blasted to pieces by men being systematically trained in violence.'

The timeless magic of Dartmoor *can* still be experienced, perhaps after climbing to the top of a gaunt, granite tor which, standing aloof, has witnessed 40 centuries of Man's insignificant attempts to tame this last wilderness, or else in the fairy-tale, lichen-encrusted woodland of Wistman's or Black Tor Beare.

It is at moments and in places like these that you realise what stands to be lost if Dartmoor is allowed to go the way of the rest of southern Britain.

THE NATURAL LANDSCAPE: A GRANITE FIST

Dartmoor is the last and largest 'knuckle' in a series of five which extends from Land's End across the south-west peninsula of England, like an enormous clenched fist of granite.

The granite bosses of Land's End, Carnmenellis, St Austell, Bodmin Moor and Dartmoor are the visible remains of a huge volcanic intrusion known to geologists as a batholith. Formed 290 million years ago when molten granite forced its way up through softer and younger sedimentary rocks, the coarse-grained rock is responsible for all of Dartmoor's dramatic scenery, including its distinctive tors.

The tors of Dartmoor – the name is thought to derive from the Celtic *twr* or tower, or from the Anglo-Saxon word for rock – are the region's best-known physical features. There has been much dis-

Dartmoor tor country. Hay Tor from Hound Tor.

cussion about the origin of these upstanding rock formations, which seem to crown every gently rising hilltop on the rolling moor. Up to 170 have been recorded, of which about 30 are named on the map. The most famous, and popular, are Hound Tor, Hay Tor, Yes Tor and Great Mis Tor; but it would take a lifetime to explore every one of these strangely-evocative blocks of rock, which have weathered into fantastic forms over countless centuries.

Vixen Tor, near Merrivale, for example, is an incredible pile of lichen-encrusted granite, standing 100 ft (30 m) high at its topmost point above a shallow, marshy depression in the moor. And the celebrated, entirely natural, 20 ft (6 m) tall rock sculpture of Bowerman's Nose on the other side of the moor near Manaton provides evidence of the amazing power of erosion on this hardest of rocks.

Bowerman's Nose, said to be named after a man who lived on the slopes of nearby Hound Tor, looks like a pile of children's building bricks, constructed on a Cyclopean scale. One block seems to be stacked on top of another in a crazily-sloping tower of grey granite, topped by an incongruous 'Andy Capp' style hat. Arthur Mee saw him as 'a good-humoured man in a cardinal's hat', while other writers have sensed a more primitive, Neanderthal presence.

It is now generally accepted that these fantastic structures are the unrotted remains of slightly more resistant granite, which have survived the twin attacks of chemical and frost action on the large horizontal and vertical cracks or joints in the rock.

The land surface of Dartmoor was once much higher than today's 700–2,000 ft (205–610 m) plateau, rising perhaps to Alpine heights. Centuries of erosion by the insidiously powerful agencies of wind, rain and frost (the glaciers of the Ice Age never reached Dartmoor) began the process of wearing down the surface and breaking down the rock into the gritty 'growan' or gravelly soil – leaving the harder tors as isolated stumps.

As the rainwater, chemicals and frosts ate deeper into the joints of the rock, huge blocks broke away to tumble downhill in chaotic heaps around the free-standing tors. These ankle-twisting piles of loose rock take the local highly descriptive name of 'clitter', which is exactly the sound they make as you slip and slide over them. A good example of a clitter slope is at Hen Tor, near Shaugh Prior.

The granites of the eastern part of Dartmoor were eroded differently, to form the dissected area of the Teign, Bovey and Dart valleys which characterise 'lowland' Dartmoor. In this softer, more-wooded landscape, a patchwork quilt of stone-walled and hedged fields and deep, narrow lanes spreads across to the red sandstones of eastern Devon.

Dartmoor's rivers flow out like the spokes of a wheel from the wild heart of the northern moor. The main rivers are the West and East Dart which combine at Dartmeet to flow southeast through Buckfastleigh; the Teigns (North and South); the Bovey which flows east to Bovey Tracey and the Tavy which flows southwest through Tavistock. But the West and East Okements and Taw are the only Dartmoor rivers to head north, to enter the Bristol Channel at Bideford Bay.

Woods are few and far between on the high open rough-grass and heather moorlands of Dartmoor's heart. But Dartmoor was well-wooded in the past, as can be proved by the large areas of peat, formerly cut for fuel, which contain the pollen of oak and elm dated to about 5,000 BC.

So it is perhaps not so odd, then, that one of the best places to get the 'feel' of Dartmoor is in one of the few remnants of that primeval woodland. The enchanted wood of Wistman's, on the clitter-clad slopes of Longford Tor in the valley of the West Dart above Two Bridges, is a magical place – a place where it is easy to believe in Dartmoor's celebrated pixies.

Stunted and gnarled oaks, mostly between 300 and 500 years old, grow straight from the chaotic mass of moss-covered clitter. And hanging from their weirdly contorted branches are wreaths and trails of moss, ferns and similar plants. It is like a scene from a fairy tale illustrated by Arthur Rackham, and one of the most haunting and atmospheric places in Britain. Needless to say, the wood is now strictly protected.

Somehow, Wistman's Wood (perhaps the name comes from that old Dartmoor word, wisht) seems to epitomise the brooding spirit of the moor, as does the similar relict woodlands of Black Tor Beare in the West Okement valley above the Meldon reservoir, and Pile's Copse on the Erme above Harford.

If the old woodland epitomises the spirit of the moor, then the skylark's soaring golden spiral of song and the soft mewing cry of the gliding buzzard give it voice. J C Bellamy's *Natural History of South Devon*, published in 1839, showed the moor to be the domain of eagle, bustard, goshawk, kite and raven. Today, of these, only the raven remains, and birdlife is dominated by those skylarks and the ubiquitous meadow pipits. Game birds are surprisingly scarce on Dartmoor, considering the enormous amount of heather cover, but the reservoirs, especially Burrator and Fernworthy, have attracted new populations of waterfowl to the delight of ornithologists.

Out on the open moor, purple moor grass, cotton

grass and heather dominate to give Dartmoor its distinctive patina. Here – where the heather is regularly burned or 'swaled' to produce the fresh young green shoots so beloved of grazing stock – the skylark's song, the deep-throated barking call of a raven, or the spine-chilling bubbling cry of a curlew are often the only sounds to break the deep silence.

Dartmoor's famous quaking bogs are revealed by

Hound Tor.

the vivid green patches of sphagnum moss, but despite their evil reputation these swamps are seldom fatal to the well-equipped walker. Indeed, there is a certain childish pleasure in wading out on to their springy surface and watching the cushion of plants quaking and undulating under your feet.

Insectivorous sundews are found in these quaking bogs, their sticky petals invitingly open to tempt the unwary fly. Here too you might chance upon the beautiful golden-yellow stars of the rare bog asphodel or the shy blooms of the marsh St John's wort, another lover of these wild, wet places.

Bracken, a beautiful plant in its brilliant range of colours through the seasons, has spread over much of the moorland fringes in recent years, to the despair of farmers. It can grow rapidly up to waist height in some places, and has robbed much of the moor of its grazing potential.

It does, however, provide cover for birds and animals like the fox and badger, which are both fairly common, but are unlikely to be seen by any but the most patient visitor because they are mainly nocturnal in their habits.

In the wooded valleys and the gentler, more sylvan landscapes to the east of the moor, bird life is much richer. Chaffinches are almost tame in some places, where they congregate in large, cheeky flocks to be fed by picnicking visitors.

Nuthatches skip headfirst down the trunks of the trees in these quiet woods, seemingly defying the law of gravity in their search for nuts and other delicacies. The raucous laugh of the green woodpecker, living up to its country name of the 'yaffle', can often be heard ringing through the branches.

On the fast-flowing rivers, the vivid sulphur-yellow tail of the falsely-named grey wagtail can often be seen, dipping up and down in the family tradition. The dipper, on the other hand, bobs with the whole of its wren-like body, usually from a favourite rock in the middle of a rushing stream. With a flash of its white bib it flits off under the water in its search for food. So common is the dipper on Dartmoor's rivers that it has been adopted as the emblem of the Devon Trust for Nature Conservation.

A strange omission from Dartmoor's list of fauna is deer, especially as for much of the mediaeval period, the moor was part of the Royal Forest of Dartmoor, converted to a chase in 1239 when Henry III granted it to Richard, Earl of Cornwall. It seems the farmers of Dartmoor were less tolerant of the red deer than their counterparts on Exmoor, for they arranged for the deer to be exterminated by the Duke of Bedford's stag hounds towards the end of the 18th century. Apart from isolated sightings of Exmoor immigrants, there are no deer on Dartmoor today.

There have been feral ponies on Dartmoor from at least the first century AD, when they were mentioned in the will of the Saxon Bishop Aelfwold of Crediton. Although today's Dartmoor ponies are a far remove

Above: Stone row, Down Tor, above Burrator reservoir.

Right: Hay Tor.

from that original stock, probably being first released on the moor during the Dark Ages, these small, sturdy little animals are still one of the sights of the moor. Apart from the annual autumn 'drifts', when the ponies are rounded up and branded, they live wild off the poor moorland vegetation for the whole year. So closely associated are the ponies with the moor, that the silhouette of one was chosen as the emblem for the Dartmoor National Park in 1951.

The many 'warrens' of the moor, for example, Trowlesworthy Warren and Ditsworthy Warren, show where Norman lords set up areas for another introduced species – the rabbit – which was hunted alongside the deer. Cigar-shaped 'pillow mounds' were artificially constructed to encourage the rabbits to settle and breed. And Dartmoor is still one of the last strong-holds of that increasingly rare but beautiful predator, the otter.

But as you stride across the open moor, or drive across it in your car, you are likely to agree with the poet, N T Carrington, whose 1826 poem, *Dartmoor*, went into several editions and encapsulated the wild, desolation of the place.

Nothing that has life
Is visible; – no solitary flock
At will wide ranging through the silent moor,
Breaks the deep-felt monotony....

Only the hardiest cattle, such as these Belted Galloway and South Devon, can thrive on Dartmoor's rough pasture.

MAN'S INFLUENCE: STEPPING BACK IN TIME

In his first report back to Sherlock Holmes from Baskerville Hall, in Conan Doyle's novel *The Hound of the Baskervilles*, the famous detective's loyal lieutenant, Dr Watson, painted an accurate picture of Dartmoor's brooding sense of prehistory.

On all sides of you as you walk are the houses of these forgotten folk, with their graves and the large monoliths which are supposed to have marked their temples. As you look at their grey stone huts against the scarred hillsides you leave your own age behind you, and if you were to see a skin-clad, hairy man crawl out from the low door, you would feel that his presence there was more natural than your own.

Watson's keenly observant eye led him to the conclusion that the occupants of Dartmoor's many pre-historic hut circles must have been an 'unwarlike and harried race', forced out on to this inhospitable moor where no one else would settle. Of course, in Watson's day, pollen analysis of Dartmoor's peat had not yet revealed that the climate of Bronze Age Britain was several degrees warmer and much drier than it is today.

But as you pick your way through the foundations of a settlement like Grimspound, near Manaton, it is not difficult to share the good doctor's uncanny feeling about the close proximity of the past and those pioneering first farmers.

Grimspound, on the wild and windswept combe between Hameldown and Hookney tors, is the most complete and accessible of Dartmoor's Bronze Age village settlements. The wall surrounding the four-acre site is almost complete and still 6 ft (1.8 m) high in places, and the remains of two dozen hut sites can be clearly seen. It is the nearest thing England has to Orkney's Skara Brae settlement, and a place where the past seems very close.

Nearly 2,000 hut circles have been identified on Dartmoor, as well as extensive field systems which show that agriculture was well developed 4,000 years ago. Unfortunately the acid, peaty soil of the moor destroys most of the evidence that modern archaeologists seek to date precisely these settlements. Pottery, wood, metal and bone rot very easily in these conditions, and it is only because these early settlers used the virtually-indestructible granite moorstone for the walls of their timber and turf-roofed homes that so much is still left to see.

Pre-dating these hut circles and settlements by up to 1,000 years are the megalithic tombs or cromlechs, and the stone rows and circles – Dr Watson's temples of prehistoric man.

Most famous of Dartmoor's cromlechs is Spinster's Rock tomb, its massive four stones standing over 6 ft (1.8 m) tall in pleasant farmland at Shilstone, near Drewsteignton. The cromlech gets its name from a local legend that it was erected by three spinsters of that parish one morning before breakfast – a labour of truly Amazonian proportions!

The cromlech is probably the denuded remains of a Neolithic (New Stone Age) burial mound, with a great capstone perched delicately on three uprights, but it is known that the monument was re-erected after collapse in 1862, so its original form is uncertain.

It was the first metal users of the early Bronze Age (known as the Beaker Folk from their distinctive pottery), who are thought to be responsible for Dartmoor's wealth of ritual and religious monuments, the stone circles and rows. The moor must have been a very sacred place indeed, judging by the number and scale of these remains.

No fewer than 12 stone circles have been counted on the moor, and more than 70 stone rows, sometimes known as 'avenues' or 'alignments'. The stone rows, which can be single, double or triple, often extend in straight lines over considerable distances across the moor (2.5/3.4 km in the case of one miles row in the Erme valley). Nearly all are associated with burial cairns, so it is thought they were used in some sort of funeral ceremony, and one can picture the

Grimspound Bronze Age village site.

solemn processions marching between the low stones across the moor.

Of Dartmoor's stone circles, the best known is probably the Grey Wethers, a pair set side-by-side on the 1,500 ft (457 m) col between the South Teign and East Dart valleys above the conifers of Fernworthy Forest and below Sittaford Tor. Like so many of these prehistoric monuments, it has attracted its own legends, and that descriptive name refers to the old story of trader who showed a farmer these stones from a distance – and sold them to him as a flock of sheep!

Another famous Dartmoor henge is at Scorhill above the Teign-e-Ever clapper bridge on nearby Gidleigh Common. The Walla Brook, which runs down from the clitter-strewn slopes of Hangingstone Hill into the North Teign near here, is thought to take its name from the Saxon word *Weala* which meant 'Welsh' or 'foreigners'.

Some scholars have taken this to indicate a folk

memory of the older, Celtic inhabitants of the moor, some of whom may have survived in their turf huts to give rise to the legends of the Dartmoor pixies who lived beneath the earth. Who knows? It is certainly an attractive theory.

By AD 710, the fair-haired Saxon invaders had penetrated far into Devon, and by the late 9th century King Alfred of Wessex had ordered the construction of four 'burghs' or fortified positions in the county to defend his kingdom against invasion by the Danes. One of these, according to the 10th century *Burghal Hidage*, was at Lydford, where a mint was also established. Even today, the grid-iron plan of Alfred's township can be recognised in Lydford's streets, and his defensive banks and the ditch where a Danish attack was later repulsed in AD 997 are still visible.

An improvement in the climate at about this time resulted in settlements again spreading up on to the moor, and a deserted village from about this period has been discovered below Hound Tor. The well-preserved strip 'lynchets', showing where Saxon and mediaeval oxen teams ploughed the moorland slopes

Spinster's Rock cromlech, Drewsteignton.

St Michael's Church, Brentor.

into long, stepped terraces, are seen on Challacombe Down, not far from Grimspound.

By the time the Domesday Commissioners moved down to Dartmoor in 1086, between 4,000 and 5,000 people were living on the moor, with one plough team per square mile.

Agriculture was not the only industry on Dartmoor at this time. For half a century, from 1100, Dartmoor became the largest producer of tin in Europe, and the great Dartmoor 'tin rush' was on. At first, the tin – thought at the time to have been deposited by 'Noah's Floode' – was streamed, that is panned from the fast-flowing rivers and streams like gold.

Later, adit mines and refining 'blowing houses', and water-powered crushing mills were installed and between 300 and 400 tons/tonnes of tin were produced every year from the Dartmoor mines. Tin was a royal metal, valued almost as highly as gold in mediaeval times, and its extraction was governed by a strict set of stannary laws (from the Latin *stannum* – tin). The stannary towns of Tavistock, Chagford, Ashburton and Plympton collected the coinage dues, and weighed and stamped the tin produced by the industry, and the four stannary areas were admin-istered by the Great Court or Parliament of Crockern Tor, near Two Bridges, where their boundaries met.

So powerful was this court that the tinners had their own gaol at Lydford Castle, where even the MP for Plympton, Richard Strode, was imprisoned in 1512 for non-payment of a £160 fine imposed by the Crockern Tor Parliament.

The stannary laws echoed the ferociousness of the earlier forest laws which had governed the Royal Forest of Dartmoor, which extended over all of the present National Park. Indeed, the infamous practice of 'Lydford Law' – executing the prisoner and then passing sentence as an afterthought – may have originated from the Forest's Court of Swainmote, rather than the later Stannary Courts.

Since 1239, the Forest of Dartmoor and the Manor of Lydford have been held by the Duke of Cornwall – currently the Prince of Wales. Many lovers of the moor were heartened by Prince Charles's announcement that future management of his 69,070 acre (27,952 ha) estate – which makes him easily the largest single landowner in the National Park – would be sympathetic to nature conservation.

Other extractive industries on the moor have included lead and silver from the Cornish-sounding Wheal Betsy engine house, east of the Mary Tavy to Lydford road, and now cared for by the National Trust. Dartmoor granite, long famed for its durability and attractiveness, was used for Nelson's Column and the former London Bridge which was transported to Arizona in 1970. The stone for this last enterprise was quarried at Haytor, and the stone sets of the horse-drawn tramway which took the stone down to be shipped out from Teignmouth can still be followed through the sheep-cropped grass.

Dartmoor's 'clay corner' around Lee Moor is an alien landscape of dazzling white cone-shaped waste tips and milky-white streams. The Lee Moor pit, so jarringly obvious from the heights of the southern moor, is one of the largest china clay pits in the world, over 300 ft (90 m) deep and covering over 100 acres (40 ha). Work on extracting the decomposed felspar in the granite began in 1830, and today it is still a very important and valuable commodity. It is said that every newspaper published in Britain contains a tiny particle of Dartmoor – but use as a paper filler is just one of a hundred uses for china clay.

It is farming, however, which is still the number one industry on Dartmoor, and the grey-faced, long-wooled Dartmoor sheep and the huge red South Devon cattle – the largest breed of cattle in Britain and increasingly used as a beef sire – are the native breeds. Ashburton, Buckfastleigh, Tavistock and Okehampton are the major market centres and convenient bases for exploring the moor; all have a good range of accommodation.

Smaller market towns include Moretonhampstead, South Brent, Ivybridge and Lydford; these also have good shops and support a thriving farming community.

The traditional Dartmoor farmhouse – an increasing number of which are now taking visitors – is built from the grey moorstone and typically has a two-storey porch. Today, not many are thatched like the perfect example at Lower Tor, near Poundsgate.

Many of these typical farmhouses date from the period of the Enclosures, and Dartmoor's equivalent of Exmoor's Knight family was Thomas Tyrwitt, friend of the Prince of Wales and auditor to the Duchy of Cornwall. Between 1785 and 1798 he enclosed some 2,300 acres (930 ha) around Two Bridges

Wistman's Wood.

and formed a new settlement on the Yelverton road which he called Prince's Town in honour of his patron.

This later became known as Princetown, but Tyrwitt's dreams of turning Dartmoor's wastes into fertile acres of corn, flax and root crops were doomed to failure. Instead, Tyrwitt built Dartmoor's most famous building, the prison at Princetown, originally to take 9,000 French prisoners from the Napoleonic War who had previously been confined to hulks at Plymouth and Hamoaze. The building was converted to a criminal prison in 1850, seventeen years after Tyrwitt died, with Princetown the only memorial to his attempted 'improvement' of Dartmoor.

The age of the Dartmoor visitor really began when the railway reached Exeter in 1844; and Chagford became one of the earliest centres for exploring the moor, thanks to the initiative of the rector, the Reverend Hayter Hames. James Perrott of Chagford was one of the earliest guides and carriage operators, a century ago.

One of the best-known and most representative townships of the moor is Widecombe-in-the-Moor, remembered all over the world because of a famous folk song about Uncle Tom Cobley and his companions who rode to the fair on Tom Pearce's grey mare.

The much photographed, 14th century church of St Pancras at Widecombe, with its pinnacled, 120 ft (36.5 m) tower, is known as the Cathedral of the Moor, and was built largely on the wealth won from tin mining and wool.

Manaton is a marvellous centre for the exploration of prehistoric Dartmoor, convenient for Grimspound, Hound Tor village and the Challacombe lynchets. Natural attractions include Becky Falls, Bowerman's Nose and Hound Tor.

On the other side of the moor, historic Lydford, with its great stone keep built in 1195, and Saxon defences, is a good resort, handy for visiting the remarkable Lydford Gorge and the amazing volcanic hill of Brentor, crowned by its mediaeval church with superb views in all directions.

The thatched roofs and moorstone cottages of Buckland-in-the-Moor are most people's dream of a West Country village, set in a well-wooded landscape above the valley of the Webburn.

What to do

HOW TO GET THERE

BY ROAD Most holidaymakers from the north and south east will come to Dartmoor via the M4 and M5 motorway. The M5 now reaches past Exeter. Alternatively, the A30 or A303 also lead to the Exeter bypass. Leaving the motorway at Junction 31, the motorist has the choice of taking the still motorway-standard A38 which skirts the south of the National Park to Ashburton, Buckfastleigh and Ivybridge on its way to Plymouth, or turning north on the A30 to Okehampton. Alternatively the B3212 from Exeter takes you through to Moretonhampstead and the centre of the National Park at Two Bridges.

BY RAIL Exeter is just over two hours away from London (Paddington) by Inter-City express, and Plymouth an hour more. Local trains still run to Buckfastleigh via Totnes. The Transmoor bus link from Exeter to Plymouth gives you the unique experience of seeing the Park from the top of a double-decker, and other bus services run from Newton Abbot and Torquay.

WHERE TO STAY

Although the National Park authority does not produce its own accommodation guide, as most of the others do, there is a perfectly good alternative published by the Dartmoor Tourist Association, available from National Park information centres. The information centres at Okehampton and Tavistock will also help with accommodation bookings.

YOUTH HOSTELS Dartmoor is not too well served with hostels, but that is perhaps one of the costs of a true wilderness. There are hostels at Tavistock, Gidleigh (near Chagford), Bellever (near Postbridge), Steps Bridge (near Dunsford) and, just outside the Park boundary, at Plymouth, Exeter and Lownard (near Dartington).

CAMPING AND CARAVAN SITES Most of Dartmoor's camping sites are situated on the edge of the moor itself 'where the weather is better and access by vehicle is easier', according to the National Park authority. Most of them are well-signposted and information about each can be obtained from information centres. To be sure of your chosen site, the authority advises campers to book in advance, especially in summer.

Caravan owners are advised not to take their vans further into the moor, but to leave them in the peripheral sites and just use the car for day trips into the 'interior'. The roads across the moor are very narrow, steep in places and often congested, so caravan owners are asked not to use these roads as through routes. Details of sites can be obtained in the same way as for camping sites.

PLACES OPEN TO THE PUBLIC

BECKY FALLS A popular 50-acre (20 ha) beauty spot off the B3344 road between Bovey Tracey and Manaton. The fast-flowing Becka Brook tumbles down over enormous granite boulders ending with a 70 ft (21 m) drop into a delightful wooded glade.

BUCKFAST ABBEY, BUCKFASTLEIGH Originally founded by King Canute in 1030, the abbey was dissolved by Henry VIII and remained a ruin until exiled French Benedictine monks purchased it a hundred years ago. The abbey was rebuilt entirely by the monks themselves and the work was completed in 1938. Nowadays it is famous for the unique tonic wine produced by the monks and sold all round the world.

DART VALLEY STEAM RAILWAY, BUCKFASTLEIGH Visitors can recapture the great days of the GWR on this carefully restored line travelling down the Dart valley to Totnes in genuine chocolate-and-cream coaches.

FINCH FOUNDRY MUSEUM, STICKLEPATH A Museum of Rural Industry in which the water-powered machinery is the main attraction. Four of the original five wheels are still turned by the River Taw, producing edge-tools as they have done for 100 years.

CASTLE DROGO, NEAR DREWSTEIGNTON The last great country house to be built in Britain, Castle Drogo was designed by Sir Edwin Lutyens and built between 1911 and 1930. The locally-quarried granite pile is a masterpiece of the period, and commands a superb view of Dartmoor and the Teign gorge from its promontory. Now in the care of the National Trust.

LYDFORD CASTLE, LYDFORD A late 12th century keep, now in the care of the Department of the Environment, which was used to imprison offenders against the ancient stannary laws.

LYDFORD GORGE, LYDFORD This contains Dart-

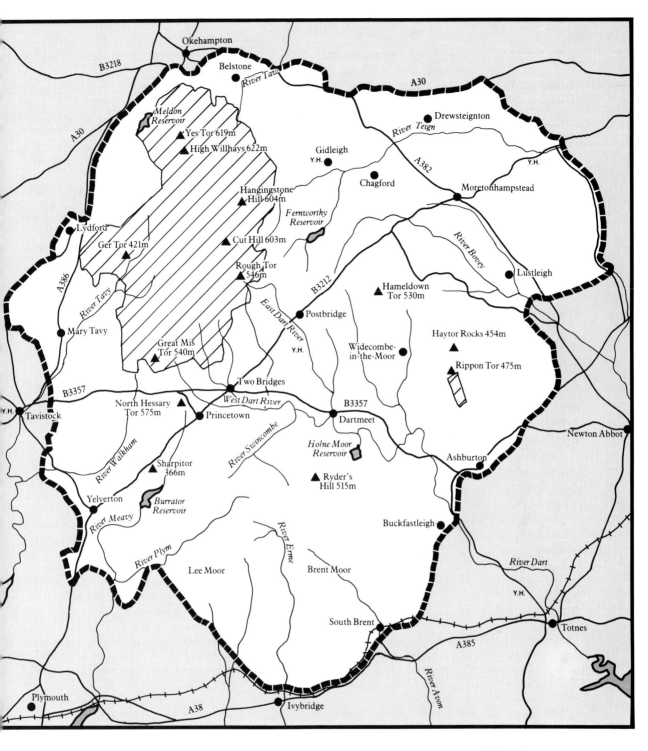

Okehampton

B3218

Belstone

River Taw

A30

A30

Drewsteignton

Meldon
Reservoir

River Teign

Yes Tor 619m

High Willhays 622m

Gidleigh
Y.H.

Y.H.

Chagford

A382

Moretonhampstead

Hangingstone
Hill 604m

Fernworthy
Reservoir

Lydford

River Bovey

Lustleigh

Ger Tor 421m

Cut Hill 603m

River Tavy

Rough Tor
546m

B3212

Hameldown
Tor 530m

Haytor Rocks 454m

Mary Tavy

East Dart River

Postbridge

Rippon Tor 475m

A386

Great Mis
Tor 540m

Y.H.

Widecombe-
in-the-Moor

B3357

Two Bridges

West Dart River

B3357

North Hessary
Tor 575m

Dartmeet

Newton Abbot

Y.H.

Tavistock

Princetown

River Swincombe

Ashburton

River Walkham

Sharpitor
366m

Holne Moor
Reservoir

Yelverton

Burrator
Reservoir

Ryder's
Hill 515m

Buckfastleigh

River Meavy

River Erme

River Dart

River Plym

Lee Moor

Brent Moor

Y.H.

Totnes

South Brent

Plymouth

A38

Ivybridge

A385

River Avon

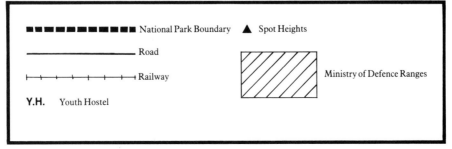

▬▬▬▬▬▬ National Park Boundary   ▲ Spot Heights

——————— Road

⊢–⊢–⊢–⊢–⊢ Railway

////// Ministry of Defence Ranges

Y.H.   Youth Hostel

moor's finest waterfall, the 90 ft (27 m) White Lady, in a ferny chasm formed by the River Lyd. There is also a series of potholes, including the Devil's Cauldron, to be explored on a 1.5 mile (2.4 km) walk through the woods.

There are museums at Ashburton, Moretonhampstead, and Okehampton.

ANCIENT MONUMENTS

	Grid reference
Grey Wethers Stone Circles, Postbridge	(SX 596797)
Scorhill Stone Circle, Gidleigh	(SX 655873)
Spinster's Rock Tomb Chamber, Drewsteignton	(SX 700908)
Challacombe Stone Rows & Standing Stones	(SX 591670)
Ditsworthy Warren Stone Rows & Cairns, Drizzlecombe	(SX 590670)
Foales Arrishes Settlement, Widecombe	(SX 737758)
Grimspound Settlement, Manaton	(SX 700809)
Broadun Ring Settlement, Postbridge	(SX 637802)
Trowlesworthy Warren Settlement	(SX 573644)
Cranbrook Castle Hill Fort, Moretonhampstead	(SX 739890)
Prestonbury Hill Fort, Drewsteignton	(SX 746900)
Fingle Bridge, Dunsford	(SX 743899)

MAPS

The whole of the Dartmoor National Park is covered by the Ordnance Survey's excellent one inch to one mile (1 : 63,360 scale) Tourist map of Dartmoor. This contains most of the information anyone could want when visiting the area, and the attractive shading and colouring still reminds us of the old pre-metricated maps. The National Park is also covered by the 1 : 50,000 Landranger maps, nos 191,201 and 202.

FURTHER READING

Crossing, William, *Guide to Dartmoor*, David & Charles, 1965.

Gill, Crispin (ed), *Dartmoor: A New Study*, David & Charles, 1970.
Gill, Crispin, *Dartmoor*, David & Charles, 1976.
Hansford Worth, R, *Dartmoor*, reprinted David & Charles, 1967.
Harris, Helen, *The Industrial Archaeology of Dartmoor*, David & Charles, 1968.
Harvey, L A, & St Leger Gordon, D, *Dartmoor*, Collins, 1953.
Hoskins, W G (ed), *Dartmoor National Park*, HMSO, 1957.
Perkins, J W, *Geology Explained: Dartmoor and the Tamar Valley*, David & Charles, 1972.
Pettit, Paul, *Prehistoric Dartmoor*, David & Charles, 1974.
St Leger Gordon, Ruth, *The Witchcraft and Folklore of Dartmoor*, Hale, 1965.
Tourists Guide to the Dartmoor and Exmoor National Parks, Regional Publications, n.d.

The National Park authority produces an extensive and inexpensive range of booklets on all aspects of Dartmoor life and history, which are available from information centres.

DRIVING

Two roads cross in the centre of Dartmoor at Two Bridges, like a huge St Andrew's cross. They are the B3212 from Exeter and Moretonhampstead to Yelverton and the B3357 (formerly A384) from Ashburton to Tavistock.

Both offer the careful motorist (they both start as fairly narrow, stone-walled country lanes and have several steep hills) a rewarding glimpse of wildest Dartmoor. But, as always, there is no real substitute for stopping the car, parking it sensibly, and walking. In just a short distance from the car, you can feel you have the moor to yourself.

The B3212 runs across Steps Bridge and up to Doccombe, a granite hamlet which seems to grow from the hillside. Across Mardon Down, it leads on to Moretonhampstead and then up on to the real moor at Bush Down, 1,500 ft (457 m) above the sea. Down again on an exciting switchback to Postbridge where the remains of a clapper bridge cross the East Dart. The West Dart is met at Two Bridges at the boundary between the great wildernesses of the north and the south. The road leads on across the moor to Princetown and its dismal prison and then to Sharpitor and Peek Hill – the aptly-named eminence with commanding views across Cornwall – before dropping steeply to Yelverton.

Widecombe-in-the-Moor.

The B3357 from Ashburton is shorter and in some ways more dramatic, taking in the well-known but sometimes crowded beauty spot of Dartmeet where the East and West Dart rivers converge at the foot of a steep hill. Up over Huccaby Tor to Two Bridges again, the road runs on past the 700 ft (212 m) BBC-tv mast of North Hessary Tor to the left opposite Rundlestone. The descent off the moor at Merrivale is marked by a large concentration of prehistoric remains and clitter slopes, with convenient car parks for their exploration.

WALKING

Still the best walkers' guide to Dartmoor is William Crossing's 1909 *Guide to Dartmoor*, as valuable and comprehensive a guide as has yet been produced. It also includes some common-sense advice on the desirability of carrying a compass if the walker is straying off the beaten track (not recommended for the inexperienced rambler).

There are still tragedies on Dartmoor almost every year among those who ignore Crossing's sound advice. Any walker venturing on to the northern moors, where the Army has extensive live-firing training areas, must first check that access is allowed. Weekends and the period between mid-July and mid-September are usually clear, but when warning signals are displayed – red flags by day and red lights by night – then entry to these red-and-white-posted danger areas is forbidden. Details of firing times are advertised at local post offices, police stations and in newspapers every week, or you can use the telephone answering service on the following numbers: Torquay 24592, Exeter 70164, Plymouth 701924 or Okehampton 2939.

An easy 6 mile (9.5 km) walk from the B3212 near Moretonhampstead takes in the best-preserved and most evocative Bronze Age settlement on the moor at Grimspound. From the car park six miles south-west from Moretonhampstead, make for Hookney Tor. The granite-walled hut circles of Grimspound lie on the hillside below, an oasis in the heather-covered moor. Further on, on Challacombe Down, the remains of 16th century tin mining can be seen in the excavated gullies in the hillside above Headland Warren Farm.

The more lush, well-wooded eastern fringe of Dartmoor is perhaps best seen in the 4 mile (6.5 km) walk, previously described, in the valley of the Becka Brook at Manaton to the romantic Becky Falls. There are also gentler way-marked walks around Burrator reservoir and Bellever Forest near Postbridge.

Highest and wildest Dartmoor can be tasted by the more serious 9 mile (14.5 km) walk from Sticklepath via Cawsand Beacon to the impressive triple-topped Hound Tor and back via Belstone Common to Belstone itself. Another classic walk on the high moors is the 13 mile (21 km) excursion from Gidleigh to Cranmere Pool, which is usually a disappointingly dismal swamp, but is nevertheless a goal for Dartmoor wanderers.

Cranmere Pool saw the start of a time-honoured Dartmoor walkers' tradition. Here in 1854, a Chagford guide named James Perrott left a small box where visitors could leave their visiting cards and sign a visitors' book. This custom later developed into the modern one of leaving post cards, stamped and addressed, for the next visitor to post. About a dozen of these letter boxes, usually with a visitors' book and stamp pad, now exist at popular walkers' destinations on the moor.

The National Park authority also runs an excellent and extensive programme of guided walks in all parts of the Park during the summer. All you have to do is turn up at the appointed venue (details from information centres listed below) for an informative walk of one to six hours, led by one of 50 approved guides. In fact, Dartmoor's comprehensive programme of guided walks is unrivalled by the other Parks and should serve as a model to them.

CLIMBING, TREKKING AND FISHING

Climbing is limited to a few suitable crags well-known to the West Country climbing fraternity, who generally find greater challenges on Cornish sea cliffs.

Dartmoor is well served with riding establishments for the growing number of pony trekkers. There are stables at Belstone, Buckland-in-the-Moor, Lydford, Moretonhampstead, North Bovey, Peter Tavy, Princetown, South Brent and Widecombe. You can get further details from information centres.

Fishing normally requires a licence, and permission from the owner of the rights. However, combined permits to cover the licence as well on the Meldon, Venford and Avon reservoirs are available from the South West Water Authority, address below.

There are golf courses at Moretonhampstead, Wrangaton, Roborough Down and Okehampton Park. Swimming pools, if you dare not brave the moorland pools, are provided at the River Dart Country Park near Ashburton, Bovey Tracey, Okehampton, Chagford and Ashburton.

H.M. Prison, Princetown.

Useful Addresses

Dartmoor National Park Authority,
Parke
Haytor Road
Bovey Tracey
Newton Abbot
Devon, TQ13 9JQ.

(tel. Bovey Tracey 832093)

The Secretary
Dartmoor Tourist Association
8 Fitzford Cottages
Tavistock
Devon PL19 8DB.

South West Water
Peninsula House, Rydon Lane
Exeter EX2 7HR.

(tel. Exeter 219666)

West Country Tourist Board
Trinity Court
Southernhay East
Exeter.

(tel. Exeter 76351)

Devon Trust for Nature Conservation
75 Queen Street
Exeter, EX4 3RX.

Dartmoor Preservation Association
The Hon. Membership Secretary
7 Bouchiers Hill
North Tawton
Devon EX20 2DG.

National Park Information Centres

Guildhall
Bedford Square, Tavistock.

The Car Park, Postbridge.

Town Hall, Princetown.

West Street, Okehampton.

Steps Bridge, Near Dunsford.

New Bridge, Near Ashburton.

There are tourist centres with Dartmoor information in the
Civic Centre, Paris Street, Exeter (tel. Exeter 72434) and
the Civic Centre, Royal Parade, Plymouth (tel. Plymouth 264850).
Information is also available from Dartmoor National Park
Authority, Bovey Tracey (tel. Bovey Tracey 832093).

Exmoor National Park

DEER, DOONES AND DAMAGE

The three Ds epitomise Exmoor, one of the smallest and most intimate of Britain's National Parks.

They represent respectively three key features which put this 265 square mile (686 sq km) National Park, set up in October, 1954, apart from the other nine.

The deer are Exmoor's famous herds of red deer (Cervus elaphus) Britain's largest land mammal and the emblem chosen by the National Park authority for its badge. The herds on Exmoor, which are thought to contain a total population of up to 800, constitute the largest stronghold of those noble beasts outside the Scottish Highlands, and they are believed to be directly descended from the prehistoric deer which once grazed much of Britain's forests.

They are still vigorously hunted and therefore tolerated by local farmers who are said to grow an extra acre or two of roots 'for the deer', which often feed on farm crops especially in a bad winter. The deer share their forage with the shy Exmoor ponies, perhaps the nearest thing we have in Britain to truly wild horses.

For most people, Exmoor is synonymous with the Victorian novel *Lorna Doone* by R D Blackmore, which was subtitled *A Romance of Exmoor* and published in 1869. This tale of thwarted love, bloodthirsty villains and high, melodramatic passion has fired the imagination of successive generations of readers, and inspired thousands of 'Dooneland' pilgrims, who arrive seeking the sites described in Blackmore's novel.

Richard Doddridge Blackmore was educated at Blundell's School, Tiverton, just as John Ridd was in the book, and he knew the moor very well, although like most novelists, he adapted the scenery to fit his plot.

He later wrote 'If I had dreamed that it ever would be more than a book of the moment, the descriptions of scenery – which I know as well as I know my garden – would have been kept nearer to their fact.

The Harbour, Lynmouth.

I romanced therein, not to mislead any other, but solely for the uses of my story.'

Many people do not realise that Blackmore's tale was based on well-documented legends common among the people of Exmoor. There was a notorious band of outlaws named Doone in the Badgworthy valley in the mid-17th century, and they did commit atrocities such as those described in the book; Blackmore states in one footnote, 'This vile deed was done beyond all doubt.'

The Exmoor that Blackmore remembered was much more like that described by the Parliamentary Commissioners of 1651, 'A mountenous and cold ground much be Clouded with thick Foggs and Mists ... overgrown with heath, and yielding but a pore kind of turf ...' than it is like today's well-ordered, tidy landscape of field and farm with the moorland 'outover'.

Which, sadly, brings us to the third 'D' of Exmoor – the irreparable damage done to the shrinking moorland heart by ever-increasing agricultural improvement and reclamation. This is no new phenomenon, despite the modern outcry which followed the discovery that piecemeal reclamation had reduced the moorland heart of the National Park from about a third of the total area of the Park in 1954 to about a quarter today.

The reclamation was begun in earnest by John Knight, a Midland ironmaster who bought 15,000 acres (6,070 ha) of the former Royal Forest in 1818, after an Enclosure Act had been passed to free it for agriculture.

During the next few decades, Knight and his son Frederic who succeeded him, established 15 new farms within the 29 mile (47 km) perimeter Forest Wall they built round their property, and thus changed the landscape of Exmoor dramatically. The waterlogged peats, silts and clays of the moor were transformed into well-drained soil, not quite good enough for the arable crops John Knight had intended, but eminently suited to the root crop/grassland rotation still practised on the moor to this day.

The mark of the Knights is still to be seen almost

everywhere on Exmoor. More than anyone else, it was this pioneering Shropshire family who shaped the Exmoor visitors now know and love. The subtle mix of a patchwork of fields in the valleys, lined by the beech-planted earthen banks erected by the Knights, the woodlands in the deep combes and the moorland on the hilltops are the very essence of Exmoor.

Before the Knights arrived, there was only one house in the forest at Simonsbath, where the Warden James Boevey lived. The Knights made Simonsbath their moorland capital and created the thriving little township of today.

There are only about 47,000 acres (19,000 ha) of heather moorland left now, mainly in the western and central areas of the ancient Royal Forest – a tract of hunting ground preserved for Royal use. It is centred on the boggy ridge of The Chains, which rises to nearly 1,600 ft (477 m) at Chains Barrow and Hoaroak Hill, and around the Park's highest point at Dunkery Beacon (1,704 ft/519 m).

What is left has been increasingly fragmented, a process actively encouraged by Ministry of Agriculture grants of 50 per cent or more of the cost of reclamation or other improvements. The matter came to a head in 1976, when 250 acres of moorland on the Glenthorne Estate and another 375 acres at Stowey Allotment near Glenthorne were threatened with reclamation. This was within a mile of the centre of Exmoor's moorland heart, and after the National Park authority had found it would be faced with a £9,000 a year management agreement to save the moorland from destruction, the Government stepped in and ordered an inquiry.

The Porchester Inquiry, headed by Lord Porchester, recommended a more rigid regime of conservation for the fast-disappearing heartland of Exmoor, coupled with a more sympathetic attitude by the Ministry of Agriculture.

It also produced two maps which showed the total area of existing moorland and areas where a 'flexible' approach to reclamation could be made, and where the moorland was such an important element of the National Park's landscape that it should be 'conserved so far as possible for all time', and within which there would be 'the strongest possible presumption against agricultural conversion'.

Moorland conservation orders were introduced, under which farmers would be paid a lump sum in compensation for *not* improving moorland, aided by a 90% grant from the Government. But in these times

Hoaroak Water, above Watersmeet.

36

of shrinking budgets and ever-increasing pressure from farmers on the moorland fringe, the question is how long can the nation afford this kind of compensation to keep a National Park in the state for which it was originally designated?

Of course, there is much more to Exmoor than the high moorland of the west and centre. To the east of the broad and fertile Vale of Porlock and the wooded valley of the Exe, the Brendon Hills, heavily forested on their northern flanks, present a much more settled and lived-in landscape of gentle valleys and prosperous farms.

Many people get their first introduction to Exmoor on day trips from the popular seaside resorts of Minehead, Lynton and Lynmouth or Porlock. And indeed the 29 miles of spectacular hogs-back cliffs which form this part of the North Devon and Somerset coast are one of the National Park's greatest assets. The rocky headlands of Hangman Hill, Duty Point, and Foreland Point offer superb views both across the Bristol Channel to the dim, distant Welsh hills, and inland across the moor itself.

The magnificent coast can be best admired from the North Devon Coast Path, which contours in an exciting switchback along the cliff tops. Rivers rising on the moors make their sudden and spectacular rush to the sea down deep, wooded cleaves such as Heddon's Mouth, Woody Bay and the valleys of the West and East Lyn.

The East Lyn is joined by the Hoaroak Water at Watersmeet, a justly popular, if crowded, beauty spot. Both streams rise on the moorland wastes of The Chains where, on August 15, 1952, nine inches (23 cm) of rain fell in five hours to create the terrible floods at Lynmouth.

The scars of this appalling natural disaster can still be seen in the uprooted trees and boulders in the Glen Lyn Gorge, and rebuilt roads and bridges in the little town beneath. It has been estimated that a staggering 3,000 million tons of rainwater fell in the 38 square miles drained by the East and West Lyn rivers that night.

About 40,000 tons of boulders, some weighing more than 10 tons, were swept down into Lynmouth by a wall of water 50 ft/ 15 m high, and the delta caused by the flood still extends well out into Lynmouth Bay.

It is hard for visitors to imagine the enormous force of the water, as they wander up the tree-lined banks of the babbling West Lyn on a dry summer's day, but then that is the magic and mystery of Exmoor – a seemingly soft and gentle place where the elements have combined to create a beautiful, fragile, yet still ultimately untamed landscape.

THE NATURAL LANDSCAPE:
HIGH COUNTRY OF THE WINDS

Exmoor takes its name from the fact that Devon's mightiest river, the Exe, rises on the boggy, barrow-studded moor of The Chains above Simonsbath. From the bleak swamp of Exe Head, where the tawny moor grass is tossed incessantly by the wind, the river takes an extraordinary course, turning to the south, instead of heading north to where the inviting blue waters of the Bristol Channel lap a mere five miles away.

The Exe prefers to swing south east, away from the sea, and rushes down its deepening cleave (valley) to join the Barle below Dulverton on its seemingly perverse 54 mile (87 km) journey to the English Channel at Exeter.

Its sister river, the Barle, follows a similar course, rising from the Winaway col between Wood Barrow and Chains Barrow on The Chains, where the Knights constructed Pinkworthy (locally Pinkery) Pond. Other Exmoor rivers, like the East and West Lyn, the Heddon, the Hoaroak Water, Farley Water and Badgworthy Water, behave more logically, pursuing their rapid course down to the nearby Bristol Channel through deep, heavily-wooded cleaves cut into the rocks. The West Lyn, in fact, drops 400 feet (122 m) in its last headlong dash to the sea, and the 1952 flood bears witness to its potential power.

To find the reason for the inconsistent behaviour of Exmoor's rivers, we must look at the geology of the region. The upland block we know as Exmoor consists almost entirely of a succession of Devonian and Carboniferous rocks of about the same age as the old red sandstones which form the Brecon Beacons across the Bristol Channel.

The slates and grits of these Ilfracombe Beds all dip uniformly towards the south-east, which is the reason for the direction taken by the Exe and Barle in their early courses. The shorter, northern streams were able to cut their violent, narrow passage across the grain of the land by sheer brute force.

The moors above the coast attract a considerable rainfall – up to 60 in (150 cm) a year. And their poor, peat-bogged drainage turns them into enormous heather-topped sponges, soaking up the rain and then releasing it into the infant water courses. It is easy to see how this latent water power could cut the deep valleys which characterise the river valleys of the north coast. It has been estimated that the West Lyn has been responsible for the deposition of 200,000 cubic yards of boulders and other debris on the right bank of the East Lyn in Lynmouth.

The best way to see the succession of rocks which make up the National Park is to take the coastal path. Exmoor is not the place for towering crags or outcrops of rock inland, so we must study their exposures on the coastal cliffs, which rise up to 1,000 feet (305 m) from the waves below.

The only exception to this rule is the popular picnic spot of the Valley of the Rocks, near Lynton, a dry valley with a curious collection of craggy outcrops running parallel to the coastline but separated from it by a narrow, rocky ridge. Geologists believe that this was the original watercourse of the East and West Lyn rivers, which created the strangely wild valley with its velvety-grassed floor. Coastal erosion by the pounding waves eventually cut off and captured the valley, and its rivers, so that they now flow out to the sea at Lynmouth, leaving the Valley of the Rocks high and dry.

Along the coast path, where Lynmouth is the only settlement at sea level in 17 miles/27 km of rugged coastline, the different rock types give rise to a variety of cliff forms. The harder, more resistant red sandstones of the Hangman Grits give us the distinctive, sharply dipping symmetrical headlands of the Great and Little Hangmen above Combe Martin. The softer, grey Lynton slates have been more easily worn away by the waves to create the aptly-named Woody Bay further east along this entrancing coast.

One of the best descriptions of wildest Exmoor, apart from Blackmore's famous quote in *Lorna Doone* where he wrote 'the land lies softly', is from another famous work of fiction which was partly based on the moor. Henry Williamson's best-seller *Tarka the Otter* was based on his experiences when he lived in a 1s 6d (7½p)-a-week cob-built cottage on the North Devon coast.

'Exmoor', wrote Williamson, 'is the high country of the winds, which are to the falcons and the hawks; clothed by whortleberry bushes and lichens and ferns and mossed trees in the goyals, which are to the foxes, the badgers, and the red deer; served by rain clouds and drained by rock-littered streams, which are to the otters.'

His use of the word 'goyals' – a pure Exmoor expression also used by Blackmore to denote a deep moorland valley – shows the intimacy of his local knowledge. And his keen powers of natural history observation are illustrated by the accuracy of his catalogue of moorland habitats.

Although falcons, hawks, foxes, badgers and red deer are still quite common in Williamson's 'high country of the winds', you would be fortunate indeed

Porlock from Bossington Hill.

to spot a relative of Tarka the Otter or White-Tip his mate on the moor today. Exmoor is a little too populous and populated to provide the undisturbed wilderness required by these shy but charming predators.

The lone walker is much more likely to see Williamson's falcons and hawks, particularly kestrels and buzzards, riding the winds above the bog and bracken of the moor. The sight of a pair of buzzards, wheeling effortlessly on broad, motionless wings on the thermals rising from the moor is one of the thrills of Exmoor.

And you might be lucky enough to see the fast-flying powerful shape of a peregrine falcon, or the smaller, more nimble merlin, beating low across the heather to swoop on its prey.

The deep, wooded cleaves are the usual nesting places for these elegant raptors, but the black grouse, red grouse, curlew and ring ouzel breed on the open moor. The blackcock (male black grouse) is a handsome bird, with glossy blue-black plumage and flamboyant lyre-shaped tail, seen to best effect at the time of the lek. These are the traditional display grounds used by males at breeding times, usually between March and April.

The typical sounds of the moor are the haunting 'cour-li, cour-li' of the curlew and the croaking bark 'go-back, go-back, back, back,' of the red grouse, Britain's exclusive game bird.

Foxes and badgers frequent the deep woodland cleaves, and the foxes are hunted by four packs which cover the moor, notably the Exmoor Foxhounds. But if we mention hunting on Exmoor, the controversial staghounds which have the moor's noble red deer as their quarry are most likely to come to mind.

The Exmoor red deer are descended from those which were hunted when Exmoor was still a Royal forest, and strict laws were imposed to protect them for Royal sport. No longer protected by forest laws, the red deer which are numbered between 500 and 800 head, roam freely between Bridgwater and Barnstaple Bay, but are seldom seen by the passing motorist.

The hunters, usually local farmers who tolerate the sometimes extensive damage caused by the deer, say hunting is an effective form of control and the killing is selective with only old or sick animals left to the hounds.

The best time to see, and hear, Exmoor's most famous mammals is during the October rut, as the

Crock Point, Woody Bay.

stags gather harems of hinds around them in preparation for mating. Their roaring challenge to other males, so descriptively known as 'belling', is one of the most thrilling sounds in nature, echoing across the combes and goyals of the open moor, just as it has for long centuries before Man came to Exmoor.

Next to the red deer, Exmoor's most famous wild mammals are the shaggy-coated Exmoor ponies, a truly wild species unlike the feral, gone-wild, ponies of Dartmoor, the New Forest and the Shetlands.

They are descended from wild horses which managed to survive the Arctic conditions of the last Ice Age, and modern Exmoors seem to have inherited that sturdy hardiness. They are agile, lively animals usually bay, dun or brown in colour with the muzzles, inside of the ears, and around the eyes a characteristic oatmeal. In fact, the Exmoor pony – an officially recognised rare breed because of its scarcity – is better suited than either the red deer or native white-faced Exmoor Horn sheep to living outdoors all the year round on the most meagre diet of moorland roughage. A thick outer coat of wiry hair sheds the rain water and keeps the pony dry and warm, and the extra-strong curved jaw bone is well adapted for grinding the toughest forage.

That forage on the moor consists mainly of purple moor grass – purple only in late summer like the heather – and cotton grass, bent grass and sedges in the swampy places. Gorse, bracken and heather (ling, bell and cross-leaved heath) are dominant on the drier uplands and present an ever-changing kaleidoscope of colour and tone.

MAN'S INFLUENCE: RATHER A THING OF PLEASURE THAN PROFIT

The best known of Exmoor's 'prehistoric' remains – the primitive-looking clapper bridge of Tarr Steps across the River Barle – may not be prehistoric at all.

Despite the fact that it seemed to receive official recognition as a prehistoric monument from the Postmaster General in 1968, when a series of postage stamps was issued showing British bridges, modern scholars are not so sure. Fords and stepping stones certainly preceded bridges in prehistoric times, and similar clapper bridges on Dartmoor have been dated at not earlier than AD 1400.

There is no evidence that Tarr Steps, with its 15 'arches' and 20 stone piers supporting the large stone slabs which form the 180 foot (55 m) footway, is any earlier. Certainly, it has often been destroyed by flooding when the Barle was in spate, and rebuilt several times, most recently in 1948 and 1953. And

Dunster Castle.

E T MacDermot, the historian of the Royal Forest of Exmoor, records that in 1279 the Barle was crossed at Three Waters, about a mile downstream, with no mention of Tarr Steps.

But whether Tarr Steps, one of the most popular beauty spots in the National Park, five miles (8 km) north of Dulverton on the B3223, is as old as it looks or not, there is plenty of evidence of the works of prehistoric man on Exmoor.

Perhaps the most enigmatic and fascinating are the mysterious standing stones, like the nine-foot-tall (2.7 m) Long Stone standing sentinel on the moors above Challacombe, where there is a whole system of barrows, tumuli and stones.

A glance at the Ordnance Survey map of this wild, windswept heart of the moor shows the enormous importance it must have held for prehistoric man, the first inhabitants of Exmoor. A string of the star-shaped representations on the map of tumuli, each with its name in Gothic lettering – Holwell, Roe, Longstone, Wood, Chains and Chapman Barrows – are spaced along the desolate, boggy ridge of The Chains. There are estimated to be between 300 and 350 of these round barrows or burial mounds on Exmoor, showing where these first settlers were laid to rest.

Where they may have lived is shown by the dots signifying the remains of hut circles, above the valleys of the West Lyn, Hoaroak Water and Farley Water. But although the sites are still clearly marked on the map, many are now thought to be natural groupings of stones or man-made cairns, so the story of the everyday lives of these Bronze Age people remains an enigma to baffle archaeologists and fascinate visitors.

Certainly Challacombe's Long Stone, with its attendant barrow, belongs to this period, somewhere between 2300 and 1300 BC. The very presence of these monuments indicates the organisational skill of these 'primitive' people, but the question 'why?' remains unanswered, although it is safe to assume they held some ritual or religious significance.

The Iron Age inhabitants of Exmoor were the Dumnonii, and they built the still-impressive hill forts, such as the six acre (2.4 ha) one at Shoulsbury, on a 1,500 ft (457 m) western spur of the moor on the other side of Old Close Bottom from the Long Stone at Challacombe. Wind Hill, Countisbury is probably the most formidable defensive earthwork on Exmoor. This linear ditch is now thought to have been dug by an Iron Age invasion force which must have landed in Lynmouth Bay and constructed this earthwork to defend its tenuous position against attack from the east.

Roman influence on Exmoor was confined to excursions along the coast of the Bristol Channel, during the mid and late 1st century, and there is no evidence that the Imperial legions ventured far inland apart from slight traces of iron-working on the Brendon Hills. An often mist-shrouded square Roman 'fortlet' above the cliffs at Old Barrow just along the coast from Countisbury is one of the few reminders of their presence. Is it too far-fetched to suggest that the Wind Hill earthwork might have been constructed by the tribes to repel attacks from the legionaries of Old Barrow? It has also been suggested that it might be the site of the battle of Arx Cynuit, when Danish invaders was repelled by Odda in AD 878.

Another fortlet, which was probably a fairly temporary affair, like Old Barrow, has been excavated at Martinhoe on a height still known as The Beacon, close to the North Devon Coast Path. The Roman beacon cairn can still be seen between the two ramparts in the north-eastern corner, from where signals would have been passed to patrolling ships of the Imperial navy in the Bristol Channel 800 ft (240 m) below.

Evidence that the Roman influence never extended far inland is provided in most positive form by the Caratacus Stone, enclosed in its protective shelter just off the B3223 on Winsford Hill. The inscription, *Carataci Nepus* (kinsman of Caratacus), has been dated to the fifth to seventh century, and it is tempting to believe it commemorates a relative of the Caratacus of the Silures who so vigorously opposed the Roman

Selworthy village is largely cared for by the National Trust.

Woody Bay.

yoke before his final defeat and transportation to Rome in AD 50. Another similarly inscribed stone of about the same age is kept in the garden of Six Acres Farm, Lynton, and commemorates Cavudus, son of Civilis. It was 'rescued' after serving as a gatepost near Caffin Cross for many years.

Apart from Dunster's 11th century tower, the Norman influence is seen at Holwell Castle near Parracombe, where there is a classic and well-preserved grass-covered motte and bailey earthwork – the earliest form of castle built by the first emissaries of William the Conqueror.

The Royal Forest of Exmoor, never a tree-covered expanse in the modern sense but an open area of moor and heath preserved for Royal hunting of deer and other prey, dominated the mediaeval life of the region. Villages like Dulverton, Winsford, Exford and Dunster kept very much to the edge of the moor or the river valleys, and the harsh forest laws ensured that the deer had a more or less free run, tempting only the bravest poachers.

The laws were administered by a warden, foresters and gamekeepers, and the payment for grazing rights was made at six-monthly Swainmotes held at Hawkridge and Landacre, where a fine mediaeval bridge crosses the Barle. Latterly, as the forest laws were relaxed, up to 30,000 sheep were grazed during the summer on the moor, and the bordering commons were extensively used for growing corn.

By 1652, the freehold of the forest had been bought from the Parliamentary Commissioners by James Boevey who made the first inroads into the moorland waste by building a forester's lodge and a few enclosures at Simonsbath. Boevey's wardenship overlapped the reign of terror of the Doones by 40 years, so it is surprising that this diminutive but dynamic former London merchant does not figure in

the Doone legends, or indeed in Blackmore's famous novel.

By 1690, the Attorney General was able to describe the forest as 'a Chase, which is esteemed rather a thing of pleasure than profit . . . and what profits may arise upon this mountainous, barren and Boggy Ground are casuall and uncertaine.'

All that was to change with the advent of the Knight family who, as described earlier, made the profits of the moor much less casual and uncertain by initiating a systematic programme of reclamation.

You can still see the Knight farms like Warren Farm, on the southward-facing slopes of Dry Hill above the Exe Cleave, built from the grey moorland stone and standing four-square against the elements. They are surrounded by a network of high earthen

Tarr Steps.

Farming improvement, Brendon Hills.

banks crowned by spindly beech hedges enclosing rectangular fields carved straight from the moor.

The Knights reclaimed something like 2,500 acres (1,000 ha) of moorland, metalled over 20 miles (32 km) of roads across the moor, and created their moorland 'capital' of Simonsbath.

John Knight moved into what had been James Boevey's forester's lodge and it became the family headquarters for their great pioneering enterprise over nearly 80 years. Simonsbath, with its Knight-built church and sheltering beech wood (also planted by John Knight) is a perfect centre from which to explore the magnificent surrounding moorland scenery, particularly the barrow-studded heights of The Chains and the headwaters of the Exe and Barle.

The later prosperity of Exmoor has been founded on sheep and cattle, notably the local breeds of the Exmoor Horn, a curly horned, white-faced down sheep, and the 'Red Ruby' Devon breed of beef cattle.

Certainly, the foundations of villages like Dunster were laid by a flourishing mediaeval woollen industry, as can be seen by the sturdy, octagonal Yarn Market, built in 1609. The little township, watched over by the massive tower of the de Mohuns, once produced its own exclusive type of Kersey cloth known as 'Dunsters'.

It is both a gateway to the National Park and a centre for exploring the north coast and the little-visited, gentle Brendon Hills.

The much-photographed Yarn Market stands at the end of the broad main street near the Butter Cross, opposite the 16th century Luttrell Arms, which is said to be a former residence of the Abbots of Cleeve.

Dulverton, modern administrative headquarters of the National Park, is a well-appointed centre for the exploration of south east Exmoor and the sylvan valleys of the Exe and Barle. It was granted its Thursday market as long ago as 1306 by Edward I, and the five-arched bridge over the Barle may have been used by Lord Tennyson in 1891, when he so accurately described Exmoor as 'the land of bubbling streams'.

If the Doone Valley is your objective, Brendon, a straggling village with an oddly-isolated church, the tiny hamlet of Malmsmead, at the foot of the Badgworthy Valley, or Oare, where Blackmore set the tragically-interrupted wedding of Lorna Doone and Jan Ridd in the 15th century church, are the best centres. Oare is Mecca for Doone pilgrims in the summer months, so be warned, you are unlikely to have it to yourself.

Allerford, with its famous twin-arched packhorse

bridge and thatched schoolhouse, is an Exmoor gem, just off the A39 and handy for the rewarding ascents of the Bossington and Selworthy Beacons.

The twin villages of Lynton and Lynmouth are well-known holiday resorts, with the larger, Victorian creation of Lynton lording it over its smaller, coastal neighbour. The cliff top site of the parish church of St Mary is surely unrivalled in England and just to the west of the village lies the dramatic little Valley of the Rocks, a strangely wild place.

A cliff railway, opened in 1890, links the two towns, and takes the visitor down to picturesque Lynmouth, now thankfully largely recovered from the disastrous floods of 1952. You can see where the water came from, with such savage force, in the Glen Lyn gorge, a 40-minute walk from the town. The harbour, with its rebuilt colour-washed fishermen's cottages and Rhenish Tower, has been carefully restored, and a new deep, wide river channel now carries the flood waters safely out to sea.

Lynmouth shares the distinction with Porlock

Valley of the Rocks, Lynton.

Dunster's main street, with the castle in the background.

Weir of being the only place in the National Park where you can drive your car down to the sea wall. Porlock, the village at the foot of the infamous hill, has a church dedicated to St Dubricius, one of the many Welsh missionaries said to have crossed the Bristol Channel on improvised rafts to spread the Christian word.

Culbone, set deep in the coastal woods west of Porlock, boasts another; St Beunos is the smallest parish church in England, dates back to Saxon times and is well worth the effort of finding it in the woods which once sheltered a leper colony.

Winsford (birthplace of Ernest Bevin), Exton and Exford are all charming, thatched villages along the valley of the Exe and convenient for the highest and wildest parts of the moor to the west.

The wise visitor to this small but beautiful National Park will try to avoid the 'honeypots' of Tarr Steps, Lynmouth, Dunster and Porlock on summer weekends, and seek the *real* Exmoor on the bare moorland skylines, before it is too late.

THE PICNIC CAFE

What to do

Signpost, Brendon Hills.

HOW TO GET THERE

BY ROAD From London and the south east, the M4 motorway is the great highway to the south west, and joining the M5 from the Midlands at Junction 20 north of Bristol and turning south, the motorway network will take you as far as Bridgwater (Junction 23) or Taunton (Junction 25).

It is less fast but probably more pleasant to leave the M4 at Junction 17 (Chippenham) and join the A350 and A361 to Frome, Glastonbury and Taunton. The A30 and A303 is another quieter route from the Home Counties, and there are long-distance coach services to Taunton, Barnstaple, Ilfracombe and Minehead from most regional centres.

BY RAIL Taunton, the eastern gateway to Exmoor, is just under two hours from London (Paddington) by Inter-City express, on the Exeter/Plymouth/Penzance line.

WHERE TO STAY

The National Park authority produces its annual *Accommodation Guide*, providing a comprehensive list of places to stay, from hotels and country inns to guest houses, farmhouses (a highly recommended way to enjoy this country) and self-catering establishments. Any of the information centres listed later should

be able to provide visitors with accommodation details when they arrive, although in the summer months it is advisable to book in advance.

YOUTH HOSTELS There are youth hostels at Instow (near Barnstaple), Lynton, Exford and Minehead, and Holford and Crowcombe to the east of the National Park.

CAMPING AND CARAVAN SITES A camping leaflet is produced by the National Park, but the best plan, once again, for both campers and caravaners is to call in to a convenient information centre for the details.

PLACES OPEN TO THE PUBLIC

DUNSTER CASTLE The 11th century tower of the castle frowns over the bustling village street. The building, home of the de Mohuns and Luttrells for 800 years, has been much altered through the ages, and survived a six-month siege in 1646 during the Civil War. It was remodelled during the 19th century and is now in the hands of the National Trust.

ARLINGTON COURT Six miles south of Combe Martin on the A39, this stately Regency house stands in beautiful grounds which include a lake and heronry. It is now owned by the National Trust and includes an exhibition of horse-drawn vehicles.

PILES MILL, ALLERFORD Another National Trust property, this mill used to make 'scrumpy' – the strong cider drunk in these parts. It houses an exhibition of restored farm machinery.

CLEEVE ABBEY, WASHFORD Ruins of a 12th century Cistercian abbey, dissolved by Henry VIII and later used as a farm. Much remains to be seen, including the cloisters, refectory, chapter-house and common room. Now in the care of the Department of the Environment.

LYN AND EXMOOR MUSEUM, LYNTON Housed in St Vincent's Cottage, one of the oldest houses in Lynton, it contains an amazing variety of exhibits in a tiny space, from farm and household equipment to antique maps and prints.

WATERSMEET COTTAGE, WATERSMEET 1.5 miles (2.4 km) east of Lynmouth on the A39, this early 19th century fishing lodge is at the confluence of the East Lyn and Hoaroak Water. A National Trust property, with walks through Trust woodland to Scoresdown.

When visiting the twin villages of Lynton and Lynmouth, many visitors use the Cliff Railway, built

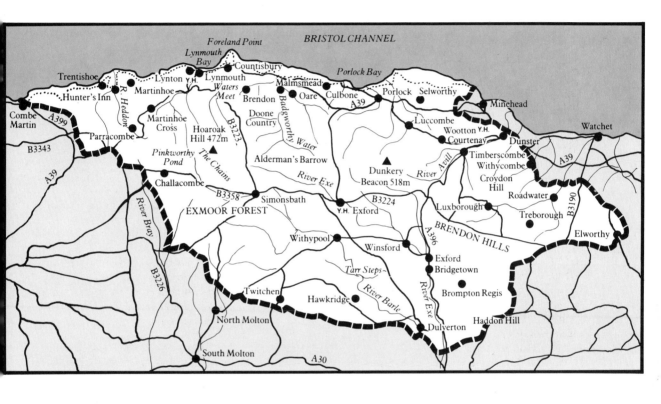

BRISTOL CHANNEL

Foreland Point

Lynmouth Bay

Countisbury

Porlock Bay

Lynton Y.H.

Lynmouth

Malmsmead

Trentishoe

Waters Meet

Oare

Culbone

Porlock

Selworthy

Hunter's Inn

Martinhoe

R. Heddon

Brendon

A39

Minehead

Combe Martin

A399

Martinhoe Cross

Doone Country

Badgworthy Water

Luccombe

Wootton Y.H.

Parracombe

Hoaroak Hill 472m

Courtenay

Dunster

Watchet

B3343

A39

Pinkworthy Pond

The Chains

B3223

Alderman's Barrow

River Exe

Dunkery Beacon 518m

River Avill

Timberscombe

Withycombe

A39

Challacombe

River Bray

B3358

Simonsbath

B3224

Croydon Hill

Roadwater

B3190

EXMOOR FOREST

Y.H. Exford

Luxborough

Treborough

B3226

Withypool

Winsford

A396

BRENDON HILLS

Elworthy

Twitchen

Tarr Steps

River Barle

Exford

Bridgetown

River Exe

North Molton

Hawkridge

Brompton Regis

Haddon Hill

South Molton

A30

Dulverton

━━━━━━━ National Park Boundary ▲ Spot Heights

──────── Road ·················· South West Peninsula Coast Path

Y.H. Youth Hostel

in 1890, which links the two, and played a vital role in rescue operations during the 1952 flood.

ANCIENT MONUMENTS

	Grid reference
Stone Circle, Porlock Common	(SS 845446)
Stone Circle, Withypool Hill	(SS 836343)
Chapman Barrows, Parracombe	(SS 696435)
Five Barrows, North Molton	(SS 733368)
Long Stone, Challacombe	(SS 705431)
Setta Barrow	(SS 726380)
Alderman's Barrow	(SS 838423)
Shoulsbury Hill Fort	(SS 706391)
Oldbury Castle Hill Fort	(SS 909282)
Bat's Castle Hill Fort	(SS 988422)
Old Burrow Roman Fort	(SS 788494)
Caratacus Stone, Winsford Hill	(SS 890335)
Holwell Castle, Parracombe	(SS 670446)
Tarr Steps, Withypool	(SS 867321)
Butter Cross, Dunster	(SS 989438)
Yarn Market, Dunster	(SS 992437)
Oare Bridge	(SS 802474)

Lorna Doone country, Badgworthy Valley.

MAPS

The one inch to one mile (1 : 63,360) Exmoor Tourist map from the Ordnance Survey is essential and is your best guide to the National Park and, incidentally, to much of central Devon also. Sheets 180 and 181 cover the Park in the 1 : 50,000 Landranger series. These two maps also show the walker rights of way in the National Park.

FURTHER READING

Allen, N V, *The Birds of Exmoor*, Exmoor Press, 1974, *o/p*.

Allen, N V, *Exmoor Handbook and Gazetteer*, Exmoor Press, 1974, *o/p*.

Blackmore, R D, *Lorna Doone*, Nelson, 1869.

Burton, S H, *Exmoor*, Hodder & Stoughton, 1969.

Coleman-Cooke, John (ed), *Exmoor National Park*, HMSO, 1970.

Grinsell, L V, *Early Man: Exmoor's Archaeology*, Exmoor National Park, 1982.

Lloyd, E R, *The Wild Red Deer of Exmoor*, Exmoor Press, 1974.

Orwin, C S, *The Reclamation of Exmoor*, David & Charles, 1971, *o/p*.

Peel, J H B, *Portrait of Exmoor*, Hale, 1970, *o/p*.

Tourists Guide to Dartmoor and Exmoor, Regional Publications, n.d.

Williamson, Henry, *Tarka the Otter*, Putnam, 1927.

Right: Packhorse Bridge, Allerford.

The Exmoor National Park authority publishes a limited, but very good, range of booklets on the Park, and those describing its excellent system of waymarked walks are particularly recommended. Other booklets, available from information offices, cover Exmoor's archaeology and the nature trails at North Hill, Minehead and Cloutsham.

DRIVING

Most visitors approach Exmoor from the east, from Taunton on the A361 turning north at Bampton on the B2222 for Dulverton. From here, the A396 follows the Exe valley north, eventually to Dunster, with views of Dunkery Beacon to the west.

The trunk road, A39, from Dunster to Minehead and on to Porlock via the notorious hill which climbs to over 1,200 ft (365 m) at the White Stones, is the best way to appreciate the coastal nature of the National Park. Its exciting switchback provides extensive views across the Bristol Channel and the wooded cleaves which run down to the sea in one direction, and across the bleak brown moors of the interior. The road runs west to Lynton and Lynmouth and then strikes inland to Parracombe.

Exmoor is well served with cross-park routes, thanks mainly to the 19th century enterprise of the Knight family. The B3224 from Wheddon Cross to Exford joins with the B3223 which runs north from Dulverton and Winsford Hill at White Cross and then runs across the moor to Simonsbath. From this centre of the real Exmoor, the B3223 runs due north over The Chains to Lynton and Lynmouth.

West from Simonsbath the B3358 runs through the ancient hunting forest to Challacombe, with plenty of convenient parking or picnic places en route.

WALKING

Exmoor is perhaps the gentlest of our ten National Parks for the walker, although that does *not* mean that the central moorland core should be underestimated. Storms can whip in with tremendous ferocity from the Bristol Channel, and damp, clinging mist can hang over the moors, combes and cleaves to baffle the most experienced navigator.

The National Park authority has pursued a vigorous footpath waymarking policy, linked with an excellent series of booklets complete with Ordnance Survey-based maps.

Summit-baggers will probably want to make first for Dunkery Beacon, at 1,704 ft (519 m) the highest point of the Park. And although by the quickest route, from Dunkery Gate on the road from Wheddon Cross, this is less than 200 yards (183 m) from the road, the views from its heather-clad summit are surprisingly rewarding, extending, according to legend, over 15 counties. Certainly it is a climb well worth making, but perhaps a better and more enjoyable route is from Webber's Post near Luccombe – via the lower slopes of Robin How – taking in the Rowbarrows, Stoke Pero Common and Stoke Pero Church (still lit by candles) on your return. (About 6.4m/10.5 km.)

The other great objective for Exmoor walkers must be the 'Lorna Doone Trail' into the so-called Doone Valley of Badgworthy Water. Most paths start from Malmsmead where the Badgworthy Water is followed south, passing Hoccombe Combe and the possible site of the Doone Gate of Blackmore's novel. There is a memorial stone to the author on this route, and a café for refreshments.

Exmoor farming country, near Oare.

For nearly 20 miles (32 km), the North Devon Coast Path – part of the South West Peninsula Coast Path – runs through the Park between Minehead and Combe Martin. From Minehead, where a number of cliff-top routes have been waymarked on North Hill, the path runs over Selworthy Beacon to Porlock and tiny Culbone Church. Hugging the well-wooded coastline the path heads west towards Countisbury Common, where other paths take the walker out to the spectacular viewpoint of Foreland Point with its lighthouse flashing across the grey waters of the Bristol Channel.

On to Lynton and the Valley of the Rocks, the path skirts the well-named and beautiful Woody Bay to descend the dramatic cleave of Heddon's Mouth. Climbing again across Trentishoe Down to the rocky coastal headlands of Great and Little Hangman the path leads down to leave the Park at Combe Martin. It can be joined or left at various points, and in places it rivals the wonderful coastal path of Pembrokeshire.

TREKKING, BOATING AND FISHING

As elsewhere, pony trekking has become a major growth industry on Exmoor (once called 'the riding playground of England') and some bridlepaths, especially on the fragile moorland soil, are beginning to suffer from overuse. One of the finest pony routes is from Lynton to Withypool via Saddle Gate and Kinsford Gate, and there is no shortage of hiring stables for the holiday maker. The National Park authority produces a special riding leaflet, as it also does for angling.

Many of the mountain streams and rivers support good stocks of brown trout, but care must be taken to ensure that fishing is not done on private waters. Salmon are caught in the lower reaches of the Exe and Barle, and there is sea fishing from Minehead, Lynmouth and Porlock.

Most of the boating opportunities are to be found at the coastal resorts of Minehead, Porlock and Lynmouth. There is canoeing on the Exe and Barle.

Useful Addresses

Exmoor National Park Offices
Exmoor House, Dulverton
Somerset TA22 9HL.
(tel. Dulverton 23665)

National Park Information Centres
(Open Easter – September)

County Gate
Near Malmsmead, North Devon.
(tel. Brendon 321)

Information Centre
Cross Street, Combe Martin
North Devon.
(tel. Combe Martin 3319)

Under Pavilion
The Esplanade, Lynmouth
North Devon.
(tel. Lynton 2509)

Information Caravan,
Dunster Steep Car Park
Dunster, Somerset.
(tel. Dunster 821835)

Other Information Offices

The Publicity Officer
Combe Martin
North Devon.
(tel. Combe Martin 3319)

The Information Office
Lee Road
Lynton
North Devon.
(tel. Lynton 2225)

Minehead and West Somerset
    Publicity Association
Market House
Minehead
Somerset.
(tel. Minehead 2624)

Information Centre
Doverhay
Porlock
Somerset.
(tel. Porlock 862427)

Brecon Beacons National Park

THE BECKONING BEACONS

Mention South Wales to most people and a picture of smoky valleys, filled by slate-grey terraces and watched over by the stark outline of whirling pithead winding gear is the one still most likely to come to mind.

This is the Wales of the Rhondda, the Wales of black-faced miners who spent most of their lives delving hundreds of feet below ground, only to emerge with joyful voices to match those of the song birds they carried underground with them.

It is also the Wales of bible-thumping non-Conformist preachers, where chapel on Sunday was an essential way of life, and where the miners were taught to lend their mighty voices to the praise of God's endless bounty. And despite the inky black hell of their everyday subterranean existence, many of those South Wales miners needed no reminders of that bounty. For perched on the grimy shoulders of the mills and mines of the South Wales coalfield was the loveliest and most spectacular mountain scenery in Southern Britain.

The Brecon Beacons have beckoned generations of people from the tightly-packed terraces of Tonypandy, Treorchy and Tredegar, not to forget Merthyr Tydfil, Aberdare and Swansea. Their bold, challenging summits represented a perfect escape from the claustrophobic confines of their working life; a chance to clear the choking, clinging coal dust from long-suffering lungs and replace it with the clean fresh air of the mountains.

The proximity of the teeming industrial conurbations of South Wales was one of the major reasons for the creation of the Brecon Beacons National Park in April, 1957. It was the last British National Park to be designated: and the long-awaited recognition of the importance of these green hills to those who valued them came six years to the day after the first National Park had been founded in the Peak District, for very similar reasons. But unlike the Peak District, the Beacons had enjoyed a long tradition of free access to their extensive common land, which still occupies 35 per cent of the total area.

The Brecon Beacons National Park covers 519 square miles (1,344 sq km) of Dyfed, Gwent, Mid-Glamorgan and Powys, and takes it name from the crowning sandstone peaks at its heart, above the township of Brecon.

The Beacons – Corn Du (2,863 ft/872 m), Pen-y-Fan (2,907 ft/886 m) and Cribyn (2,608 ft/795 m) – stand like a massive tidal wave, petrified on the point of breaking over the green, hedged lowlands of the Usk valley. Seen from the north, it is a dramatic and highly distinctive skyline, and the gently-sloping, reservoir-dotted southward dip-slopes and steep northern scarps represent one of the classic examples of this type of landform.

The imposing sweep of the sandstone scarp-face of Pen-y-Fan, russet-red strata glowing among the steep screes and green gullies, is the spectacular reward for climbers approaching from the ridge of Bryn Teg,

Left: Sgwd Clun Gwyn waterfall, Mellte valley.

Right: Memories of a forge disaster in the churchyard at Llanelly.

and presents a perfect picture of mountain majesty.

From the 'knuckles' of the upstanding flat-topped summits, four long finger-like ridges point north towards Brecon, with green, glaciated cwms in between.

But there is much more to this National Park than just the Beacons themselves. Bracketing the Beacons to the east and west are two other distinct mountain masses, both confusingly prefixed by the adjective Black.

The Black Mountain (singular), or in Welsh, Mynydd Du, in the west is a seldom visited landscape of shifting mists and remote mountain summits, where legends of the old days still exert a powerful influence.

One of the abiding folk tales of the Carmarthen Fan, as the area is usually known, is that of the Lady of the Lake, a member of the *Tylwyth Teg* (the Fair Community or Fairy People) who lived beneath the mysterious wind-flecked waters of Llyn-y-Fan Fach below the 2,460 ft (750 m) summit of Bannau Sir Gaer.

She emerged to show herself to a farm lad called Rhiwallon, who immediately fell in love with her captivating and alien beauty. The courtship progressed and eventually her fairy father agreed that the young man could marry her if he successfully selected her from his five daughters, all of whom were identically beautiful. Fortunately, the Lady of the Lake gave him a sign, and he won his bride and the dowry of as many cattle and sheep as he could count.

As always, there was a catch. If she was touched by cold iron three times (the number varies with the telling), she would return to the lake forever. The inevitable happened, and the dark-haired beauty went back beneath the cold waters, taking her dowry with her. It has been suggested that this mediaeval story is a revival of an ancient folk memory of the

arrival of the Iron Age Celts in this part of Wales, and that the Lady was a member of the older, Stone Age community.

Between the Black Mountain and the Beacons is the ancient Royal hunting ground of Fforest Fawr – a great expanse of moorland and deep woodland valleys – which today contains the important National Nature Reserve of Craig Cerrig Gleisiad, a cragbound hollow in the hills where rare arctic and alpine flowers bloom.

Beyond the Beacons and the broad valley of the Usk to the east, lie the other Black Mountains (plural), a self-contained block of sandstone hills stretching north from Abergavenny, with its twin guardians of the Sugar Loaf and Skirrid Fawr, to Hay-on-Wye.

These Black Mountains are the last bit of Wales before England; and the ancient boundary ditch of Offa's Dyke marches along their eastern crest. The

mountains' distinctive darrens, cliffed exposures rising from the valleys in long ridges, are one of their most typical features and these ridges offer magnificent walking. Below the hill, Llangorse Lake, the largest natural lake in the National Park, now suffers from overuse by powerboats, and its clear waters are gradually being polluted.

To the south of the mountain masses, where the heights drop down towards the towns of the coal field, a startlingly different landscape exists, where the rivers of the Tawe, Taf Fawr and Fechan flow through, over, and often beneath white-grey limestone.

This is the country of the caver, where some of the longest cave systems in Britain have been explored and where show caves like those at Dan-yr-Ogof offer the visitor a taste of this esoteric adventuring. Spectacular waterfalls, like those in the heavily wooded Mellte and Hepste valleys south of Ystradfellta, add another exciting element to the ever-changing scene, where the limestone gives way to a narrow belt of millstone grit.

With such a large number of visitors, most of whom just come for the day, the Brecon Beacons National Park was duty bound to cater for their interests and help them understand and enjoy their visit to the full. This was the thinking behind the setting up in 1966 of the excellent Mountain Centre near Libanus, a visitor centre which offers a pleasant introduction to the varied landscape of the National Park in a marvellous setting.

The centre, on the moorland slopes of Mynydd Illtud with fine views of the Beacons to the south, was established with financial help from the Carnegie Trust, and rivals the Lake District's Brockhole Centre in the range of activities and possibilities presented to its many thousands of visitors each year. The Craig-y-Nos Country Park serves a similar purpose in the valley of the Tawe to the south west.

The Brecon Beacons are nearer to the metropolis than most of the other National Parks, and the completion of the M4, M5 and M50 motorways and the opening of the Severn Bridge brought the Park that much closer for millions of day visitors from the south east and the Midlands. This pressure has added to that already being felt from South Wales – the Park is only 25 miles (40 km) from Cardiff and 14 miles (22 km) from Swansea.

The pressures show themselves in many of the usual ways; erosion on the too-popular paths and congestion on narrow moorland roads. But the Brecon

The Beacons from Mynydd Illtud Common.

Beacons, and especially the eastern Black Mountains, seem to suffer most from overuse by the increasingly popular pastime of pony trekking. Many popular routes are being churned into quagmires by the pounding, sure-footed hooves of the ponies, and new centres seem to spring up almost overnight in the valleys. Along some narrow roads, specially constructed pony tracks have been put in before footpaths, and the valley in which Llangorse Lake lies has become the biggest pony-trekking area in Wales, with over 20 centres in the national park.

The other serious threat to the Park appears to be another all-too-common one – commercial coniferous afforestation. The case of the Cnewr Estate in a cwm below the summit of Fan Gihirych, the highest point of Fforest Fawr, illustrates what can happen: the National Park committee was forced to accept a compromise plantation after pressure from forestry interests was backed by the Government. This area, especially in the lower valleys, is already extensively forested, and the reservoirs of the Taf Fawr and Taf Fechan complete a virtually man-made landscape.

Despite their comparatively modest altitude and southerly latitude, the Brecon Beacons are not to be underestimated. Every year people die in these deceptive mountains, even fit and capable Special Air Service commandos from the Sennybridge camp, who use the area for endurance training.

A simple stone obelisk on the shoulder of Corn Du above Lyn Cwm Llwch, reminds the modern walker of the dangers. It commemorates five-year-old Tommy Jones, who was lost on a short walk on the night of August 4, 1900, and whose body was found only after a search which attracted national concern and publicity and lasted a full month.

For little Tommy Jones, son of a miner from Maerdy in the Rhondda, the Beacon's beckoning had been fatal.

THE NATURAL LANDSCAPE: THE BRECON ALPS

When the widely-travelled Daniel Defoe passed through South Wales in his *Tour Through the Whole Island of Great Britain* in 1724, he equated the mountains of Brecon with the Alps or the Andes.

This was not a compliment. The soaring Beacons filled Defoe with unimaginable horror. 'Sometimes,' he wrote, 'we see these mountains rising up at once,

Left: The Gatehouse, Llanthony Priory.

Right: Llangorse Lake.

from the lowest valleys, to the highest summits which makes the height look horrid and frightful, even worse than those mountains abroad...' Although the Alps were much higher, he explained, they rose one behind another, 'so that the ascent seems gradual, and consequently less surprising.'

Approached from the lush, neatly-hedged pastureland of Herefordshire or the flat expanses of the Severn Estuary, the Brecon Beacons can come as a bit of a surprise. But for today's taste, the change is usually a cause for excitement, even exhilaration, as you realise that once again you have left the Lowlands behind for Highland Britain.

The most spectacular sight is still that of the north-facing scarp slopes of the Beacons themselves, one of the most distinctive hill forms in Britain and a powerful magnet to walkers from afar. The ever-changing, brilliant colours are perhaps the feature which most impresses the first-time visitor to these airy summits.

At times, they form a purple, even black backdrop to the patchwork-quilt landscape of the valley of the Usk, and at other times they glow bright rosy red or crimson in the rays of the sinking sun. And when snow cloaks their precipitous northern slopes, the horizontal strata give the impression of a gigantic sandwich cake, sliced through by some celestial knife.

The chief components of the colourful 'sandwich' are alternating layers of old red sandstone or brownstones laid down in the shallow waters or desert-like coastal plains of the Devonian period between 400 and 280 million years ago. The redness of the rocks is caused by the amount of iron oxide in them, and this is also the cause of the sometimes startlingly red marl soils which characterise the fields in the broad Usk valley.

The old red sandstones occupy most of the northern parts of the Park, which contain all the highest hills. But they are not the oldest rocks in the area, because a narrow band of Ordovician and Silurian rock runs along the Trichrug ridge between Llandeilo and Llandovery in the extreme north west.

Later, Carboniferous limestones and millstone grits were laid above the old red sandstones and earth movements compressed and buckled the area to form the large downfold in which the South Wales coalfield now lies. These younger rocks were worn away, leaving a narrow rim on the extreme southern edge of the National Park, adding a vital element to the scenic attraction of the area.

The surface of the limestone is often pitted with solution holes – funnel-like depressions where water

Carreg Cennen Castle, overlooking the Cennon valley.

Ponies on the Cwm Cynwyn bridleway.

has filtered through the porous joints of the rock to create an underground wonderland of caves and caverns for which this area is famous. And as rivers like the Mellte and Hepste – which later form the Neath – come off the impervious sandstone and on to the limestone, they dive underground in swallow holes only to re-emerge further downstream. It is a magical landscape of disappearing rivers and pearly-grey crags thrusting through lush woodlands.

As the same streams cross the next band of more resistant millstone grit, they tumble over a series of spectacular waterfalls near Pontneddfechan which have been given beautifully descriptive names by local people. Perhaps the most charming, and spectacular, is the 50 ft (15 m) Sgwd Yr Eira (fall of snow) on the Hepste a mile north of Penderyn, where a public right of way actually runs *behind* the waterfall on a ledge so broad that shepherds used to drive their flocks along it.

Another famous series is on the Mellte near Ystradfellte, where the Sgwd Clun Gwyn and Sgwd Isaf Clun Gwyn (white field falls and lower white field falls) are appropriately named because of the surrounding expanses of flat limestone pavements.

The massive natural arch of Porth-yr-Ogof (gateway of the cave) is another showplace of the limestone area near Ystradfellte. Flat, water-worn slabs lead to the vast, low-roofed cave where the Mellte vanishes underground for about 400 yards (365 m). If the river is low, and you have a torch and are sure-footed and brave enough, you can explore the cave to the underground lake. Across the pool, in the black wall of rock opposite, you may be able to pick out, in the white calcite veins, the form of a white horse, which gives the cave its other name. But do not be tempted to go further without an experienced guide – many fatalities have occurred here among those who went too far unaided.

It is far safer and probably more enjoyable to visit the well-lit and award-winning Dan-yr-Ogof (under the cave) show caverns adjacent to the Craig-y-Nos Country Park in the Tawe valley near Abercrave.

The steep-sided ravines, caves and waterfalls of the limestone area were probably cut and enlarged by powerful melt waters from the retreating glaciers of the Ice Ages. Even then the north-facing, steep scarps of the highest mountains held the greatest accumulations of ice and snow, as they do today in the harsh winters which occur here.

The classic, semi-circular cwms, which contain lakes like Llyn Cwm Llwch in Cwm Llwch below Pen-y-Fan and Corn Du in the Beacons, or Llyn-y-Fan Fach and Fawr below the Carmarthen Black Mountain scarp were gouged out by those Ice Age glaciers. The tarn-like lakes were formed when the glaciers left moraines which created effective dams to impede the escaping water. Llangorse Lake was

formed in a similar way in a shallow rock basin scooped out by the ice.

Another, more unusual Ice Age feature of the Black Mountain is a long, straight 50 ft (15 m) high ridge lying parallel to the foot of Fan Hir, which was left by a long-lasting snow bank.

Where a lake was not formed in these glacial hollows, boggy areas were often left, like the botanists' paradise of the Craig Cerrig Gleisiad National Nature Reserve, in the rocky heart of Fforest Fawr in the Nant Cwm Du valley. Here, an arctic-alpine vegetation clings to the tiered cliffs of the high, secret valley.

The north-facing cliffs are the haunt of the sinister, coal-black raven, the largest and most powerful member of the crow family. Their soaring, effortless flight almost matches the graceful, wide spirals of the Park's most typical bird of prey, the buzzard. No longer persecuted in the way they were, these majestic masters of the air can often be seen wheeling above the scarps of the Beacons or Black Mountains, their razor-sharp eyes picking out prey.

Wildlife thrives in the secret, secluded valleys of

Right: The Beacons from the valley of the Usk.

Below: Mist rises below the Beacons.

the National Park in places like the Cwm Clydach National Nature Reserve, between Gilwern and Brynmawr, where a relict beechwood supports a rich and rare flora. A rare species of whitebeam tree, relative of the rowan or mountain ash, is also found here, and other rarities of this National Park include those two small, ferocious hunters, the polecat and the pine marten.

In mediaeval Welsh law, the rich, chestnut fur of the marten could be used only on the monarch's robes. One saving grace of the ever-spreading coniferous plantations is that they may be one reason for the increase in the area of the numbers of the polecat.

MAN'S INFLUENCE: LAND OF MYTHS AND LEGENDS

Folk tales, such as the one about the mysterious Lady of Llyn-y-Fan Fach, often have a germ of truth in them. Perhaps the story was, as has been suggested, a distant folk memory of an older people who inhabited the remote valleys of the Mynydd Du. In these lonely, misty hills, legends stick, and somehow the gloomy atmosphere lends credence to them.

A similar story surrounds the reed and alder fringed expanse of Llangorse Lake, or Llyn Syfaddan as it is known in Welsh. This shallow, glacier-formed lake in the shadow of the other Black Mountains is a famous haunt of wildlife – water fowl in particular – although, today, its serenity and purity is under attack by power boats.

The story is that Llangorse Lake covers an ancient city, flooded in retribution after a local man married a noble woman from there. To gain the gold she demanded before she would wed, he killed and robbed another man, thereby bringing a curse on his family which would exact its vengeance after nine generations. The couple soon forgot the curse, but sure enough, it was fulfilled at a feast, and the city and all its inhabitants were drowned.

Tradition has it that at times the church steeple can still be seen above the waters of the lake, with a woman – the old woman of Llangorse – perched on top waiting to lure disobedient children beneath the waves.

Of course, no ancient city has been discovered in the shallow waters of Llangorse Lake. But, about a century ago, a pile of stones was discovered which, on investigation, proved to be the foundations of an artificial island, or crannog, probably dating from the New Stone or early Bronze Age. Not a city, perhaps, but the primitive huts built on wooden piles above the lake's surface must have supported a small population of lake dwellers, perhaps related to the people of the Lady of Llyn-y-Fan Fach on the other side of the National Park.

As usual, the most positive evidence we have of the earliest settlers in the Brecon Beacons are tombs, long or round cairns or barrows, situated on the hilltops. Here the leaders of the communities of the Neolithic and Bronze Ages were buried with a few simple possessions and jewellery to help them in the hereafter.

A group of stone circles, or henges, found on the western side of Fforest Fawr constitutes one of only

two Welsh concentrations of these sites, which must have served a religious or ceremonial purpose. A score of Iron Age hill forts – once occupied by a tribe known as the Silures, who gave their name to one of the oldest rock types found in the area – have also been identified in the Park. The most impressive of these, and the largest in Wales, is Carn Goch (red mound) covering 30 acres (12 ha) on a bracken-covered hill near Llangadog in the Towy valley. Castell Dinas at the head of the Rhiangoll valley is another. From these lofty vantage points, the fur-clad chieftains surveyed their lands. Chief of the Silures was the legendary resistance leader, Caratacus. He began a tradition of fierce independence against foreign aggressors which was to start with the Romans and continue against the Normans and later the English.

The great Roman regional headquarters was just outside the present 'capital' of Brecon. Known simply as Y Gaer (the fort), its typical rectangular defences were excavated by Sir Mortimer Wheeler in the 1920s and are believed to have housed a 500-

Inside Porth-yr-Ogof cave, near Ystradfellte.

strong cavalry unit recruited in far-off Spain. Y Gaer was the hub of a local network of Roman roads, such as Sarn Helen, which can still be followed as it marches across Mynydd Illtyd through Fforest Fawr to Coelbren.

During the so-called Dark Ages, most of the area of the present National Park fell into the princedom of Brycheiniog, an Irish-based dynasty which exhibited many manorial, even feudal, features. But when the yoke was felt of the Norman conquerors based in their aggressively superior stone-built castles (like those at Hay, Brecon, Trecastle, Tretower and Crickhowell) Welsh nationalism flared again. Twm Shon Catti was a kind of Welsh forerunner of Robin Hood, sheltering in the mountain fastnesses near here; and nowhere is the presence of the alien Norman invader felt more obviously than in the imposing, crag-top ruins of Carreg Cennen Castle, on the extreme west of the National Park.

Three hundred feet (91 m) above the wooded valley of the Cennen river, near Llandeilo, Carreg Cennen was built in the 12th century by Lord Rhys of nearby Dynevor. It features a 230 ft (70 m) long sloping passage cut through the living rock to a natural cave, which may have been a dungeon in the past. The castle, which was attacked by the last great Welsh resistance leader Owain Glyndwr in 1403, was finally 'slighted' by 500 Yorkists during the Wars of the Roses, using 'bars, picks and crow-bars of iron' – at a cost of £28 5s 6d!

In mediaeval times, the Breconshire landscape was dominated by Fforest Fawr, a hunting forest reserved for royalty. Among the quarry was wild boar, whose name is remembered in Cwm Twrch (valley of the wild boar) and the Afon Twrch (Boar river) in the Upper Tawe valley.

The forest, also known as the Great Forest of Brecknock, was protected by severe laws enforced by 'regarders' or rangers and was not enclosed until 1815–1819. In a way, the forest was a forerunner of the present National Park, being a protected area, although for vastly different reasons. Today's wardens are unlikely to maim or put to death offending visitors!

The romantic ruin of Llanthony Priory, an Augustinian foundation of the 12th century, is beautifully sited in the sylvan vale of Ewyas in the Black Mountains. Somewhat incongruously, it now houses the Abbey Hotel within its cloisters, and was previously the home of poet Walter Savage Landor.

Mercifully, industry has left few scars in the Brecon

Hay-on-Wye.

Beacons landscape, being mostly contained in the coalfields to the south. The promise of good money to be made in the coalfields of Dyfed did, however, lead to large-scale depopulation of some of the upper mountain valleys, where abandoned farmsteads and cottages can still be found today. Small water-powered woollen mills and charcoal-burning forges in the Clydach valley are the only major industrial incursions, and the well-restored Monmouthshire and Brecon canal, built between 1797 and 1812 to serve the small local ironworks and bring in coal from Newport, now takes pleasure cruisers 32 miles (51 km) through the National Park between Brecon and Pontypool.

The little Georgian township of Brecon is the centre of the National Park, and an excellent and convenient centre for exploring the breath-taking grandeur of the north-facing scarps of the Beacons. The County Museum is here, with the motte and bailey remains of Brecon Castle and the former priory church of St John, which became Brecon Cathedral in 1923.

Eastern gateway to the modern National Park is Abergavenny, with its surrounding highly-individual hill shapes of Blorenge, the Sugar Loaf and Skirrid Fawr and Fach. There are the ruins of a mediaeval castle and an interesting museum as well as a comprehensive range of accommodation to suit most visitors.

Hay-on-Wye, at the northern extremity of the Black Mountains, is today best-known as the country's biggest centre for second-hand bookshops. Richard Booth's book empire was formerly administered from the ruined confines of the 11th century castle, until a disastrous fire destroyed it. Hay is an important agricultural market centre, and the former cheese and butter markets are also remembered in the street names.

Crickhowell is another busy little market town on the slopes of Crucywel (or Table Mountain) above the valley of the Usk. Table Mountain is a detached block which has slipped from the main mass of Pen Cerrig Calch (literally, a limestone capped peak) and which was utilised as an Iron Age hill-top fort.

George Borrow in his wanderings through *Wild Wales* in 1862 had no hesitation in calling Llandovery 'about the pleasantest little town in which I have halted in the course of my wanderings'. The town is an ancient borough, with a 13th century shell keep, and is an ideal centre, along with Trecastle, for exploring the rarely-visited north-west corner of the National Park, which includes the myth-haunted cwms of the Mynydd Du and the Carmarthen Fans.

What to do

HOW TO GET THERE

BY ROAD The opening of the Severn Bridge and the M50 Ross Spur off the M5 has made the Brecon Beacons easily accessible from the major centres of population in London and the West Midlands. The M4 takes the motorist round Newport from where the A4042 leaves on Junction 26 to Abergavenny. From the terminus of the M50 at Ross-on-Wye, the A40 also takes the motorist through to Abergavenny and on to Brecon itself.

BY RAIL Inter-City trains from London (Paddington) go to Newport, Cardiff and Swansea. There are rail links from these major stations to Abergavenny in the east and Llandeilo, Llangadog and Llandovery in the west. The narrow-gauge Brecon Mountain Railway runs for 2 miles/3.2 km on the track of the former Brecon and Merthyr Railway from Pant station, north of Merthyr, to Pontsticill on the Taf Fechan reservoir.

Beech roots in the Clydach Gorge Nature Reserve.

WHERE TO STAY

The National Park authority publishes a comprehensive holiday accommodation leaflet, as does the Wales Tourist Board, available from its local information centres including those at Abergavenny and Brecon, where a bed-booking service operates for visitors.

YOUTH HOSTELS There are youth hostels at Ty'n-y-Caeau (Brecon), Llwyn-y-Celyn (Libanus), Ystradfellte, Capel-y-Ffin (near Llanthony) and Llanddeusant (near Llangadog).

CAMPING AND CARAVAN SITES An annually up-dated leaflet is produced by the National Park authority, with prices and facilities listed for the whole of the National Park area. Details of basic overnight camp sites can be obtained by telephoning the National Park office on Brecon 4437.

PLACES OPEN TO THE PUBLIC

MOUNTAIN CENTRE, LIBANUS An excellent introduction to the National Park, in a superb setting with magnificent views of the Beacons. There is a spacious lounge, picnic and refreshment areas and lecture rooms for visiting groups. Regular film or slide shows are given, as well as guided walks based on the centre.

CRAIG-Y-NOS COUNTRY PARK In the grounds of the former home of Adelina 'Home Sweet Home' Patti; there is water and woodland, and places to picnic and a range of summer demonstrations of country skills.

DAN-YR-OGOF AND CATHEDRAL SHOW CAVES Britain's largest and longest show caves are adjacent to the Craig-y-Nos Country Park. They have won several major tourism awards. The caves are dry and brilliantly-lit. Among the above-ground attractions are a restaurant, a geological museum and a Dinosaur Park, a great favourite with children. A recently-opened Bone Cave gives the visitor an idea of what life was like for the earliest cave dwellers.

BRECKNOCK MUSEUM, BRECON Situated in Captain's Walk, Brecon, this fascinating museum in the old county town has displays illustrating local wildlife and archaeology.

Y GAER ROMAN FORT, NEAR BRECON Part of the walls, and the foundations of some gates and towers are open to the public. The fort is of the typical,

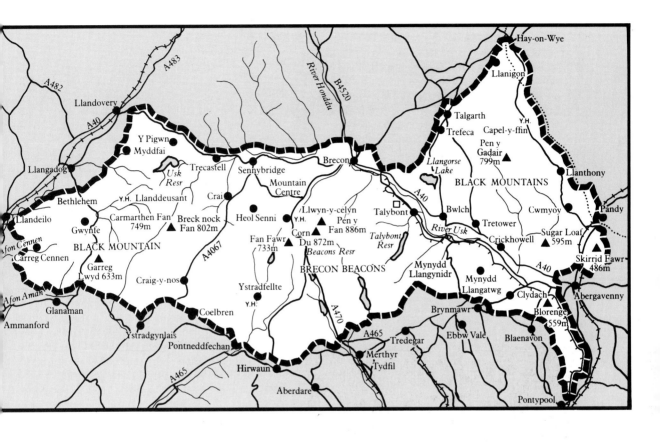

▰▰▰▰▰▰ National Park Boundary	▲ Spot Heights
—————— Road	············· Offa's Dyke Long-distance Path
⊢⊢⊢⊢⊢⊢⊢ Railway	⊢⊢⊢⊢⊢⊢ Canal
Y.H. Youth Hostel	☐ National Park Centre

rectangular plan adopted by the Romans everywhere, from Brecon to Housesteads.

LLANTHONY PRIORY This Augustinian priory, founded in 1107 by William de Lacy, is set in green meadows below the craggy slopes of Bal Mawr (1,991 ft/600 m) in the valley of the Honddu. It is the most picturesque ruin in the Park and just up the valley at Capel-y-Ffin are the pseudo-gothic remains of another religious house founded in 1870 by the eccentric Reverend Joseph Leycester Lyne, who called himself 'Father Ignatius'.

CARREG CENNEN CASTLE Certainly the most impressive castle in the Park, situated on a limestone crag high above the Cennen river, 3 miles/4.8 km southeast of Llandeilo. Most of the remains, including the rockcut passage, date from the 14th century, but such an imposing defensive site was undoubtedly used long before that. Carreg Cennen is a fascinating and awe-inspiring place.

TRETOWER CASTLE AND COURT Tretower, near Crickhowell, represents a complete record of mediaeval fortified and domestic architecture. Picard's Tower is a unique building, with a 13th century round keep inside the remains of an earlier, square structure. Close by is Tretower Court, a 14th and 15th century house which shows perfectly the transition to a more domestic style of architecture as the times became more settled and peaceful.

GARWNANT FOREST CENTRE In the Taf valley, the centre demonstrates the work of the Forestry Commission within the National Park, and has some very interesting exhibits.

ANCIENT MONUMENTS

	Grid reference
Ty-Isaf Long Barrow, Talgarth	(SO 182291)
Ty-Illtud Long Barrow, Llanhamlach	(SO 098263)
Ffostyll Long Barrows, Llaneleu	(SO 179349)
Carn Goch Hill Fort, Llangadog	(SN 690244)
Castell Dinas Hill Fort, Talgarth	(SO 179301)
Y Gaer Roman Fort, Brecon	(SO 002296)
Maen Madoc Standing Stone, Ystradfellte	(SN 919158)
Brecon Castle	(SO 042288)
Crickhowell Castle	(SO 217183)
Hay Castle	(SO 228424)
Trecastle Motte and Bailey	(SN 882292)

Above: Cast-iron bridge at Clydach Gorge.

Right: Llangasty Church, on the shore of Llangorse Lake.

MAPS

The Brecon Beacons National Park is fortunate in being largely covered by three of the Ordnance Survey's excellent Outdoor Leisure maps (1 : 25,000 scale). The three sheets cover the western area (Llandeilo and the Black Mountain), the central area (Brecon and the Beacons) and the eastern area (Abergavenny and the Black Mountains). Landranger (1 : 50,000 scale) maps, nos 146, 159, 160, 161 and 171 also cover the National Park, although most of the area is on sheets 160 and 161.

The National Park authority also produces an introductory map to the Park (scale $\frac{1}{2}$ in to 1 mile).

FURTHER READING

Barber, Chris, *Exploring the Brecon Beacons National Park*, Regional Publications, n.d.

Davies, Margaret (ed), *Brecon Beacons National Park*, HMSO, 1967.

Emlyn Evans, D, *Brecon Beacons National Park Scenery: A Geological Interpretation*, Brecon Beacons National Park, 1973.

Godwin, Fay, & Toulson, Shirley, *The Drovers Roads of Wales*, Wildwood House, 1977.

Mason, Edmund J, *Portrait of the Brecon Beacons*, Hale, 1975.

Massey, M E, *Birds of Breconshire*, Brecknock Naturalists' Trust, 1976.

Poucher, W A, *The Welsh Peaks*, Constable, 1962.

Cribin from Pen-y-Fan.

The National Park authority also publishes a wide range of cheap, specialised leaflets ranging from walks and caving, to birds, geology and guides to the towns of Brecon and Crickhowell.

DRIVING

The Brecon Beacons is well served by half a dozen good north-south roads which cross the National Park, each of which can be used to show the varied character of the main physical divisions. Perhaps the best known is the A40 which follows the Usk valley between Abergavenny and Brecon before skirting the northern edge of the Black Mountain via Senny-bridge and Trecastle to Llandovery. The A479 from Tretower to Talgarth gives tantalising glimpses of the eastern Black Mountains.

From the A465 'Heads of the Valleys' road, which forms a convenient, southern boundary between coalfield and National Park, three main routes cross the Park. The A470 from Merthyr Tydfil follows the Taf valley to the Storey Arms, a convenient starting point for the ascent of Pen-y-Fan, to Libanus and Brecon.

The A4067 from the unpronounceable Ystradgyn-lais to Sennybridge, snakes over desolate moorland between Fforest Fawr and the Black Mountain, while the A4069 crosses the western heights of the Black Mountain between Brynaman to Llangadog.

WALKING

The National Park authority runs an extensive pro-gramme of guided walks led by part or full-time wardens during the summer months. They start from popular locations such as Llanthony Priory or the Mountain Centre, and are an ideal introduction to the beauties of the country as interpreted by an expert.

Perhaps the best excursion in the Black Mountains starts from Llanthony and follows the right of way eastwards to the ridge along which runs the Offa's Dyke long distance path. Follow the scarp along this ancient boundary – constructed by the King of Mercia in the 8th century to mark the division be-tween his kingdom and Wales – to Hay Bluff, return-ing along the long ridge on the western site of the

Honddu valley to Cwm Bwchel and back to your car at Llanthony. A shorter walk is the ascent of Skirrid Fawr or Holy Mountain, outside Abergavenny, from Crowfield on the B4521 (2.5 miles/4 km).

The classic ascent of the Beacons themselves goes up from Bailea to the north and climbs the grassy, eroded spur of Bryn Teg to Cribyn with its breath-taking views of the precipices of Pen-y-Fan. Take the path to the reigning summit and, if you are still feeling fit, go down to the col known as Arthur's Seat to ascend Corn Du, the westernmost Beacon.

Return via the Cefn Cwm Llwch ridge, with the glacial tarn of Lyn Cwm Llwch nestling like a glittering sapphire in the cwm below. This is a long and strenuous walk, and should be attempted only in good weather and with the right equipment.

CLIMBING, CAVING, TREKKING AND BOATING

Most of the rock climbing in the Brecon Beacons is on the southern limestone, where quarry faces have produced some exacting routes. The generally loose and friable nature of the brownstones and sandstones of the main mountain masses makes them unsuitable for climbing.

The limestone area is also a Mecca for cavers or pot-holers. It is one of the richest areas for caving in the country, with the deepest and longest systems yet found in Britain. Most visitors, however, will be content with the excellent show caves of the Tawe valley.

Boating, canoeing and sailing take place on the British Waterway Board's Brecon-Pontypool canal (one of the few to go through any of our National Parks) or on the River Usk at Brecon, or else on Llangorse Lake.

There are swimming pools at Abergavenny, Brecon and Sennybridge, and the rivers at Brecon and Hay are also sometimes used, but this use of the reservoirs is frowned upon by the water authorities.

A licence is required for fishing in the salmon rivers of the Usk and Wye, and in the reservoirs or at Llangorse Lake.

USEFUL ADDRESSES

The Brecon Beacons National
   Park Office
6 Glamorgan Street
Brecon
Powys, LD3 7DP.

(tel. Brecon 4437)

NATIONAL PARK INFORMATION CENTRES
(Open April–September)

Watton Mount
Brecon, Powys LD3 7DF.

(tel. Brecon 4437)

Monk Street
Abergavenny
Gwent NP7 5NA.

(tel. Abergavenny 3254)

Broad Street
Llandovery
Dyfed SA20 0AR.

(tel. Llandovery 20693)

The Mountain Centre
Near Libanus
Brecon
Powys LD3 8ER.

(tel. Brecon 3366)
(Open daily, except Christmas day)

Danywenallt Study Centre
Talybont-on-Usk
Brecon
Powys LD3 7YS.

(tel. Talybont-on-Usk 677)

Wales Tourist Board
Brunel House
2 Fitzalan Road
Cardiff CF2 1UY.

(tel. Cardiff 499909)

Forestry Commission Information Centre
Garwnant
Near Merthyr Tydfil.

(tel. Merthyr Tydfil 3060)

Pembrokeshire Coast National Park

A PLACE APART

Pembrokeshire thrusts out its clawed hand into the blue, storm-wracked Celtic Sea; the last windswept outpost of Wales and the first landfall for seabirds and invaders.

It is a land of sharp contrasts, from dizzy cliffs to secluded, sandy coves – known for good reason as havens – and from wild tumuli-studded moorland heights to deep estuaries winding inland for many miles where ancient oakwoods tumble down to the water's edge.

That most poetic of languages, Welsh, had a special description for this land where the sea dominates. In *The Mabinogion*, an 11th century collection of Welsh folk legends, it is known as *Gwlad hud a lledrith* – the land of magic and enchantment.

But perhaps the landscape's greatest protagonist was a widely-travelled and much-quoted Welshman of Norman stock who knew the area like the back of his hand. Giraldus Cambrensis (Gerald the Welshman) was born at Manorbier Castle on the south coast in about 1146 – a spot he described as 'the most delectable in Wales'.

Gerald's *Itinerary through Wales*, written in 1188, not only provides us with a vivid picture of the principality as it was in the late 12th century, but also establishes Gerald's love for his own homeland.

'Penbroch [Pembroke]', he wrote, 'is the finest part of the province of Demetia. And Demetia [Dyfed] is the most beautiful part of Wales.' Those generations of visitors and tourists who have made Pembrokeshire a popular holiday destination over the past 200 years, have shared Gerald's unequivocal views on the attractions of this land, where history and legend are often inseparable.

The fact that Pembrokeshire – in its new 'super-county' of Dyfed, once again reverting to its ancient name – is different, a place apart, was illustrated by its designation, in February, 1952, as the fifth British National Park.

It is also the smallest (225 square miles/583 sq km)

Strumble Head from Garn Fawr.

and the only one which is predominantly coastal in its scenery – a strange fact for a small island like Britain.

Indeed, when people think of Pembrokeshire today, it is usually the incomparable 230 mile (370 km) serrated coastline which springs to their minds. The 168 mile (270 km) Pembrokeshire Coast long distance path, which opened in 1970, threads its tortuous but spectacular route along this fine and varied shore, and is undoubtedly the best way to get to know the National Park.

The influence of the sea is ever present. Nowhere in this mainly linear National Park is more than 10 miles (16 km) from the sea, and most of it is only 3 miles (5 km) from the tang of salt water.

There are two major inland incursions in the National Park's boundary, taking in two widely-contrasting landscapes quite different from the coastline.

The area known as Daugleddau takes in the drowned estuaries of the two Cleddau (Western and Eastern), the Carew and the Cresswell rivers.

The National Park authority appropriately calls this sector 'the inner sanctuary', and it certainly has a secret, secluded nature. Small, intimate communities, many with a fascinating industrial history, nestle along the well-wooded river banks, and the extensive reed banks and mudflats are in sharp contrast to the sea cliffs of the coast.

All the rivers flow into the broad natural harbour of Milford Haven which is excluded, like Pembroke, from the National Park because of its heavy industry based on the many oil refineries and associated works.

The other major inland area of the National Park is the Presely Hills, a self-contained moorland block in the north of the Park, rising to a 1,760 ft (536 m) summit, Foel Cwm Cerwyn, above Bryberian.

These wild moorland heights – which are increasingly suffering from the blight of insensitive forestry plantations – were the home of prehistoric man. A glance at the map shows the tell-tale signs of stone circles, cromlechs (tombs) and hill forts.

However, the Presely Hills are best remembered by the historian as the source of the famous 'blue stones'

Cat Rock and Dinas Head from Careg Germain, Newport Sands.

which form the inner circle of the most celebrated prehistoric monument in Britain – Stonehenge on far-off Salisbury Plain.

How they got there, whether by a prodigious feat of prehistoric engineering or by the carrying force of a long-forgotten glacier, no one really knows but there is no doubt Stonehenge's 'foreign' stones originated from the rocky, eastern coast of the Presely at Carn Meini.

The rounded, rolling moors of Presely are a blaze of royal-hued heather and golden gorse in the late summer, echoing the brilliant colours of the coastal cliff tops.

Here in spring and early summer the ground is smothered in a carpet of wild flowers – sea campion, thrift, vetches and celandines – making it almost a crime to walk on such beauty.

The kind, oceanic climate, warmed by the gentle influence of the Gulf Stream and a sunshine and rainfall record unequalled in Wales, makes the Pembrokeshire Coast a rival to the holiday hot-spots of England's south coast 'Riviera'.

But while most of the human visitors flock to the popular holiday haunts of Tenby, Saundersfoot, Fishguard, St David's and Poppit Sands, many thousands of other visitors seem to have even more trouble finding a place to enjoy the sun on the sea cliffs.

These visitors are, of course, the vast flocks of sea birds which find the temperate climate ideal for breeding and nesting. The Pembrokeshire Coast is justly famous among ornithologists for its amazing variety and abundance of sea birds, which seem to nest or roost on every available crevice and ledge on the cliffs, sea-stacks and off-shore islands, many of which are bird reserves. A good reason, at least, for the Pembrokeshire Coast National Park authority to choose the dumpy razorbill as its emblem.

Overcrowding is also a problem in the human centres of the Park, especially where caravan sites have been allowed to spread in unsightly ranks across the cliff tops.

The National Park authority estimates there are about 150,000 holiday-makers and 8,000 day-trippers in the Park on an average August day. That is about six times the number of full-time residents.

But the one million tourists who come annually contribute something like £20 million to the local economy, which still depends largely on agriculture, with arable and dairy farming predominating. As tourism is a trend which can only increase, this is a fact of life which will have to be faced, while always bearing in mind the interests of the people who live in this relatively densely-populated area.

One of the finest stretches of limestone sea-cliff scenery in Britain, from St Govan's Head to Linney Head, is barred to the public as it lies in the Castlemartin Artillery Ranges. The ranges, among the most important NATO training areas in Europe, cover 5,880 acres (2,390 ha) and include many interesting historic sites inland, and sea stacks, blow holes and caves on the coast.

Access to the charming little chapel of St Govan's is sometimes restricted, and visitors should refer to the posted times of live firing before entering this area. It is quite dangerous enough to walk too close to these vertiginous cliff tops, without getting one's head blown off in the process!

With the presence of modern industry, in the shape of the enormous supertankers which are a common backdrop to views from the south coast, and the obtrusive military occupation of Castlemartin Artillery Ranges, the Park can never be said to be immune from the ravages of the 20th century.

The Three Chimneys, Marloes Sands.

77

THE NATURAL LANDSCAPE: SHAPED BY THE SEA

Despite the fact that it contains some of the finest coastal scenery and sea cliffs in Britain, the predominant horizon of the Pembrokeshire Coast is flat.

A broad plateau covers most of the National Park at an average height of 200 ft (60 m) above the sea. This platform dominates the whole Pembrokeshire peninsula – with the exception of the higher block formed by the Presely Hills – but it is regularly indented by steep-sided river valleys which snake inland for several miles.

This famous 200 ft (60 m) erosion surface, the planed-off top surface of the land, was formed about 17 million years ago at the beginning of the period geologists know as the Pliocene.

The powerful agent responsible for smoothing off the Pembrokeshire landscape is the one which formed so much of it in the first place – the sea. In those long-distant days the sea level was 200 ft (60 m) higher than it is today and the waves cut across the surface of the land.

As the sea level began to fall (about two million years ago), the wave-cut platforms were revealed. Rain fell, and new river valleys were cut through the platform, to form the deep gorges of places like the Gwaun valley, Nevern, Alan and Solva.

The next major shaping effect on the ancient landscape happened about 15,000 years ago, only yesterday on the vast geological time scale, as the great ice caps of the Ice Age melted, once again raising the sea level and drowning the newly formed river valleys far inland.

So were formed the classic *rias* or drowned valleys, seen today in the wonderful natural harbours of Milford Haven, and, on a much smaller scale, Solva Harbour to the south of the St David's peninsula. Subsequent drownings of the densely-wooded land surface are graphically illustrated by the weird, fossilised landscape of the submerged forests of the Pembrokeshire Coast, revealed occasionally at places like Amroth, Saundersfoot, Manorbier, Freshwater, Newgale, Abermawr and Newport, at low water, especially after winter storms.

But what of the rocks which formed the land? They range from the earliest Pre-Cambrian system – formed at the very dawn of the Earth, when the molten ball at last began to cool – to the familiar coal measures and limestones of the Carboniferous period, laid down a mere 250 million years ago.

Those 'older-than-time' Pre-Cambrian rocks, dated at between 2,000 and 3,000 million years old, predominate around the St David's peninsula. And the pale lilac walls of the beautiful little cathedral of the Province's patron saint are partly constructed of this stone, as is the adjoining ruined Bishop's Palace. Pre-Cambrian rocks also form the ridge between Roch and Treffgarne and the cliffs of Goultrop.

Much of the northern half of the National Park is Ordovician, up to 500 million years old, left by an ancient ocean and then disrupted by volcanic forces which formed the hard, upland blocks of Pencaer and Presely, Carn Llidi and the island of Ramsey.

Considerably more recent depositions left the old red sandstone, coal measures and limestones of the southern coast, leaving a distinct, South-East/North-West boundary which, as we shall see, had such an effect on the course of human history in this area.

The great geological joy of the National Park and, after all, the primary reason for its designation, is its incomparable coastline. The contortions of primeval earth movements are graphically illustrated in the folded strata seen in such places as the coast of Dinas Island, Pan-yr-Afr, near Cemais Head, Glenbeach at Saundersfoot, and in the classic up-ended ribs of the Three Chimneys, rising vertically like the buttresses of a cathedral from the beach at Marloes.

The sea still has not finished its architectural shaping of the landscape, and there are spectacular examples of coastal erosion all along the coast path. Perhaps the most famous formation is the Green Bridge of Wales, a huge, soaring natural arch of limestone jutting out from the cliffs of Flimston Down on the south coast. Eventually, this spectacular feature will collapse, and form tooth-like sea stacks like those of the nearby Stack Rocks and Elegug Stacks. Blow-holes (where sea-level cave roofs have collapsed and where the surging storm waves can shoot spray up to 40 ft/12 m in the air), caves, rocky headlands and golden beaches, like those at Newgale, Freshwater and Marloes, bring a never-ending variety to this finest of all coast paths.

Usually the only residents of the largely inaccessible sea stacks are the sea birds, for which the Pembrokeshire Coast is justly famed. Several of their nesting sites are protected areas, accessible only by permit, and even the hard men of rock-climbing, who enjoy dangling precariously above the pounding waves, respect the birds' nesting season by a self-imposed ban.

The great gannet colony of Grassholm, 12 miles off the west coast, is reckoned to be one of the biggest in the world, and is an important RSPB reserve. With

Across Raggle Rocks, Marloes, towards Gateholm Island.

a breeding population of more than 20,000 birds, the total, counting youngsters, can be as many as 60,000.

The tiny, rock-bound island often appears to have a white 'halo' when viewed from the mainland in late summer, as the thousands of gannets wheel and cry endlessly above its craggy cliffs.

Watching the creamy-white gannets feed is one of the most spectacular sights in nature, as they plummet vertically in a 100 foot power-dive into shoals of herring, folding their 6 ft (1.8 m) wings at the very moment of impact.

Storm petrels – the sailor's 'Mother Carey's Chickens' – nest on the island of Skokholm, alongside 35,000 pairs of Manx shearwaters, in a West Wales Naturalists' Trust reserve which was the first bird observatory in Britain.

Boat trips run from Dale, Marloes, and Solva on the mainland take many hundreds of binocular-armed birdwatchers out to the famous National Nature Reserve of Skomer, off the Dale-Marloes peninsula.

The 722 acre (292 ha) island supports one of the finest seabird colonies in Europe, with the elegant, gliding fulmars sharing cliffspace with shags, kittiwakes, razorbills, herring and great and lesser black-backed gulls. There is also a 100,000 strong colony of the mainly nocturnal Manx shearwater, and the island is also home to a British rarity, that elegant crow, the red-beaked-and-legged chough. Puffins and shearwaters nest in burrows, often ones vacated by rabbits. The absence of the birds from the mainland and Ramsey is thought to be entirely due to the presence of rats.

All round the shores, the sinister, almost reptilian black shape of the cormorant is seen much more often than its close relative, the shag.

Ramsey Island, off St David's, is a favourite breeding ground for the grey seal. It is the birthplace of about 200 white-furred, liquid-eyed pups every year, and tagging has shown that these creatures may swim as far as Ireland, Brittany or Spain within a few months of their birth in Pembrokeshire. A worrying factor has been the excessive amount of effluent poison found in their blubber in recent years, due to industrial pollution.

The clear, translucent waters of the Pembrokeshire Coast allow the careful observer ample opportunity to see these clumsy land mammals in their true element of the sea, where they display a grace of movement which belies their bulk.

Elegug Stacks, near St Govan's Chapel.

St Govan's Chapel.

MAN'S INFLUENCE: THE GREAT DIVIDE

Both the last successful and the last unsuccessful invasions of Britain left their mark on the face of Pembrokeshire.

William of Normandy's all-conquering expedition which began in 1066, the date that every school-child remembers, was directly responsible for the main social division in the county and the National Park.

North of a line running from the Brandy Brook at Newgale in the west to Amroth in the east, the language generally spoken today is Welsh. The farms and place names are Welsh and even the architecture of the buildings and churches have a spartan 'Welshness' about them. Headlands on the coast are 'pens' and estuaries are 'abers'.

South of the line, which some historians have dubbed the 'landsker' or 'landscar' from the Norse word for frontier, there is an equally definite English feel to the country, with English being the most common language. The farms and settlements have anglicised names, and the churches have English-looking square towers. On the coast here, bays are 'havens' and headlands are 'points'.

The ancient boundary is marked by a line of military frontier castles, from Llanstephan in the south east, through Laugharne, Narberth, Llawhaden, Wiston and Haverfordwest, to Roch overlooking St Bride's Bay in the north west.

Spreading out from their strategic base at Pem-broke, the Norman warlords quickly consolidated their gains with this line of fortresses – and effectively split the county into two. To the north of the line lay the harder, older rocks of St David's, and the harsh mountains of Presely. And here the Celtic Welsh retreated, taking their customs, tradition and language which can still be observed nine centuries later.

The south became 'Little England beyond Wales', a kinder, softer and more fertile land, more akin to the West Country than the wild mountains of the Principality.

It is said that the division between the 'Englishry' and the 'Welshry' was so strong at one time that if a girl married across the landscar she would never be received back on her own side again.

The Normans built over fifty castles in Pembroke-shire, an indication of the need to subdue an obdurate native population. Today the castles are a popular tourist attraction, especially the ruins of Tenby Castle, Manorbier Castle – which is often compared with the Crusader castles of the Middle East – Newport, Nevern, Picton, romantic Carew and Upton – the grounds of which are now maintained by the National Park authority. Splendid castles just outside the Park boundary exist at Cilgerran, Haverfordwest, Pembroke and Roch.

The other, farcically unsuccessful invasion took place on February 22, 1797, at Carreg Wastad, a small headland below the hamlet of Llanwnda just outside the present National Park boundary near Fishguard.

A motley army of 1,400 men, mainly convicts from French prisons, commanded by the Irish-American General William Tate, landed with 100 rounds of ammunition per man and four days food, with the intention of marching to Chester and Liverpool as a diversion timed with a rebellion in Ireland. Unfortunately for them, this ill-assorted rabble chanced on a shipload of wine recently wrecked (a lucrative local pastime) and were in no fit state to defend themselves when the Pembroke Company of Gentlemen and Yeomanry Cavalry advanced. Two days later, the 'landing of the French' was over with an unconditional surrender at nearby Goodwick Sands, where a pub now proclaims the fact. The Pembroke Yeomanry has to this day worn the name of Fishguard as a battle honour, the only British regiment to carry an honour won on British soil.

The French and Normans were only the last two in a succession of invaders who found the natural harbours and sandy coves of the Pembrokeshire Coast tempting ports of call.

Looking south-west towards St David's Head from Pwllderi.

The first were probably Stone-Age cave dwellers and Mesolithic flint chippers who left their detritus at many sites along the coast, notably on the Nab Head, near Dale and on the banks of the Nyfer at Newport.

The first Neolithic farmers probably came ashore in simple wood-and-skin boats not unlike the coracles still seen at Cilgerran on the Teifi, and, although it is hard to trace where they lived, no one can be in any doubt as to where they buried their leaders. The cromlechs or burial tombs of these long-dead chieftains are one of the most impressive features of the historic landscape of Pembrokeshire. It is interesting to speculate that some so honoured may have been the masterminds behind the transportation of the Presely bluestones 180 miles (290 km) to Stonehenge.

The best known cromlechs are at Pentre Ifan, on the northern slopes of Presely, where an enormous, 16 ft (4.8 m) capstone is supported with amazing grace by three, 7 ft (2.1 m) uprights, and at Carreg Samson (the grave of Sampson's finger) longhouse above the cliffs at Abercastle, where the capstone weighs 12 tons. These stones are really only the skeletons of the tombs, which were originally covered in a mound of earth and stones which has weathered away over the past 5,000 years.

The Presely was also the home of the first metal-users of the Bronze Age, and their round cairns can be seen on the bald, rocky hilltops of Foel Drygarn, and at Crugiau Cemais, on a knoll above the Nevern valley. Many are found along prehistoric ridgeways, like the Fleming's Way (named after mediaeval immigrants) across the Preselys from St David's, and the Ridgeway in the south from Angle through Pembroke to Penally.

Scattered at regular intervals along the coast are the Iron Age hillforts often known locally as 'raths'. This is an Irish word and found nowhere else on the mainland but Pembrokeshire, perhaps indicating the strength of the trading ties between the two cultures on either side of the Irish Sea. In the northern, Welsh area they are known as 'castells' and perhaps the best example is the so-called 'Warrior's Dyke' which separates the promontory of St David's Head from the mainland. Carn Ingli, above Newport, and Foel Drygarn in the Preselys are more typical, isolated hill top examples.

Pembrokeshire is one of the few parts of Britain which escaped major Roman influence, but in the 5th and 6th centuries, the Age of the Saints, the early missionaries of the Celtic Church spread their gospel all along this coast. Where they made their

Above: Carew Castle.

Right: Bishop's Palace and Cathedral, St David's.

landfall, the site was usually marked by a chapel. So we find places like the cell of St Govan's Chapel, reached down a steep stairway through the limestone cliffs near Bosherston, and the group of chapels; St Patrick's, St Justinian's and St Non's, around the spiritual capital and cathedral city of St David's.

Dewi Sant, or St David, is of course the Patron Saint of Wales, and he founded his tiny cathedral at Glyn Rhosyn on the St David's peninsula in the 6th century.

So important was St David's as a place of pilgrimage during the Middle Ages that two pilgrimages here were deemed to be equal to one to Rome. The present cathedral, on the site of St David's monastery, was built about 1180 and the adjoining Bishop's Palace in 1340. The town, smallest city in Britain, still retains its town walls and the Porth-y-Twr gate.

The tiny church, one of the finest in Wales, was built to be out of sight of the marauding Viking sea raiders, but this did not prevent it from being attacked no fewer than ten times.

The Vikings are remembered, appropriately for such brilliant seafarers, in the names they gave the small islands, or *holms* as they knew them. Thus we have Skokholm, Grassholm and Gateholm, while

Grey seals are often seen off the coast.

Ramsey, Caldey and Skalmey (Skomer) include the *oy* element which refers in Norse to a larger island. *Vik*, which means a bay with a safe anchorage, is found in Goodwick, Musselwick and Gelliswick; and Dale, a common name here as elsewhere for a valley, is also pure Norse.

After the days of the Norman 'Great Divide', Pembrokeshire settled down to a busy mediaeval period of trading with the people of almost every cove and haven trading some commodity across the Bristol Channel, the Irish Sea or to the coasts of Europe. Many lime kilns, like the carefully-restored examples at Porth Clais, near St David's, sprang up to make lime to fertilise the soils of the area, and collieries, especially in the Saundersfoot area, exploited the high quality anthracite found in the southern coal measures.

Today's industry is concentrated on farming, and the mild climate and fertile soils make Pembrokeshire's early potatoes, grown mainly in the Dale-Marloes peninsula, justly famous. Tourism is increasingly important; and thousands are also employed in the giant Milford Haven refineries and in the oil port – the largest in Britain.

Tenby (population 5,000), is not only the largest town in the Pembrokeshire Coast National Park, it is the largest in any of the National Parks of Britain. A traditional holiday destination since Dr John Jones of Haverfordwest first promoted its health-giving sea waters in 1781, its colour-washed Regency houses and castle-topped hill manage to retain their charm and character despite the many visitors.

Tenby is a fine centre for exploring the south, and the embarkation point for monastery-topped Caldey Island, famous for its perfumery.

The real 'capital' of the National Park, Haverfordwest, actually lies outside the boundary. Its busy trading past, at the tidal limit of the Western Cleddau, is reflected in the name of the quayside inn, *The Bristol Trader*, and in the fact that the Mayor is still known as the Admiral.

Another fine centre just outside the Park boundary is Pembroke, with one of the best preserved castles in a land of castles. Henry Tudor, later Henry VII, was born here, and the circular keep is one of the finest in Wales. Fishguard, where the harbour was blasted out of the rock to provide a terminus for the 'greyhounds of the Atlantic' but which now only takes the Irish cross-channel ferry, is ideally placed for exploration of the northern coast and the Presely Hills.

St David's may be the smallest city in Britain, but it is also one of the most charming. It is still a place of pilgrimage for many homecoming Welshmen, for whom it is simply Ty Ddewi – the house of David. Boats go from here round the bird-filled cliffs of Ramsey Island across the treacherous tide races of Ramsey Sound.

The popular golden sands of Saundersfoot were only 'discovered' by tourists relatively recently, and the fine little harbour which is now thronged by pleasure craft of all descriptions, was originally constructed for the export of coal from the mines of Begelly, Kilgetty and Stepaside. The coal mines are all closed now, but walkers on the Pembrokeshire Coast Path still use the narrow-gauge railway track – including tunnels – built to get the coal to the sea.

The Harbour, Tenby.

86

What to do

HOW TO GET THERE

BY ROAD The M4 now brings visitors to within an hour of the National Park, and as it snakes ever westwards, the Park will become even more accessible to motorists using the motorway network. The main artery inside the Park is the A40 Carmarthen-Haverfordwest-Fishguard road, with the A477 going south to Pembroke and the A487 reaching out to the St David's peninsula.

BY RAIL Inter-City services go from London (Paddington) as far as Swansea, from where local lines go to Carmarthen through to Fishguard and Haverfordwest.

WHERE TO STAY

The Wales Tourist Board publishes an annual *Where to Stay in Wales* guide, and separate local accommodation guides are produced by the tourist associations of Haverfordwest and St Bride's Bay, St David's and District, Fishguard and Goodwick and District, Tenby and South Pembrokeshire, and Saundersfoot Chamber of Trade. The tourist information centres at Kilgetty (tel. Saundersfoot 813672/3), Cardigan (tel. Cardigan 3230), Fishguard (tel. Fishguard 873484), Haverfordwest (tel. Haverfordwest 66141) and St David's (tel. St David's 392) also have up-to-date details of available accommodation, and operate a bed-booking service.

YOUTH HOSTELS All conveniently sited on the coast for the long-distance path walker, at Poppit Sands (St Dogmael's), Pwllderi (Strumble Head), Trefin, Whitesand, St David's, Broad Haven, Marloes and Pentlepoir.

CAMPING AND CARAVAN SITES As already mentioned, the Pembrokeshire Coast is over-endowed with caravan parks, which tend to get overcrowded in the summer. Camp sites are also fairly plentiful, but it is always best, in the summer season, to get advice and information from the nearest tourist information centre. These are given later.

PLACES OPEN TO THE PUBLIC

TUDOR MERCHANT'S HOUSE, TENBY Tucked away in one of the many backwaters of Tenby, this 15th century building is now a museum and in the care of the National Trust.

THE MUSEUM, CASTLE HILL, TENBY Part of the living quarters of the 13th century Tenby Castle, which stands on a headland 'which the sea peninsulateth'. The museum, founded in 1878, is very popular, and a visit should be combined, if possible, with an exploration of the Five Arches, the only remaining gate of the old walled town.

MAÑORBIER CASTLE A splendidly-sited, 12th and 13th century castle, on a low promontory overlooking the blue waters of Manorbier Bay. The birthplace of Gerald de Barri, alias Giraldus Cambrensis (Gerald the Welshman) it is an impressive sight when viewed from the beach.

ST GOVAN'S CHAPEL Reminiscent of the tiny chapels of the West of Ireland, St Govan's is romantically situated in a cleft in the limestone cliffs near Bosherston. But access is limited to certain times only (check with information centres) because of the military use of the adjacent Castlemartin ranges. The chapel was once believed to have been the cell of St Gawaine.

ST DAVID'S CATHEDRAL/BISHOP'S PALACE The ancient town gate, Porth-y-Twr, leads to what has been described as 'the finest church in Wales'. The bones of St David and St Justinian are believed to be buried in these purple, pinnacled walls. A special delight are the 'joyously irreverent' misereres (misericords) carved in the choir stalls by a 15th century craftsman with an evident sense of humour. Early Christian monuments include one to Hedd and Isaac, sons of Bishop Abraham who was killed by Viking raiders in 1080. The roofless Bishop's Palace, arcaded and still impressive, stands in the close to the west of the cathedral.

PICTON CASTLE Near Haverfordwest, this castle has been in the Phillips family since the 15th century and has been extensively restored from its 14th and 15th century shell in recent years. It is probably best known today for its collection of Graham Sutherland paintings, housed in a separate range of buildings. Sutherland found much of his inspiration in the Pembrokeshire countryside.

CAREW CASTLE An impossibly romantic ruin on the Carew estuary, sometimes regarded as the most beautiful castle in the county. It dates from about 1270 as a

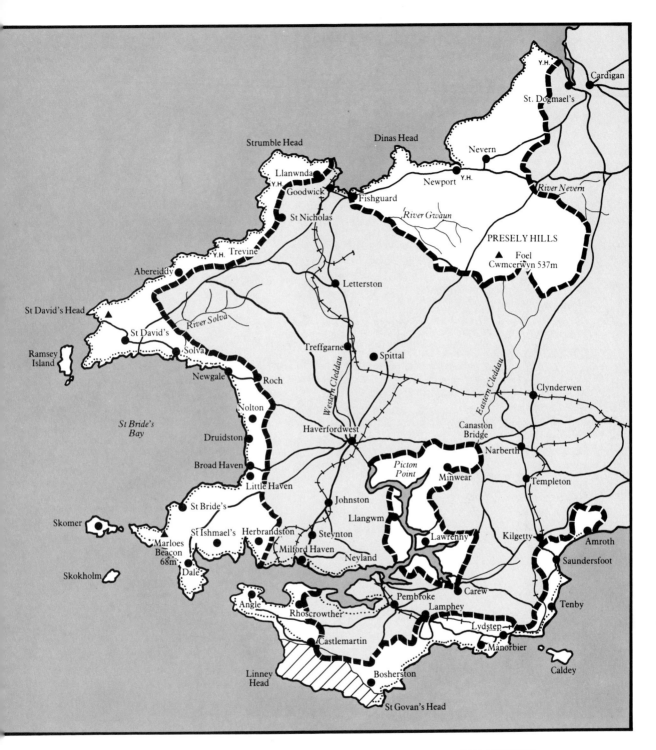

simple rectangle with massive round corner towers. But the mullioned windows and oriels, which were inserted in the 16th century, show how fortresses were later converted into homes.

CAREW FRENCH MILL Recently restored by the National Park authority, this tidal corn mill is now a museum and in some ways is similar to the East Anglian mills which also relied on the tides. A nearby picnic site is convenient for both castle and mill.

CALDEY ABBEY, CALDEY ISLAND Thousands of Tenby-based holidaymakers make the short boat trip to Caldey Island to visit the Cistercian abbey and Norman priory church. The whitewashed, pantiled roofed abbey has a definite French feel about it, and the monks' manufacture of scent is famous.

Just outside the Park, but musts for visitors to the region, are the historic town of Pembroke, with its splendid round-keeped castle and town walls; the county town of Haverfordwest, headquarters of the National Park and home of the County Museum and Records Office (appropriately sited in the 13th century castle); and the coracle centre of Cilgerran, with its own mighty castle above the Teifi.

ANCIENT MONUMENTS

	Grid reference
Pentre Ifan Cromlech	(SN 099370)
Carreg Samson Cromlech	(SM 848335)
Devil's Quoit Cromlech	(SM 886008)
Crugiau Cemais Burial Cairns	(SN 125414–126417)
Warrior's Dyke Camp, St David's	(SM 722279)
Carn Ingli Hill Fort, Newport	(SN 062372)
Foel Drygarn Fort	(SN 157336)
Nevern Cross	(SN 081400)
Solva Lime Kilns	(SM 804241)

MAPS
Ordnance Survey 1 : 50,000 Landranger maps, nos 145 (Cardigan), 157 (St David's and Haverfordwest) and 158 (Tenby) cover the National Park at a scale of about $1\frac{1}{4}$ in to the mile.

Unfortunately, there is no $2\frac{1}{2}$ in to the mile Outdoor Leisure map covering the area although 1 : 25,000 sheets are available.

Heather, gorse and thyme, Cemaes Head.

FURTHER READING
Barrett, John H (ed), *The Pembrokeshire Coast Path*, HMSO, 1974.

John, Brian, *Pembrokeshire*, David & Charles, 1976.

Miles, Dillwyn (ed), *Pembrokeshire Coast National Park*, HMSO, 1973.

Owen, T R, *Geology Explained in South Wales*, David & Charles, 1973.

Pembrokeshire Coast National Park Handbook, The, Pembrokeshire Coast National Park, 1981.

Rees, Vyvyan, *Shell Guide to South West Wales*, Faber, 1963.

Saunders, David, *Birds of Pembrokeshire*, Five Arches Press, 1976.

The National Park authority publishes a range of publications on the area, and particularly recommended are their junior series and booklets on birds, castles, coastal scenery and butterflies. The series of site cards based on villages or settlements in the Park are also very good value.

DRIVING
Roads in the Pembrokeshire Coast National Park mainly step back a respectful distance from the spectacular coastline, which can only be explored satisfactorily on foot.

To get a taste of the place, however, a drive along the A487 from the centre of Haverfordwest north to the charming little harbour of Solva, then on to the spiritual centre of St David's, skirting the coast to Fishguard, would take some beating. In the south the limestone Linney Head/St Govan's Head peninsula is best explored by the B4319, and the Marloes peninsula is reached by the B4327 from Haverfordwest. Access to the wild moorland routes across the Presely Hills is by the B4329 from Haverfordwest or the A487 from Fishguard.

WALKING
If you cannot manage the whole of the 168 mile (270 km) Pembrokeshire Coast path, the National Park authority has published a useful mileage chart which shows the distances between the main points, so you can break up the walk quite easily. Self-guided trails have also been provided at places like Dinas Island (3.5 miles/5.6 km), St David's (2 miles/3.2 km) and the Dale peninsula (7 miles/11.2 km), and various nature trials also exist.

Other recommended walks include the 6 mile (9.6 km) round of rocky headland overlooking Ramsey

The church of St Brynach, Dians Island, destroyed by a storm in 1859.

USEFUL ADDRESSES

The Pembrokeshire National Park Office
County Offices
Haverfordwest
Dyfed SA61 1QZ.

(tel. Haverfordwest 4591)

Wales Tourist Board
Brunel House
2 Fitzalan Road
Cardiff CF2 1UY.

(tel. Cardiff 499909)

NATIONAL PARK INFORMATION CENTRES

Kingsmoor Common
Kilgetty.

(tel. Saundersfoot 812175)

Drill Hall
Main Street
Pembroke.

(tel. Pembroke 682148)

Milford Haven refineries, from inside the Park.

Sound and Ramsey Island from St David's – one of the most spectacular sections of the coast path; or the 5 mile (8 km) trek from Rosebush, from where slate was taken to roof the Houses of Parliament, to the summit of the Preselys at Foel Cwm Cerwyn (1,760 ft/ 536 m) for breathtaking views of the northern half of the Park.

CLIMBING, TREKKING AND FISHING

Rock climbing is almost exclusively on the sea cliffs, with an added edge of excitement caused by the crashing waves below. But one word of warning – you should not venture on to the sea cliffs if you are not an experienced climber or if you are on your own. Every year there are tragic accidents, and people sometimes find themselves unexpectedly cut off by the fast-rising tides.

Pony trekking has not yet reached the level of popularity it has in the Brecon Beacons, but as every- where else, its popularity is increasing. Details can be collected from the National Park information centres. The Park produces a special leaflet on riding and pony trekking, as it does on fishing, which is mostly on private waters.

40 High Street
Haverfordwest.

(tel. Haverfordwest 66141)

The Norton
Tenby.

(tel. Tenby 2402)

City Hall
St David's.

(tel. St David's 720392)

National Car Park
Broad Haven.

(tel. Broad Haven 412)

Bank Cottages,
Long Street,
Newport.

(tel. Newport 820912)

Kingsmoor Common
Kilgetty.

(tel. Saundersfoot 813672/3)

The Croft
Tenby.

(tel. Tenby 2402)

3 Heath Fields
Pendre, Cardigan.

(tel. Cardigan 3230)

Town Hall
Fishguard.

(tel. Fishguard 873484)

West Wales Naturalists' Trust
7 Market Street
Haverfordwest.

Source of Stonehenge's bluestones – looking north from the Presely Hills.

Snowdonia National Park

THE LAST STRONGHOLD

Mediaeval English sailors plying across the Irish Sea called the often snow-capped hills of North Wales 'Snawdun' or 'Snaudune'. To them it was a strange, wild and forbidding land. A place of jagged peaks which seemed to brush the sky, where the snows of winter held the hills in their icy grip long after spring had arrived elsewhere. The mountains of Snowdonia, as they became known, were a familiar landmark, but one to be admired from a respectful distance.

The Welsh called this land *Eryri* – the abode of eagles. It is inspiring to think of the great soaring shapes of those magnificent raptors as they rode the thermals on broad, outstretched wings over the crag-fast waters of Glaslyn at the foot of the reigning peak of Yr Wyddfa. Sadly, today the eagles have gone, but the snows still linger after winter in the north-facing gullies of Lliwedd – or in the darkest recesses of Twll Du – the Devil's Kitchen – in the Glyders.

Snowdonia has always been a last refuge for the Welsh, a place where, for centuries, rebels and fugitives have felt secure amid the secret places of the mountains. The tradition goes back a long way to that mysterious half-legend, half-fact figure of King Arthur.

The long saddle between Yr Wyddfa and Lliwedd is called Bwlch-y-Saethau – the pass of the arrows. The name recalls the legendary site of Arthur's last battle with his traitorous nephew Modred. On this exposed and windswept col, Arthur received a fatal wound from a chance arrow at the very moment of his victory. He was buried where he fell, and his loyal followers raised a great cairn of rocks to mark his grave, which was known as Carnedd Arthur before it was broken down during the last century.

The story does not end there, for during the early 19th century, a young shepherd was gathering his sheep on the upper slopes of Lliwedd, close to Bwlch-y-Saethau. One of his flock escaped on to a ledge on the precipitous east face of Lliwedd, and the

Snowdon and Crib Goch from Nant Gwynant.

shepherd scrambled after the sheep, eventually finding himself opposite the mouth of a deep cave.

A dim light came from the depths of the cave, and he cautiously felt his way inside. As his eyes became accustomed to the blackness, he made out long ranks of sleeping warriors, lining the dank walls of the cave, but accidentally banged his head on a bell which was hanging by the entrance.

On the Pyg Track.

The warriors awoke with a mighty shout, and the frightened shepherd fled off the mountain in a blind panic. He told his amazing story to his friends, and then promptly, but not surprisingly, lost his reason. His fantastic story was believed, because it confirmed a legend common here as in other parts of the country, that Arthur, the once and future king, had not gone but was merely sleeping, waiting to come again when the nation was in need of a saviour.

It is a legend that Snowdonia shares with Richmond Castle in Yorkshire, Eildon Hill in Scotland and Glastonbury Tor in Somerset, but Wales, and Snowdonia in particular, has always been a stronghold of Arthurian legend.

A better-documented hero, who also sought refuge under these cloud-capped heights, was Llywelyn the Great, who styled himself *Princeps Aberfraw Dominus Snawdon* – Prince of Aberffraw and Lord of Snowdon.

He was the first of the fiercely independent Welsh princes to unite the nation in the 13th century against the English oppressors.

It was a campaign continued by his grandson, Llywelyn ap Gruffudd or Llywelyn the Last, who died fighting Edward I's armies and whose sterling resistance from his mountainous stronghold was the principal reason for Edward building a string of castles designed to subdue the troublesome Welsh.

Although strictly speaking the term Snowdonia applies only to the group of hills surrounding Yr Wyddfa, the name Snowdonia was adopted by the National Parks Commission in 1951, when the area became the third National Park to be designated.

Its 840 square miles (2,171 sq km) stretches from Penmaenmawr to the mouth of the Dyfi and takes in some 23 miles (37 km) of the best coastal scenery of Tremadog and Barmouth bays. Inland, the boundary

is the valley of the Conwy and the former county boundary of Merioneth.

Enclosed in that area is some of the grandest mountain scenery south of Skye, and the highest land in England and Wales. The ranges are well known, from the northern bastions of the Carnedds, Glyders and Snowdon Massif, to the central Moelwyns, and the featureless bleak moorland expanse of the Migneint. The heather-clad, rugged Rhinogs and Arennigs flank the Mawddach, while the southern base is constructed from the sweeping crags of Cadair Idris in the west through the Arans to the Berwyns in the east.

It is a land of grey rock, which glistens like newly-polished armour in the frequent, drenching rain storms of this exposed west-facing coast. A land of emerald green sheep-cropped grass, which turns a light straw colour as the winter winds whip across the hills. A land where bracken, apple green in spring and burnished gold in winter and autumn, cloaks the lower slopes, and where old woods hide fast-flowing torrents draining from the hills. Truly, these are the mountains of longing.

'Perhaps in the whole world there is no region more picturesquely beautiful than Snowdon, a region of mountains, lakes, cataracts and groves, in which Nature shows herself in her most grand and beautiful forms.' So wrote one of Snowdonia's earliest protagonists, George Borrow in *Wild Wales* published in 1862.

His effusive account of the ascent of Yr Wyddfa is a classic of early guide-book literature, but even when Borrow reached the summit in 1854, he was far from being the only visitor that day. Other groups, he

Slate miners' cottages, Blaenau Ffestiniog.

Llyn Idwal from the Devil's Kitchen, Twll Du.

recorded in his quaint Victorian prose, could be seen ascending or descending as far as the eye could see.

The facts of the account could equally well have been penned today, for 130 years later the popularity of Snowdon is by no means diminished. It is estimated by the National Park authority that more than half a million people walk on Snowdon every year, causing serious footpath erosion and increasing conflicts with farming and conservation interests.

Up to 1,500 walkers and 1,000 train passengers set foot on the summit on a busy summer day, with many leaving a disgusting trail of litter behind them. Indeed, Snowdon's summit with its 4.5 mile (7.2 km) rack-and-pinion railway and ugly station café has been described as 'the highest slum in Britain'.

Action was obviously needed if the situation was to be remedied, and, in 1982, the National Park embarked on a £250,000 facelift scheme, which includes a general tidying up of the summit and the acquisition of the summit buildings by the authority. Work on the badly-eroded footpaths has been going on steadily since 1979, at an annual cost of £200,000, and the results are plain to see and, on the whole, very welcome. Thankfully, however, plans formulated in the mid-1970s, to have groups fill in forms before access would be allowed to the popular paths, seem to

have been abandoned. The uproar from the outdoor movement at the news was loud and justified. If the plan is ever allowed to happen, then the principle of 'freedom of the hills' can be forgotten.

Snowdon is still the 'honeypot' of the National Park, although there are other places where visitor pressure is intense – like Cadair Idris, where legend says that a climber who spends New Year's Eve asleep on the summit will awake as a madman or poet.

Slate quarries, which once roofed the world with their hard, blue-grey rock, may still disfigure the landscape, for example, round the small excluded enclave around Blaenau Ffestiniog; and power stations, like those at Ffestiniog, or the nuclear-powered Lego blocks at Trawsfynydd, may jarringly remind us of the 20th century, but Snowdonia remains largely inviolate.

This National Park authority has always been the most doggedly independent and nationalistic of them all. Planning documents are written in Welsh first, and in English almost as an afterthought. Meetings are conducted in Welsh, with English translation through headphones for those who need it. This part of Wales has traditionally been a hotbed of Welsh nationalism, and a last refuge for the Welsh language.

That ancient *Hwyl*, an indefinable spirit perhaps best translated as a passionate Welshness, which first fired the breast of Llewelyn, still bursts to the surface on occasion, such as when an English second-home-owner's cottage is burnt down by nationalist militants.

Lack of local housing is a common problem in all our National Parks; young local people are unable to buy homes in their native villages because of inflated prices, so they move away and more 'in-comers' take their places.

Nowhere is this justifiable resentment felt more strongly than in Snowdonia. Memories are long in these savage, elemental mountains. People still remember the tales taught them by their parents, about the Red Dragon of Wales who fought the Black Dragon of the Saxons on the rocky crag of Dinas Emrys (Merlin's Fortress), in the vale of Gwynant. And it was the Red Dragon who was victorious.

THE NATURAL LANDSCAPE: WHEN HIGHEST WAS LOWEST

Nothing in Britain illustrates more clearly the fleeting impermanence of those things we sometimes regard as unchangeable, than the chance discovery a lucky

Cnicht and Moelwyn Mawr seen from the Croesor valley.

walker may make on the summit of the highest mountain in England and Wales.

Perhaps our walker has struggled up the seemingly never-ending grind of Crib Goch from Pen-y-Pass, and balanced dizzily along the shattered knife-edge of the ridge to reach the comparatively easy slopes of Crib-y-Ddysgl and Bwlch Glas. The 3,560 ft (1,085 m) summit of Yr Wyddfa – with its spectacular panorama which prompted Craddock to write in 1770, 'it is doubted whether there is another circular prospect so extensive in any part of the terraqueous globe' – is the climber's reward.

Unlike Craddock, today's visitor will probably have to share the 'wilderness experience' with as many as 2,000 other summit-baggers.

But if our walker wanders away from the milling throng around the summit cairn and restaurant, he or she may, if lucky, pick up a rock which will disclose more about the history of our island than any dusty geological textbook.

Although all around is evidence of the peak's volcanic past, the walker might find a piece of lighter, softer rock which bears the unmistakable impression of an ancient sea shell, a mollusc from the Ordovician period of perhaps 550 million years ago. Then the walker will know, as few of the other breathless summitteers will know, that this lofty peak was once at least 3,560 ft (1,085 m) lower, beneath the turbulent waters of a shallow sea, constantly showered by the fiery debris of surrounding volcanoes.

The reigning peak of Yr Wyddfa was in fact the bottom point of a downfold – or syncline – between two higher mountain masses, before unimaginably powerful earth movements reshaped the land. This fact can readily be seen in certain lights from the crest of Crib Goch or Crib-y-Ddysgl, when the sun picks out the downward-dipping strata on Clogwyn-y-Garnedd – the precipice of the cairn.

The geology of Snowdonia is more perplexingly complicated than any of the other National Parks and it is a tale of violent drama, unmatched in the imagination of any director of a Hollywood epic.

The most famous physical feature of the Snowdonia National Park is what geologists call the Harlech Dome. This great uplift in the sedimentary rocks was centred on what we now know as Harlech. The later volcanic strata, covering the muds and sands which became the slates and grits of today, have been eroded from the centre of this dome, but remain to the north, south and east. It has perhaps best been described as an enormous pie dish, with the 'filling'

Llanberis Pass from the Pyg Track.

formed by those ancient Cambrian grits and slates which give us the rugged landscapes of the Rhinogs, and the outer rim from the Ordovician volcanics.

These volcanic rocks produce the jagged, challenging outlines of the so-called 'ring of fire' which encircles the Harlech Dome; and they created the distinctive features of Cadair Idris, the Arans, the Arennigs, Glyders, Carnedds and Snowdon itself. The Snowdon of today is a huge pile of much-eroded Ordovician lava and ash nearly one mile in thickness. The careful observer may be able to make out on Lliwedd's face the rough pattern of hexagonal columns which were formed from cooling lava, as was the most famous example, Ireland's Giant's Causeway. The two isolated summit blocks on 3,010 ft (917 m) Tryfan – perhaps Snowdonia's most challenging peak – were formed in exactly the same way. Over many years, they have been nicknamed Adam and Eve by climbers, the fittest and bravest of whom will leap the gap between the two to gain the 'freedom of Tryfan'.

The finishing touches were put to this masterpiece of natural landscape by the crushing, grinding and chiselling of the Ice Age glaciers, a mere moment ago in geological time. One of the first studies of glaciation as a landscape creator was made here in 1860 by Andrew Ramsay, who published his findings in *The Old Glaciers of Switzerland and North Wales*. The glaciers of 10,000 years ago scoured out the characteristically U-shaped valleys of Llanberis, Nant Ffrancon, Nant Gwynant, Nantlle, and Tal-y-Llyn in the south, where the process was aided by a major geological fault.

The rocky, frowning cwms – basins or corries – of Cwm Glas, Cwm Idwal and Cwm-y-Cau, on Cadair Idris, were the birthplace of these glaciers, and the ferocious frosts of the same period shattered the intervening ridges into the pinnacled knife edges of Crib Goch and the Nantlle Ridge. Frost-shattering was also the cause of the fantastic, lunar landscape found on the desolate summit of the Glyders. It is perhaps the wildest, most primeval spot in Wales, completely covered with a chaotic jumble of enormous blocks of rock, some piled on top of each other, others balanced seemingly precariously out from the main mass. The most famous of these is the so-called Cantilever Stone on Glyder Fach, first noted with incredulity by Thomas Pennant in 1781. Charles Kingsley described the astonishing scene in 1857 as, 'that enormous desolation, the dead bones of the eldest born of time'.

These forbidding mountain fastnesses were a refuge for rare flora and fauna, long before they served as a refuge for man.

Not far from that amazingly desolate and seemingly barren rockscape of the Glyder summit, are flowers more often found gracing alpine or arctic hills. Mountain avens and purple mountain saxifrage cling to the dank, dark buttresses and clefts of Cwm Idwal, one of 16 National Nature Reserves set up by the Nature Conservancy Council in the National Park. But you are unlikely to find the most famous of Snowdonia's floral rarities, the delicate, drooping white head of *Lloydis Serotina*, the mountain spiderwort, commonly called the Snowdon lily. This shy flower was discovered by the Welsh botanist Edward Lhuyd in 1696, but has never been found anywhere else in the British Isles. The same distinction applies to the yellow-flowered Welsh poppy, a native of similar remote rocky ledges.

Heather is surprisingly scarce in Snowdonia, except in the rugged country of the Rhinogs and Berwyns and this is thought to be due partly to the fact that sheep grazing has always been so important, and partly because grouse rearing and shooting has never achieved the importance here that it has in other National Parks.

As if in keeping with the bloody human history of the area, Snowdonia has become a stronghold for predators, those much-maligned creatures of the animal world who do such a useful job in preserving the overall balance of nature. In the air, the commonest sight is the sinister black shape of the raven, a master of the quickly changing air currents of the highest crags. Other kings of the mountain air are buzzards, kestrels, merlins and peregrine falcons, each species now enjoying a welcome recovery after years of accidental and intentional persecution.

An ornithological oddity of the National Park is Craig-yr-Aderyn or Bird Rock, which is situated 4 miles/6.4 km inland from Tywyn. Here, on the steep, Gibraltar-like face of a cliff which, in the past, must have had the sea lapping at its foot, nest cormorants, those elegant black divers normally associated with sea cliffs.

Snowdonia has also remained one of the last strongholds of two carnivores mercilessly persecuted in lowland Britain – the polecat and the handsome but elusive pine marten.

In the tumbling, rushing mountain streams, salmon and sea trout make their uncanny, brave pilgrimages to ancestral spawning grounds, to the delight of anglers and naturalists alike. And in the over-populous Llyn Tegid or Bala Lake, exists yet another Snowdonian rarity, a strange silvery-white

Lynnau Cregennen, in the foothills of Cadair Idris.

trout known as the gwyniad, a wary fish which has never been known to take the angler's lure. It rarely leaves the depths of the lake, at the foot of the noble outline of the Aran range, sharing this type of habitat with another, even more infrequently seen denizen of Snowdonia's lake-depths, the legendary Afangc.

This fabulous monster is said to have inhabited a deep pool in the Conwy near Betws-y-Coed before being tempted out and dragged up the mountain by villagers to Glaslyn, the deep, dark little tarn at the foot of Yr Wyddfa.

And there, so the story goes, the Afangc still lives, waiting to tempt the over-ambitious angler or curious monster collector.

MAN'S INFLUENCE: AN UNTAMED LANDSCAPE

In a land where legend and tradition exert such a powerful influence, it is often difficult to separate myth from history. Fact and fiction blend inseparably, like the wreathing mists which cling to the summits as tenaciously and persistently as legends stick in the minds of men.

In fact, Snowdonia's historic past has been every bit as turbulent as the geological history which shaped the land so violently in the first place. Rebellion and war have stalked these rugged hills since time began. Even today, that fierce nationalism still simmers below the surface, reflected in the strong tradition of religious non-Conformism.

It is hard to put your finger on this intense and jealously guarded 'separateness' of the North Welsh. But it certainly goes a long way back before the Act of Union with England, passed in 1536 but formulated by the first Welsh King of England, Harri Tudor or Henry VII.

Even after Henry Tudor's victory at the Battle of Bosworth in 1485, when he was supported by large numbers of Welshmen – including Rhys ap Meredydd, his standard bearer, now buried at Ysbyty Ifan near Blaenau Ffestiniog – Snowdonia remained an isolated province ruled by the Welsh-speaking princes of Gwynedd. And Edward I's string of imposing castle towns or 'bastides' at Conwy, Caernarfon, Criccieth and Harlech merely gave a semblance of control, in the hope of attracting the civilising influences of English traders and merchants to Wildest Wales.

To find the roots of the *hwyl* of the North Welsh it is necessary to go back to the first settlers of the mountainous landscape.

Dotted here and there on what now seem such inhospitable uplands are the enigmatic hut circles where they lived. These are still called *Cytiau Gwyddelod* by local Welsh-speakers, which can be translated as 'Irishman's huts', and it gives a clue to the origins of their inhabitants.

These Neolithic (New Stone Age) pioneers swept down the great cultural highway which was the Irish Sea, settling in places such as Anglesey, the North Wales mainland, Scotland, Ireland and as far south as Cornwall and Brittany.

The majority of their settlement sites in Snowdonia are found on the coast between Bangor and Conwy, or along the shores of Cardigan Bay. Megalithic tombs or cromlechs, where they buried their chieftains, can be found at Maen-y-Bardd and Capel Garmon in the valley of the Conwy, but the richest hunting ground for searchers after the Snowdonia of prehistory must be in the extreme north east, around the area dominated by Penmaenmawr Mountain.

Left: Bwlch-y-Saethau, Snowdon.

Right: The Snowdon Horseshoe – Lliwedd, Snowdon, Crib Goch and Crib-y-Ddysgl – from Llynnau Mymbyr.

Here, on an outcrop of dolerite on the crag of Graig Lwyd, was a Neolithic and Bronze Age centre of industry which, with that of the Langdale Pikes in the Lake District, is one of the earliest centres of Stone Age technology so far discovered in Britain. The rock was used for the shaping of stone axe heads, which were transported all over Britain. They have been identified on numerous sites from Land's End to the New Forest and the Firth of Forth.

Burial cairns and round barrows are also common on this northern coastal strip, where some of these earliest British industrial workers were laid to rest. And perhaps they worshipped at the misnamed Druid's Circle on the open, bracken-covered moor above Penmaenmawr – the best preserved stone circle or henge monument in the National Park. The Druids, whose power extended over most of Britain in pre-Roman days, had their headquarters on nearby Anglesey, but they came at a much later date than the time when this isolated, evocative site was sacred.

The Iron Age followed the Bronze, and Braich-y-Dinas also on Penmaenmawr was a fine example of the hill forts so typical of the period, until quarrying unfortunately destroyed it. These hill forts probably played an important role in the stubborn resistance to the Roman invasion of the 1st century, for the Imperial armies were the first organised invaders to experience the obdurate nature of the native Welsh in the defence of their country.

The Romans, showing their formidable organisational skill, built a series of permanently garrisoned forts, linked by the first metalled roads to be pushed through the mountains. The great north-south highway through Wales, known as Sarn Helen both here and in the Brecon Beacons, was a major artery, as was the coast road between Conwy and Caernarfon, site of Segontium, perhaps the most important of Snowdonia's Roman forts. Others existed at Bryn-y-Gefeiliau near Capel Curig, Tomen-y-Mur near Trawsfynydd and Caer Gai, on the shores of Llyn Tegid (Lake Bala in English). The Romans stayed for some 300 years, but whether the shadowy figure of Arthur, as the 6th century leader of the first Welsh resistance, should be added to the list of warriors who

used Snowdonia as a stronghold is still a matter for debate. On the evidence of place names alone, there should be no dispute.

Of the documented resistance leaders, the best known are the Llywelyns who, as already mentioned, stood firm against the next wave of foreign invaders, the Norman English.

They were the most famous of the native Welsh princes, and the first, Llewelyn the Great, set up his headquarters on the impressive crag-top site of Castell-y-Bere, near Tywyn, one of the few remaining Welsh castles which owes its origin to Welsh rather than English builders. The last of these Welsh princes, Llywelyn ap Gruffudd, is commemorated by the cairn on the summit named after him, the 3,484 ft (1,062 m) height of Carnedd Llywelyn. The nearby Carnedd Dafydd (3,426 ft/1,044 m) is said to be named after his brother.

Edward I's great fortresses were all strategically placed around the coasts, but eventually even Llewelyn's stronghold of Castell-y-Bere succumbed and was remodelled by Edward. The so-called Roman Steps which march across the Rhinogs from Cwm Bychan are more likely to have been a mediaeval paved pack-horse supply-route to the castle and town of Harlech on the coast.

Harlech, a splendid example of a planned mediaeval garrison town, is an excellent centre for exploring the rough walking country of the Rhinogs – one of the wildest mountain areas in Britain. Other centres in the south include Barmouth, Tywyn and Aberdyfi on the coast. Inland, the pleasant little market town of Dolgellau is convenient for Cadair Idris and the Arans.

The northern mountains of Gwynedd around Snowdon itself are best served by the villages of Llanberis, Beddgelert, Capel Curig, Betws-y-Coed and the Ffestiniogs. Blaenau Ffestiniog was excluded from the National Park because of the obvious scars left by the slate mining industry.

This has been one of the most important modern industries of Snowdonia, and its legacy is also found inside the National Park's confines. Few people who have climbed Snowdon by the popular 5 mile (8 km) Llanberis track alongside the railway can fail to have noticed the huge stepped staircase of the Dinorwic slate quarry across Llyn Peris. Between 1850 and 1880, more than 100,000 tons (101,600 tonnes) of slate a year were produced from these open-cast quarries, some of the biggest in the world.

The slate industry of Snowdonia sparked off a remarkable cultural movement among the locally-recruited employees. The men worked hard, often in atrocious conditions, but they also studied, sang and prayed hard in their spare time away from the quarries.

Another kind of industry which utilised the mineral wealth of the mountains, were the copper mines of Snowdon itself. Walkers using the Miner's Track from Pen-y-Pass follow the footsteps of those miners, who often walked up from the pass to their place of work, the ruins of which can still be seen on the shores of Llyn Llydaw and Glaslyn.

Today, forestry has become of enormous commercial importance, as in other mountain areas. The village of Betws-y-Coed (chapel in the forest) is almost completely surrounded by the new forest of Gwydyr, which has grown since 1921 to stretch from Llyn Crafnant to Penmachno. Visitors enter the little township on the graceful single iron span of the Waterloo Bridge on the A5 Holyhead Road. It was so-named because it was constructed in 1815, the same year as the famous battle. Thomas Telford's Holyhead road – designed for stagecoaches, but today carring an ever-increasing volume of holiday traffic to Snowdonia – was a masterpiece of early 19th century civil engineering.

Gradients were reduced to 1 : 20 wherever it was possible, and although Telford made use of many parts of the old turnpike routes he also created entirely new, brilliantly engineered routes in other places. The road up the Nant Ffrancon valley, for example, is hardly changed today, and the lay-bys built to hold stone for repairing the road perform the same function for today's motor road as they did for the road of the horse-drawn coaches of a century and a half ago.

Undoubtedly, improved communications served to open up the wonders of Snowdonia to the adventurous tourist as well as to those en route for Ireland and the Holyhead ferry. Strangely, however, Snowdonia never attracted the literary genius of a Wordsworth or Ruskin to sing its praises, but the visitors have come anyway.

Perhaps the key question was posed eight years before the Park was designated, when that great conservationist and proponent of the National Park, Sir Clough Williams-Ellis was outlining his vision to the Queen Mother at Penygwryd at the foot of the Llanberis Pass.

'It's fine your preparing this splendid countryside for the people,' said the distinguished visitor, 'but are you doing anything about preparing the people to make proper use of it?'

The Cadair range seen from the estuary of the Mawddach.

What to do

HOW TO GET THERE

BY ROAD The M1–M6 is the quickest route from the south east, leaving at Junction 12 (Cannock) for the A5 Watling Street. The opening of the M54 to Telford and beyond will speed up what has traditionally been a tedious journey via Shrewsbury to Llangollen and into the National Park via Betws-y-Coed. A pleasant alternative route, often avoiding the holiday queues, is the A458 from Shrewsbury to Welshpool and Dolgellau and the southern part of the National Park.

Visitors from the north should leave the M6 at Junction 20 to join the M56 and then the A55 or A458 North Wales coast road to Caernarfon. The A470, the major north-south artery of the Park can be joined at Tywyn, just before Conwy.

BY RAIL By Inter-City service from London (Euston) to Holyhead, Anglesey. Alternatively leave the main line at Chester or Crewe, where branch lines run to Conwy and Bangor. From the West Midlands, lines run to Aberdovey and Barmouth.

WHERE TO STAY

The Wales Tourist Board's annual *Where to Stay in Wales* is an invaluable guide, available from any information centre and from many newsagents and booksellers. A bed-booking service is also provided at tourist information centres and most National Park visitor centres. In addition, the National Park authority owns a number of self-contained holiday chalets at Llanrwst, on the banks of the Conwy River. Details from the Curator, Snowdonia National Park Chalets, Glan-y-Borth, Llanrwst, Gwynedd, LL26 08B.

YOUTH HOSTELS There is a good range of youth hostels, of varying grades, at Bangor, Ro Wen (Conwy), Penmaenmawr, Colwyn Bay, Snowdon Ranger, Llanberis, Idwal Cottage, Pen-y-Pass, Capel Curig, Lledr Valley, Oaklands (near Betws-y-Coed), Byn Gwynant, Ffestiniog, Harlech, Gerddi Bluog (near Harlech), Llanbedr, Kings (Dolgellau), Dinas Mawddwy, Corris and Plas Rhiwaedog (Bala).

Dolbadarn Castle, Llanberis.

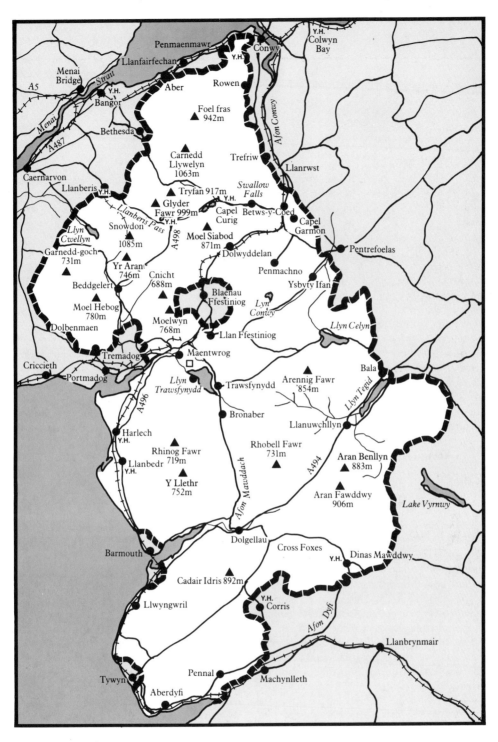

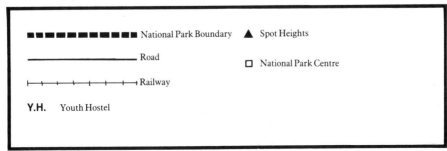

National Park Boundary   ▲   Spot Heights

———————— Road

     □   National Park Centre

Railway

Y.H.   Youth Hostel

The Dyfi estuary, Aberdyfi.

CAMPING AND CARAVAN SITES The official advice from the National Park authority is that tented camping sites are best found by going to the area and looking for camping signs. There is no shortage of sites, and visitors are urged to book directly with the farmers or landowners at each site.

Caravans are not officially encouraged in the National Park, but there are some sites, especially along the west coast. Information offices should be able to help.

PLACES OPEN TO THE PUBLIC

HARLECH CASTLE Perhaps the most dramatic of all of Welsh Edwardian castles, Harlech was even more impregnable when the waters of Tremadog Bay lapped the rocky outcrop on which it was built. The sea is now half a mile away, but the massive grey walls and imposing gatehouse are still every bit as for-

midable as they were when they were built in the 13th century. There are fine views of Snowdonia from the battlements.

DOLBADARN CASTLE, LLANBERIS Overlooking Llyn Padarn at the foot of the Llanberis Pass, Dolbadarn Castle is notable both for its precipitous location and its imposing 40 ft (12 m) ruined tower. A Welsh castle, it was built in the late 12th or early 13th century.

DOLWYDDELLAN CASTLE The traditional birthplace of Llywelyn the Great, this late 12th century castle with its rectangular keep was extensively altered in the 19th century when the upper part of the tower and its battlements were reconstructed.

GWYDIR CASTLE, LLANRWST An ivy-covered Tudor mansion, with a priest's hole, a bedroom where Charles I slept, and peacocks roaming the garden.

CASTELL-Y-BERE, ABERGYNOLWYN In a situation which rivals Carreg Cennen in the Brecon Beacons, this lonely mountain stronghold situated in the shadow of Cadair Idris was captured by Edward I but was abandoned in 1294.

CYMER ABBEY A small, ruined Cistercian abbey on the east bank of the Mawddach, now partly swallowed up by an adjoining farmyard, but with some interesting features still remaining.

LLECHWEDD SLATE CAVERNS, BLAENAU FFESTINIOG Outside the National Park but well worth a visit, these award-winning caverns show the visitor what life was like for the generations of slate miners whose subterranean labours roofed the world. An exciting underground railway with a breathtaking incline takes you to the deepest levels.

WELSH SLATE MUSEUM, DINORWIC The former workshop of this huge quarry – which is so obvious on the northern site of the Llanberis Pass – shows old machinery and equipment and informative film and audiovisual shows.

There are also museums at Porthmadog, Tywyn and Betws-y-Coed and the CEGB welcomes visitors to its power stations at Ffestiniog (Britain's first pumped storage station) and Trawsfynydd, where there is also a nature trail.

Steam buffs will need no second bidding to sample one or more of the 'Great Little Trains of Wales' and the National Park is fortunate in having several of these enthusiast-run lines passing through it. The Festiniog Railway runs 13.67 miles (22 km) between Porthmadog and Ffestiniog; the Talyllyn, 7.5 miles (11.5 km) from Tywyn to Nant Gwernod; the Bala Lake, 4.5 miles (7.25 km) along the shore and the Llanberis Lake Railway, 2 miles (3.2 km) along the eastern shore from the Padarn Country Park.

Britain's only rack-and-pinion railway, the Snowdon Mountain Railway, takes those unable or unwilling to walk to the 3,560 ft (1,085 m) summit of the highest mountain in England and Wales. The journey takes about an hour for the 4.75 mile (7.5 km) trip from Llanberis, and there's a restaurant on top.

ANCIENT MONUMENTS

	Grid Reference
Capel Garmon Burial Chamber	(SH 818544)
Maen-y-Bardd Cromlech	(SH 741718)
Pen-y-Gaer Hill Fort, Beddgelert	(SH 586458)
Craig-yr-Aderyn Hill Fort, Llanfihangel-y-Pennant	(SH 644068)
Bryn-y-Gefeiliau Roman Site, Capel Curig	(SH 747573)
Dolwyddelan Castle	(SH 722524)
Dolbadarn Castle	(SH 586598)
Castell-y-Bere	(SH 667086)

MAPS

A colourful jay adorns the cover of the four Ordnance Survey Outdoor Leisure maps (scale 1 : 25,000 or 2½ in to the mile) which cover the whole of the National Park in unmatched detail. The sheets are Snowdon, Conwy Valley, Harlech, Bala and Cadair Idris/Dovey Forest.

In addition, the whole of the National Park is covered in a ½ in to one mile Tourist map (too small for walking use), or the 5 in to one mile Landranger maps, nos 115, 116, 124, 125 and 135.

Linda, one of the Great Little Trains of Wales, on the Festiniog Railway at Tan-y-Bwlch Station.

FURTHER READING

Snowdonia is probably the worst-off of all our National Parks in the range of its 'in-house' publications; these are limited chiefly to a series of walks leaflets. But, as might be expected for such a popular area, there is an enormous commercial range of literature, some much better than others.

Beazley, E, *Shell Guide to North Wales*, Faber & Faber, 1971

Borrow, George, *Wild Wales*, reprinted Collins, 1955.

Challiner, John, & Bates, Denis, *Geology Explained in North Wales*, David & Charles, 1973.

Condry, William, *The Snowdonia National Park*, Collins, 1966.

James, Ron, *Rock Climbing in Wales*, Constable, 1970.

Lockley, R M, *The Naturalist in Wales*, David & Charles, 1970.

Lovins, A & Evans, P, *Eryri, the Mountains of Longing*, F.o.E./Allen & Unwin, 1972.

Macdonald, Colin, *A Visitor's Guide to North Wales & Snowdonia*, Moorland, 1982.

Millward, Roy, & Robinson, Adrian, *Landscapes of North Wales*, David & Charles, 1978.

Poucher, W A, *The Welsh Peaks*, Constable, 1962.

Poucher, W A, *Wales*, Constable, 1981.

Rhys Edwards, G (ed), *Snowdonia National Park*, HMSO, 1958.

Rowland, E G, *Hill Walking in Snowdonia*, Cicerone Press, 1951.

Styles, Showell, *The Mountains of North Wales*, Gollancz, 1973.

Wales – Castles and Historic Places, Wales Tourist Board, 1980.

Wales – Walking, Wales Tourist Board, 1978.

DRIVING

Snowdonia is a park where the main roads take you into the very heart of the mountains. Thomas Telford's A5, skilfully engineered to take stage-coaches from London to Holyhead, is still a spectacular route, with views of the Carnedds and Glyders and Tryfan at close quarters as the road threads through the Nant Ffrancon Pass. The A4086 from Capel Curig to Llanberis is almost as spectacular, climbing into the jaws of the Llanberis Pass between the Glyders and Snowdon via Pen-y-Pass, while the A498 turns off down Nantgwynant to Beddgelert and Porthmadog.

The A470 bisects the Park from Conwy to Betws-y-Coed, Blaunau Ffestiniog and Dolgellau, crossing the Arans to Dinas Mawddwy and Machynlleth,

The pass of Aberglaslyn.

while the A487 links Dolgellau and Machynlleth more spectacularly and directly under the shadow of Cadair Idris, via the wild mountain pass of Bwlch Llyn Bach.

WALKING

The best guide to the easy and safe ascent of Snowdonia's rugged mountains is W A Poucher's *Welsh Peaks*, but E G Rowland's *Hill Walking in Snowdonia* comes a close second. The National Park authority has a programme of guided walks each summer and publishes a selection of leaflets of recommended walks.

There are at least seven main routes to Snowdon's summit, of which the Miner's Track from Pen-y-Pass is probably the most popular, and is only steep as it climbs the zigzags at Bwlch Glas. The Llanberis route is longer, safe and easy, but can get crowded and suffers ever-present noise from the mountain railway.

Cadair Idris is another popular walkers mountain, and the easiest routes are from Tal-y-Llyn to the wild mountain cwm of Cwm-y-Cau, or from the north via the badly-eroded Foxes Path from Dolgellau. A pleasant walk through the wild heather-covered country of the Rhinogs is from Llyn Cwm Bychan to the Roman Steps (actually a mediaeval pack-horse route) and back.

The usual safety precautions should be taken on any mountain route in Snowdonia. The Mountain Rescue Service is called out all too often to save ill-equipped and unprepared walkers in these hills.

Inexperienced mountain walkers are better off on low level routes such as those trails the Forestry Commission provides in the Gwydyr Forest near Betws-y-Coed, or the famous Precipice Walk along the superb Mawddach estuary, near Barmouth.

CLIMBING, TREKKING AND CANOEING

With an estimated 3,000 rock climbing routes in the area, the Park obviously has much to offer the 'crag-hound'. Favourite spots include that Mecca for serious climbers, Clogwyn Du'r Arddu (Cloggy – as it is known to its aficionados) on the north-facing side of Snowdon, and the vertical cliffs of Craig Ddu, Clogwyn-y-Grochan, Carreg Wasted and Dinas Cromlech in the Llanberis Pass. Here, on this last named crag, brightly-coloured climbers can often be seen on such classic routes as Cenotaph Corner, one of the most famous of British rock climbs, which takes the climber up a 120 ft (36 m) crack that is as straight as the centre fold between two pages of a book. Other popular climbing areas include the cliffs of the Glyders, Cwm Idwal and Tryfan.

There are pony-trekking centres in many villages, with a variety of routes over the hills, and sailing takes place on Bala Lake (Llyn Tegid).

Beginners wishing to try climbing, canoeing or other outdoor activities are recommended to enrol for courses at the National Centre for Mountain Activities at Plas-y-Brenin, Capel Curig where they will receive skilled instruction in what can be dangerous sports for the unsupervised.

USEFUL ADDRESSES

Snowdonia National Park Information Office
Yr Hen Ysgol
Maentwrog
Blaenau Ffestiniog
Gwynedd LL41 4HW.

Snowdonia National Park Office
Penrhyndeudraeth
Gwynedd LL48 6LF.

(tel. Penrhyndeudraeth 770274)

National Centre for Mountain Activities
Plas-y-Brenin
Capel Curig
Betws-y-Coed
Gwynedd.

(tel. Capel Curig 214)

Snowdonia National Park Study Centre
Plas-Tan-y-Bwlch
Maentwrog
Blaenau Ffestiniog
Gwynedd LL41 3YU.

(tel. Maentwrog 85324)

Wales Tourist Board
Brunel House
2 Fitzalan Road
Cardiff CF2 1UY.

(tel. Cardiff 499909)

NATIONAL PARK INFORMATION CENTRES

Y Stablau
Betws-y-Coed
Gwynedd.

The Wharf, Aberdyfi.

Gwyddfor House
High Street
Harlech.

Old British High School, Bala.

Isallt
Blaenau Ffestiniog.

Beechwood House, Dolgellau.

Glan-y-Borth, Llanrwst.

And at Llanberis,
Oriel Eryri

Peak District National Park

THE INLAND ISLAND

The Peak District, that last knobbly vertebra in the backbone of England, has often been described as an island.

But the shores of this island are washed not by the cleansing waters of the sea, but by the grime of the great industrial conurbations of northern England and the Midlands.

The Peak stands out as a last green outpost amid the encircling Satanic mills of the Industrial Revolution cities which spread their smoky suburbs ever outwards.

In earlier days, however, before landscape appreciation became fashionable, Daniel Defoe in his *Tour Through the Whole Island of Great Britain* described it as 'a howling wilderness ... the most desolate, wild and abandoned country in all England'.

For many years, before it became Britain's first National Park in April, 1951, the Peak District had acted as a 'lung' for the expanding populations of those northern cities. These 'ramblers from Manchester way' fought long and hard for the right to roam the peaty summits of the High Peak, and some were even imprisoned for exercising what they believed was their rightful heritage. The 'access battles' were to be an important catalyst for the whole National Park movement in Britain.

As Britain's first National Park, the Peak authority pioneered many projects which other parks have since adopted. One of the first tasks of the newly-constituted authority was to negotiate special access-agreements for the highest and wildest parts of the moors, much to the delight of those early trespassers and the thousands of visitors who now follow them.

A total of 76 square miles (197 sq km) of moorland, including parts of Kinder Scout (at 2,088 ft/636 m the highest point of the 542 square miles/1,404 sq km of Park), Bleaklow, also topping 2,000 ft (610 m) and one of England's only true wildernesses, and areas bordering the eastern gritstone 'edges' frowning

On the western slopes of Kinder Scout.

down on the Derwent valley, are now covered by these access-agreements.

They allow free and unrestricted access to the public (subject only to a commonsense set of by-laws) for most of the year, except for a few days after the 'glorious 12th' of August when the moors are closed for private grouse shoots.

The Peak's ranger service was set up in 1954, at first merely to cover and act as a liaison between owners and visitors on these 'access' areas. But now the 12 full-time rangers cover the whole of the Park, fulfilling the same role and backed by an army of part-time volunteers at weekends.

Another important 'first' for the Peak was the setting up of the Tissington and High Peak Trails, in co-operation with Derbyshire County Council. Disused and unsightly railway lines, which ran through the pleasantly undulating landscape of the limestone White Peak (it takes its name from the predominate colour of the rock), were converted to easy walking, cycling and riding routes.

The Goyt valley, a sequestered gritstone vale on the western edge of the Park, deliberately depopulated when thirsty Stockport needed more reservoirs, had become, since the setting up of the Park, what in modern planning jargon is known as a 'honeypot'.

Thousands flocked to the lovely, wooded valley with its romantic ruined mansion of Errwood Hall, set in a sea of rhododendrons, but they were choking the narrow roads with their cars and it became obvious that something had to be done if the Goyt was to be saved from human saturation.

Backed by the Countryside Commission, the Park authority stepped in with a bold, innovative solution in 1970. The simple answer was that if there were too many cars, then cars must be excluded at peak periods and minibuses provided for those who could not, or would not, walk. The experiment was an outstanding success, and has been widely admired and repeated at other beauty spots elsewhere.

The Peak's 60-bed National Park Residential Study Centre at Losehill Hall, Castleton was also the

Hen Cloud and the Roaches.

first of its kind, opened by Princess Anne in 1972. It gives those who wish to learn more about the Park and its fascinating countryside the chance to do so among some of its most interesting geological and historical landscapes.

The fact that the Peak National Park authority has been able to do so much front-running is largely due to the fact that it alone, among all our National Parks, is constituted most closely to the original format recommended by Dower and Hobhouse. It is run by an independent board, with its own separate staff, although its elected members still represent the six counties partly covered by its boundaries. Only the Lake District has a similar independent Park board, although that Park now falls entirely within the one new county of Cumbria.

Connoisseurs of the Peak visit the Park in spring, autumn or even winter, when they have the summer-time honeypots to themselves. But early summer visitors can witness an ancient custom which is almost certainly a Christian revival of a pagan rite to give thanks for the gift of water.

'Well-dressing', as the custom is known, was first recorded at Tissington in 1758, but is certainly older. It involves the creation of intricate and delicate mosaic pictures, made entirely of natural materials, particularly flower petals, on panels which frame the well-springs. Perhaps the best known are at Tissington on Ascension Day, and Youlgreave.

Another age-old custom with origins lost in pre-history is the Castleton Garlanding ceremony, held on Oak Apple Day, involving the construction of a huge, six-stone pyramid of flowers which is worn by the Garland King on his ride through the town and which is later hoisted on to the tower of the parish church.

The rush-bearing ceremony at Macclesfield Forest Chapel has also survived the ravages of time. Once common in many churches and chapels throughout Britain the ceremony still takes place every August at this tiny hill-top chapel. The floor of the already-decorated church is strewn with rushes, in a conscious echo of the regular 'carpeting' that the building would have been given in earlier times. A similar ceremony occurs at Grasmere in the Lake District.

The Peak District is probably the most easily accessible of all our ten National Parks, with nearly half of England's population within easy day-trip distance. It is also the nearest National Park to London and the heavily populated south east.

The astonishing variety of scenery within its boundaries and its position on the transition zone between Highland and Lowland Britain, makes the Peak irresistibly attractive to visitors.

In a land of sharp contrasts, even long-time lovers of the Peak are often divided in their loyalties to landscape types.

There are limestone lovers, who find their particular heaven in the soft, green and grey pastel scenes of the White Peak and its spectacular dales. Here there is an almost feminine quality to the landscape, with its network of drystone walls spreading over softly-swelling contours. Bright flowers sprinkle the verdant green pastures, and the light takes on a breathtaking clarity.

Winnats Pass, Castleton.

The Dark Peak, sombre and foreboding, is in many ways the exact opposite. The brooding moors, watched over by weirdly shaped tors and long walls of sheer brown or metallic grey rock, are too depressing for some people, who prefer their scenery more tame and civilised.

But for others, those empty, windswept moors, where the only sound is the haunting cry of the curlew or the warning croak of the red grouse, are the *real* Peak District.

Here, especially if they come from the nearby industrial towns, visitors can find that purity of air which cleanses body and spirit alike.

THE NATURAL LANDSCAPE: WHITE AND DARK – THE TWO PEAK DISTRICTS

Many people are misled by the name of the Peak District. Although it gets its name from the Old English *peac* meaning knoll or hill, the usual modern interpretation of the word is a sharply-pointed mountain summit.

But you will look in vain for a Matterhorn or Tryfan in the Peak District. The only remotely peak-like tops are the upstanding remains of former coral reefs in the limestones of Thorpe Cloud, and Chrome and Parkhouse Hills in the Dove valley, or Losehill and Shutlingsloe on the borders of gritstone country further north. The predominate impression is of broad, lofty, but horizontal horizons, which never approach the alpine proportions of the Lake District or Snowdonia.

There are three major rock types in the Peak, all dating from approximately the same epoch in the vast geological timescale, and all shaping their own distinctive and individual type of landscape.

During what the geologists call the Carboniferous period (about 350 to 270 million years ago) what we now know as Britain was much nearer the equator and largely covered with shallow, warm, coral-forming seas. Later, muddy deltas were formed by long-forgotten rivers, and steaming swamps in this primeval ooze produced our coal measures.

The oldest exposed rocks in the Peak are the pearly white-grey limestones of the central and southern parts of the Park – the White Peak. On either side and to the north of this porous, bone-dry plateau, a horse-shoe of dark, heather-covered gritstone moorland creates what has become known, in contrast, as the Dark Peak.

Once, this gritstone cover extended over the whole of the Pennine Dome, but millions of years of erosion by wind, rain, ice and water have weathered it away to expose once again the underlying skeleton of limestone.

Between these two extremes, broad, green fertile valleys of shale, carved by rivers like the mighty Derwent and Wye, provide a soft transition zone.

The limestone area of the White Peak is a gently undulating landscape of soft contours, enmeshed by a net of silvery-grey drystone walls which provide perhaps the most lasting impression for visitors, especially those coming from the traditionally hedge-lined south.

But to many people, as John Ruskin observed, 'The whole gift of the country is in its glens. The wide acreage of field or moor above is wholly without interest; it is only in the clefts of it, and the dingles, that the traveller finds his joy.'

'Dingles', such as Dovedale, the valley of the Mani-fold, Lathkill Dale, Monsal Dale and Miller's Dale on the Wye, create some of the most spectacular river valleys in Britain, with naked walls of rock springing sheer from the native ashwoods.

Other dales, like the stupendous gorge of the Winnats Pass and Cave Dale near Castleton, are now

Lathkill Dale.

118

Peveril Castle, Castleton.

completely dry where the water has sunk beneath the porous rock to create another subterranean landscape available to the visitor through show caves like the awesome void of Peak Cavern, and the Blue John, Treak Cliff and Speedwell Caverns, all at Castleton.

Some rivers, like the Manifold, Lathkill and Hamps, disappear mysteriously into sink holes, only to reappear several miles downstream in this pot-holer's paradise.

Ash and yew provide the natural tree cover of these dales, while the river meadows and steep-sided cliff faces still shelter some of our rarest plants and flowers in carefully conserved nature reserves. Among these rare plants are the shrub-like mezereon, the yellow mountain pansy, the rock rose and a wide variety of our shy native orchids.

Most of the trees on the plateau are planted shelter-belts, and the pastures have been 'improved' to pro-vide grazing for the herds of black-and-white Friesians which cluster round the life-giving dew-ponds during summer. Curlews and lapwings nest in the open fields, while in the dales that chirpy under-water swimmer, the dipper, and the equally-cheeky grey wagtail attract the eye. Most of our common mammals are also found here.

The Dark Peak is a more severe, uncompromising landscape with large areas of water-logged peaty, or heather-covered, moorland ringed by precipitous edges of brown or grey rock. Man's influence is not so obvious here, although even in this wilderness Man has had an effect.

On the high moorland, boggy areas are covered with natural drainage channels known as 'groughs', and in the wet 'flushes' on the summits, grows bright

Kinder reservoir from Kinder Scout.

green sphagnum moss, while the nodding white heads of cotton grass bend in the wind. In the gritstone valleys, known locally as cloughs, native sessile oakwoods survive and support a rich range of wildlife.

The characteristic bird of the heather moorland is the furry-footed red grouse, Britain's only truly native game bird and the agent, through its keepers, of the patchwork quilt appearance of the heather. Golden plover and curlew also send their haunting calls across these wide and lonely places.

MAN'S INFLUENCE: A LIVED-IN LANDSCAPE

Only in the steepest and most inaccessible limestone dales and gritstone cloughs of the Peak can land-

scapes totally unaffected by Man still be found.

There is plentiful evidence that the first prehistoric hunter-gatherers found the high and dry limestone plateau to their liking. The many place names ending in 'low' indicate ancient burial places, while Arbor Low, near Middleton-by-Youlgreave, is one of the most atmospheric of Britain's unique henge monuments, dating from Neolithic times and still, even today, retaining much of its mystery.

These Stone Age men were the first to start clearing the native tree cover from the limestone and gritstone plateaux. Bronze Age tumuli, such as the remarkable collection on Stanton Moor near Birchover, are common on high ground.

Although the Romans began the exploitation of the lead-bearing limestone, and modern roads still follow Roman routes across the plateau, the only major Roman settlement yet found in the Park is an auxiliary fort at Navio, near Brough in the Hope Valley.

Iron Age hill forts, like those which crown Mam Tor, near Castleton, Fin Cop in Monsal Dale and Carl Wark near Hathersage, may have sheltered the last pockets of resistance against the Roman invaders by the native tribes of the Coritani and Brigantes.

Saxon settlers preferred the lush valleys of the Wye and Derwent, and left behind a legacy of villages and fine, vigorously-carved early Christian crosses like those at Eyam and Bakewell.

After the Norman conquest, much of the northwest and central part of the present National Park became the Royal Forest of the Peak, a strictly protected hunting reserve administered by William I's illegitimate son, William Peveril. His headquarters still provide the most imposing Norman remains in the Peak – the keep of Peveril Castle lording it on its crag overlooking the mediaeval township of Castleton.

The mysterious bumps and hollows in the velvety-green pastures of the White Peak bear evidence of the traditional dual-economy industries of this part of the Park – lead-mining and farming. There are many remains of 't'owd man' as the miners were called, but perhaps the most impressive and complete is Magpie Mine, near Sheldon, which is being restored as a lead mining museum.

Modern industry, such as limestone extraction and fluorspar mining – which has superseded lead mining on the same sites – threatens to change the landscape in a far more radical way than did the traditional small-scale industries like farming and gritstone extraction for building.

Overleaf: Remains of Magpie lead mine, near Sheldon.

The administrative centre of the Peak National Park and headquarters of the Peak Park Joint Planning Board is at Bakewell – a bustling little market town and the largest settlement within the Park boundary. There is a fine, commanding parish church, a busy cattle market, a lovely old mediaeval bridge over the River Wye, and an ancient market hall which has been converted into a National Park information centre. Bakewell, famous for its puddings, known only to in-comers as 'tarts', is a convenient centre for Chatsworth, Haddon, and the fascinating White Peak country.

Castleton is a good base for exploring the northern limestone area and the Hope and Edale valleys. It is also well served by shops, and has some fine show caverns where the exclusive mineral Blue John is found.

Castleton's regular street plan and the remains of its town ditch give clues to its origin as an 11th century 'new town', built in the shadow of the castle.

The main centre on the central limestone plateau is Tideswell, famous for its 14th century pinnacled parish church known as the 'Cathedral of the Peak'. It was founded on the wealth gained from lead mining and sheep farming, and is within walking distance of one of the most interesting nature trails in the Park, at Tideswell Dale.

Hathersage is convenient to explore the eastern edges and the Hope and Derwent valleys. Reputedly the home of Robin Hood's loyal henchman, Little John, you can still see what is taken to be his grave in the tiny, hillside churchyard. Just up the valley of the Todd Brook from Hathersage is the mediaeval tower house of North Lees Hall, thought by many to be the Thornfield Hall of Charlotte Bronte's novel *Jane Eyre*.

A good starting point for exploring the Upper Dove valley is Hartington with its fine houses grouped around a large market square complete with duck pond. The village is best-known locally for its cheese factory, one of the few left in the country still making Stilton. This king of English cheeses may be made only in the counties of Leicestershire, Nottinghamshire and Derbyshire – and Hartington just qualifies as it is only a quarter of a mile from the Staffordshire border.

Longnor, now a small village on the ridge between the Dove and the Manifold, retains an air of its previous importance. The cobbled market square and toll notice give a clue to its former commercial status, which was based on its fortunate position at the junction of turnpike routes across the open moor.

Probably the best centre for the Dove valley is outside the Park, at Ashbourne. The tourist bro-

Arbor Low Stone Circle.

chures call it 'the Gateway to the Peak' and it is a bustling old market town with a splendid church.

Matlock and Matlock Bath are also outside the Park boundary, but both are well-appointed tourist centres in their own right. Matlock Bath, situated in a dramatic limestone gorge cut by the Derwent, has its own illuminations in late summer, and some show caves, while larger Matlock is the administrative capital of Derbyshire.

Buxton, like Matlock, is a spa town with an aura of faded Georgian elegance. The Crescent, opposite St Ann's Well, can rival the best of Bath, and Buxton, one of the highest towns in England at over 1,000 ft (305 m), is a fine centre for touring the High Peak.

The town's mineral waters have long been famous. They were taken by the Romans, who had a baths at Buxton and called the place Aquae Arnemetiae. The baths later fell into disrepair but enjoyed a brief revival in the 16th century. A pump room was introduced in the late 18th century by the Duke of Devonshire, who, as the lord of the manor, spent large sums of money improving and rebuilding the town in the Doric style.

Left: Enclosure walls from Stanage Edge.

Overleaf, left: Stone walls near Chelmorton.

Overleaf, right: Chatsworth.

Below: Hartington.

What to do

HOW TO GET THERE
BY ROAD The motorway network neatly bypasses the Peak bringing it within easy reach of most parts of the country.

From the east, take the M1, Junction 29 (Chesterfield) or Junction 37 (Barnsley). From the west, M6, Junction 17 (Congleton) or Junction 19 (Knutsford). If you prefer to avoid motorways, the A6 takes you through to the heart of the National Park.

BY RAIL Main line services run to Sheffield, Chesterfield or Manchester, with local routes into the Park at Matlock, Buxton, Grindleford, Hathersage, Bamford and – on the 'ramblers route' – to Edale in the shadow of Kinder Scout.

WHERE TO STAY
The Peak National Park authority publishes its annual *Accommodation and Catering Guide* which is an essential reference on where to stay inside the Park. It ranges from modest farmhouse bed-and-breakfasts to four-star hotels.

Accommodation lists for the surrounding towns and areas are provided by their tourist information centres, or direct from the tourist boards themselves (see address list).

YOUTH HOSTELS There are youth hostels at Bakewell, Bretton, Buxton, Castleton, Crowden-in-Longdendale, Edale, Elton, Eyam, Gradbach, Hagg Farm (Ashopton), Hartington, Hathersage, Ilam, Langsett, Matlock Bath, Meerbrook and Ravenstor.

CAMPING AND CARAVAN SITES The National Park authority operates an advisory service from April to September to help visitors locate caravan sites in and around the Park. Telephone Bakewell 4341 for details.

In addition, the board produces a camping and caravanning leaflet which is updated each year. The board also maintains its own camp sites at Hagg Farm (Ashopton, near Bamford); and at Fieldhead, Edale; North Lees, Hathersage; Hayfield and Crowden; and also has camp sites available for tents and caravans at Losehill Hall, Castleton and Blackshaw Moor, near Leek.

A recent and very welcome Peak District innovation is a series of 'camping barns', which offer walkers simple basic accommodation, saving the need to carry or pitch a tent. Places can be booked by telephoning Hope Valley 20373.

PLACES OPEN TO THE PUBLIC
CHATSWORTH HOUSE (gardens and farmyard) The 'Palace of the Peak' and home of the Duke of Devonshire, Chatsworth has a wide range of attractions for the visitor. Apart from the magnificent house itself – which is a treasure-house of works of art – the gardens, laid out by Sir Joseph Paxton, and the children's farmyard and forest walk at the rear of the house are all of interest, and good examples of large estate interpretation.

HADDON HALL Home of the Duke of Rutland, Haddon Hall near Bakewell stands on a bluff above the River Wye, a perfect example of a mediaeval manor house. The romantic legend of Dorothy Vernon still pervades these ancient, rose-entwined walls.

LYME PARK, DISLEY This Palladian-fronted mansion on the edge of Manchester is famous for its herd of red deer. One of the sounds of the Peak is to hear the Lyme stags bellowing during the October rut.

THE OLD HOUSE, BAKEWELL A 15th century town house saved from demolition in 1955 by the Bakewell Historical Society, who carefully restored it as a local history museum.

PEVERIL CASTLE, CASTLETON In the care of the Department of the Environment this castle is also open to the public.

Show Caverns open to the public can be found at Bagshaw Cavern (Bradwell), Blue John Cavern and Mine (Castleton), Peak Cavern (Castleton), Speedwell Cavern (Castleton), Treak Cliff Cavern (Castleton), Poole's Cavern and Country Park (Buxton).

ANCIENT MONUMENTS
Grid reference

Arbor Low Stone Circle and Gib Hill Round Barrow, near Middleton	(SK 158633)
Stanton Moor Nine Ladies (stone circle and barrows)	(SK 248636)
Mam Tor Iron Age Hill Fort, Castleton	(SK 128837)

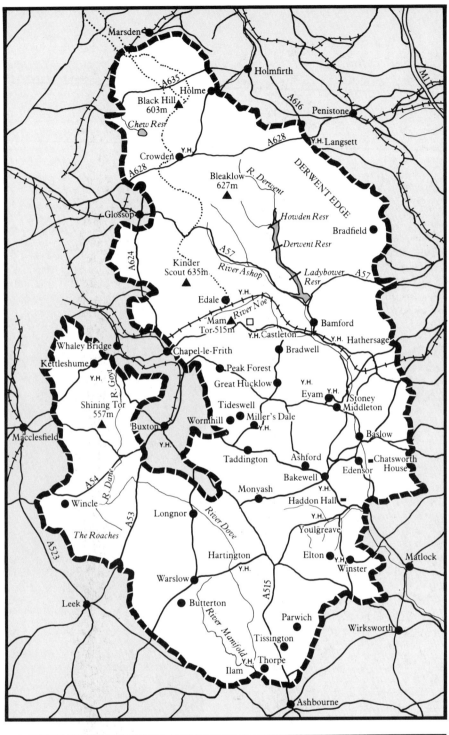

Marsden

Holmfirth

A635

Hölme

Black Hill
603m

Chew Resr

A616

Penistone

Y.H. Langsett

A628

Crowden

Y.H.

DERWENT EDGE

A628

Bleaklow
627m

R. Derwent

Howden Resr

Bradfield

Glossop

A57

Derwent Resr

A624

Kinder
Scout 635m

River Ashop

Ladybower
Resr

A57

Edale

Y.H.

River Noe

Mam
Tor 515m

Bamford

Y.H. Castleton

Y.H. Hathersage

Whaley Bridge

Chapel-le-Frith

Bradwell

Kettleshume

Y.H.

Peak Forest

R. Goyt

Great Hucklow

Y.H.

Shining Tor
557m

Buxton

Tideswell

Eyam

Y.H.

Stoney
Middleton

Wormhill

Miller's Dale

Y.H.

Baslow

Macclesfield

Y.H.

Taddington

Ashford

Bakewell

Chatsworth
House

Edensor

A54

R. Dane

Wincle

Monyash

Y.H.

Haddon Hall

Longnor

River Dove

Y.H.

Youlgreave

A53

The Roaches

Hartington

Y.H.

Elton

Y.H.

Winster

Matlock

A523

Warslow

A515

Butterton

Parwich

Wirksworth

River Manifold

Tissington

Y.H.

Thorpe

Ilam

Ashbourne

M1

============ National Park Boundary ▲ Spot Heights

———————— Road

•••••••••••••••••• Pennine Way

+—+—+—+—+—+ Railway

□ National Park Centre

Y.H. Youth Hostel

Carl Wark Hill Fort, Hathersage	(SK 260815)
Fin Cop Hill Fort, Ashford	(SK 175710)
Navio Roman Fort, Brough	(SK 181828)
Peveril Castle, Castleton	(SK 150826)
Pilsbury Castle Mounds, Hartington	(SK 114638)

MAPS

The Ordnance Survey, Peak District Tourist map (1 in to the mile, or 1 : 63,360 scale) covers the whole of the National Park in one sheet.

Better still are the OS's two Outdoor Leisure maps, the Dark Peak and the White Peak, which cover those areas in much greater detail to a scale of $2\frac{1}{2}$ in to the mile, or 1 : 25,000.

Both these maps show footpaths, bridleways and places of interest, as do the 1 : 50,000 scale Landranger maps. You will need sheet 119 (Buxton, Matlock and Dovedale) and sheet 110 (Sheffield and Huddersfield) of the Landranger maps to cover the main area of the Park.

FURTHER READING

Banks, F R, *The Peak District*, Hale, 1975.

Bellamy, Rex, *The Peak District Companion*, David & Charles, 1981.

Christian, Roy, *The Peak District*, David & Charles, 1976.

Dodd, A E & E M, *Peakland Roads and Trackways*, Moorland, 1974.

Ford, Trevor, & Rieuwerts J H (ed), *Lead Mining in the Peak District*, Peak Park Joint Planning Board, 1968.

Harris, Helen, *Industrial Archaeology of the Peak District*, David & Charles, 1971.

Millward, Roy, & Robinson, Adrian, *The Peak District*, Eyre Methuen, 1975.

Monkhouse, Patrick (ed), *Peak District National Park*, HMSO, 1960.

Porteous, Crichton, *Portrait of Peakland*, Hale, 1963.

Poucher, W A, *The Peak and Pennines*, Constable, 1966.

Smith, Roland, *First and Last*, Peak Park Joint Planning Board, 1978.

Wolverson Cope, F, *Geology Explained in the Peak District*, David & Charles, 1976.

Ladybower reservoir from Derwent Edge.

Blessing the wells, Hartington.

Bakewell Market is an important business and social occasion.

DRIVING

There are many scenic motor routes, like that which follows the Snake road via the vast Ladybower reservoir and crosses the Pennine Way to reach Glossop or, even better, the A515 which follows the line of a Roman road across the wide expanse of the limestone plateau between Ashbourne and Buxton.

In the White Peak area, a 'Routes for People' scheme provides an intricate system of scenic drives, picnic sites and car parks, waymarked footpaths, bridleways and cycle routes. You can even hire a bike from the former stations at Parsley Hay, Ashbourne, and Middleton Top on the Tissington and High Peak Trails, at Lyme Park, Monsal Head and at Fairholmes in the Upper Derwent valley, in the Peak's 'Lake District'.

WALKING

The best way to explore the Peak is undoubtedly on foot, and the Park is well served by footpaths. Many of the gentle hill and dale routes in the limestone country of the White Peak are waymarked (follow the yellow arrows) and require little in the way of equipment other than stout footwear.

Among the best of walks is that from Monyash through the entire length of magnificent Lathkill Dale, with its National Nature Reserve and remnants of former lead mining. The walk can be extended to Over Haddon or Alport (about 5 miles/8 km).

The Tissington and High Peak Trails, both former railway tracks, offer easy walking throughout their lengths and pass through some of the best of the limestone plateau scenery.

The Tissington Trail runs from Ashbourne to the quaintly-named junction at Parsley Hay, not far from Arbor Low (13 miles/21km) and the High Peak Trail, from Cromford up a steep incline to the plateau top and through to Dowlow, near Buxton (17 miles/27km).

Walking in the Dark Peak is a more serious proposition, for these dark foreboding moors should not be traversed unless you are equipped for the sudden vagaries of their climate. It comes as a surprise to many to learn that the green valley of Edale, in the shadow of Kinder, is on the same latitude as Siberia or Labrador. So the moral when walking here is, go prepared!

To get a taste of the Dark Peak, try the start of the Pennine Way from Edale to Kinder's plateau top, returning via Grindslow Knoll or the alternative Pennine Way route via Kinder Low and Jacob's Ladder.

CLIMBING AND CAVING

The gritstone edges of the Dark Peak were one of the birthplaces of the comparatively modern sport of rock climbing. The short but steep outcrops of coarse textured gritstone at places like Stanage, Laddow and the Roaches give exceptionally good holds, especially for beginners, and many of Britain's finest mountaineers cut their climbing teeth on these edges. Limestone climbing is a more recent development, in which artificial aids are used to climb apparently unscaleable vertical or overhanging walls.

Pot-holing in the underground world beneath the limestone is another popular sport for the specialist, and it centres on the Castleton area, where limestone and gritstone adjoin.

USEFUL ADDRESSES

The Peak National Park Office
Aldern House
Baslow Road
Bakewell DE4 1AE.

(tel. Bakewell 4321)

Peak National Park Study Centre
Losehill Hall
Castleton
Derbyshire S30 2WB.

(tel. Hope Valley 20373 or 20693)

NATIONAL PARK INFORMATION CENTRES

Bakewell Information Centre (T.I.C. also)
The Market Hall
Bridge Street
Bakewell.

(tel. Bakewell 3227)

Castleton Information Centre
Castle Street
Castleton.

(tel. Hope Valley 20679)

Edale Information Centre
Fieldhead
Edale.

(tel. Hope Valley 70207 or 70216)

Centres open during summer only

Fairholmes Information Centre (open daily)
Fairholmes
Upper Derwent Valley.

Goyt Valley Information Point
(sundays & bank holidays only)
Derbyshire Bridge
Near Buxton.

Hartington Old Signal Box Information Point
(weekends & bank holidays only)
Old Station
Hartington.

Torside Information Point
(weekends & bank holidays only)
Longdendale.

TOURIST INFORMATION CENTRES

Buxton Information Centre
The Crescent
Buxton.

(tel. Buxton 5106)

Matlock Information Centre
The Pavilion
Matlock Bath.

(tel. Matlock 55082)

Staffordshire Moorlands Information Centre
New Stockwell House
Stockwell Street
Leek
Staffs, ST13 6HG

(tel. Leek 385181 or 381000)

Yorkshire Dales National Park

WILDERNESS AND WARMTH

John Bigland, in his *Geographical and Historical View of the World* of 1810, wrote, 'The mountains of Craven in Yorkshire, especially Whamside, Pennygant and Ingleborough are the highest in England.'

He quoted their heights, according to Housman's tables, as Whernside – 4,050 ft (1,235 m), Pen-y-Ghent – 3,930 ft (1,197 m) and Ingleborough – 3,987 ft (1,215 m) and although today we know the heights of Yorkshire's celebrated Three Peaks should be the more modest 2,414 ft (736 m), 2,273 ft (694 m) and 2,373 ft (723 m) respectively, it is easy to understand those early geographers' exaggerations.

Such is the noble presence of these three mountain forms, which rise each in splendid isolation above the wild moorland basin of Ribblehead, that each gives the same impression of being much higher than it really is. And with the not-infrequent dustings of snow they receive each year, they seem to take on the appearance of real alpine giants.

The Three Peak country centred around Ribblehead epitomises the landscape of the Yorkshire Dales National Park.

It is a geologist's paradise of land forms not found in the same rich profusion anywhere else in Britain and the area has become the destination of many school geography field trips. It gives thousands of youngsters their first taste and understanding of the monumental forces of nature which shaped our country.

In other parts of the 680 square mile (1,761 sq km) National Park (designated in 1954 and the third largest after the Lake District and Snowdonia), crystal-clear becks disappear mysteriously into deep underground caverns, only to reappear just as unexpectedly several miles downstream.

Other rivers create a series of spectacular waterfalls as they flow over the 'steps' of harder rock, like the Ure at Aysgarth or Hardraw in Wensleydale; and up on the fell tops, acres of bare, dry, ankle-busting rock are exposed – creased and fretted like crazy paving –

Deepdale, near Dent.

above enormous dizzy gorges of sheer limestone where only the hardiest, most tenacious vegetation can survive.

The dales themselves, Swaledale, Wensleydale, Warfedale, Littondale, Ribblesdale and the smaller, westward flowing Garsdale and Dentdale, thrust lush green fingers into the heart of the hills, creating another more tranquil and settled landscape. Criss-crossed by miles of drystone walls and punctuated by clumps of trees, they contrast strongly with the fells in between.

But although the rocks were the major influence in what has happened since on the surface of these dales, the effect of Man's hand over at least 4,000 years can still be traced by a trained eye in many places on the landscape.

Man could not change the pearly-grey limestone 'scars' and gorges of Malham, Kilnsey and Gordale, where shining cliffs up to 300 ft (91 m) high sweep up in layers above the verdant, bright green sheep-cropped pastures. Although Man may be seen to be creating his own 'scars' in the quarries of Ribblesdale, they cannot match the landscapes which so influenced people like that 'artist of light' – Joseph Turner.

And there's not much sign of Man's influence either up on the millstone grit moorlands above Wensleydale and Swaledale in the north, and Wharfedale in the east, where heather and peat bog are dominant and the only form of life, apart from the white-nosed Swaledale sheep, is often the hardy fell-walker.

Elsewhere, however, and especially in the dales – where the small stone villages echo the type of rock on which they were built, seeming to grow quite naturally out of their surrounding landscape – the unique dales culture flourished.

It has received many influences over the years, from the still visible rectangular fields of the pre-historic Celts, to the Romans, the Vikings, the Angles and the Danes who left their legacy in so many of the distinctive place names of the region.

The dales also came under the sway of the great mediaeval sheep ranchers who lived in the peaceful seclusion of the monasteries and abbeys of Fountains, Bolton and Jervaulx. It was these hooded holy men who were largely responsible for introducing sheep to the fells 800 years ago, and their still beautiful, though now ruined, abbeys grew rich from the proceeds. The romantic ruins of Bolton and nearby Fountains can still give the modern visitor a kind of spiritual uplift.

Anyone who walks that length of the broad, green, stone-walled highway between Malham and Kilnsey, known as Mastiles Lane, follows in the footsteps of generations of dales folk who have used these greenways for centuries. You cannot fail to be aware of that unique sense of continuity which the dales possess as you tramp these breezy curlew-haunted upland pastures.

It is a land where Man, until recently at least, had adapted, not changed, the physical environment and the eight million visitors who throng in for day visits every year, mainly from the industrial cities of West Yorkshire and East Lancashire, come to enjoy that fine balance between the wilderness and the warmth of dales life.

Again, it is pre-eminently walkers' country, spreading across the Pennine watershed of England up which the Pennine Way wanders in one of its most rewarding and spectacular sections between Malham, Horton-in-Ribblesdale, Hawes and Keld. But there are more than 1,000 miles (1,610 km) of public footpaths and bridleways to enable you to enjoy this superb scenery, and the National Park authority has negotiated a special access-agreement covering 14,000 acres (5,665 ha) of glorious heather moorland either side of the Wharfe at Barden Moor and Barden Fell, including the wonderful viewpoint of Simon's Seat (1,532 ft/467 m) overlooking Appletreewick and the Upper Wharfe.

One of the most pressing problems facing the National Park authority, administrated by a committee of the North Yorkshire County Council, is how to reconcile its twin duties of conservation of the landscape with the provision of facilities for public enjoyment. In recent years, the interests of the local community of about 18,500 residents have taken on an increased importance, and though some dales people may resent the invasion from the towns, particularly when it interferes with their living or way of life, tourism has also brought much-needed wealth.

Perhaps the greatest headache for the authority is the large-scale extraction of limestone from the eight active quarries within the Park. One of the most worrying and illogical aspects is that of the three million tonnes taken annually, only about 20 per cent

Walls and barns, Swaledale.

is used for the purposes to which it is best suited, in the chemical industries. The vast majority of the very pure limestone is wasted in roadstone aggregate, for which almost any stone would be appropriate. Apart from destroying the very fabric of the National Park, these quarries create problems of noise, dust and heavy traffic on narrow roads. But as planning permission was given in most cases before National Park designation, and in the ludicrous absence of any national policy for mineral extraction, they are likely to remain a thorny problem in the side of the planners.

Mineral extraction, in the ancient small-scale lead mines at places like Gunnerside in Swaledale, around Upper Wharfedale, or in various village quarries for building stone, has long been a traditional industry of the area. But the sheer scale of modern quarries, whose faces can be over a mile long, threatens changes to the landscape more violent than anything seen in the past.

THE NATURAL LANDSCAPE: AN UNCONFORMING LAND

Lovely Thornton Force, at the head of what Wainwright has called, 'The most delightful walk of its kind in the country,' through the Swilla Glen at Ingleton, is one of the most famous geological localities in Britain.

Dr Arthur Raistrick, the celebrated dales historian and geologist, defied anyone to place a hand between the limestones of the upper part of the falls, over which the Kingsdale Beck plunges, and the upturned edge of the greenish Cambrian slates on which they have been superimposed, and not feel the power of the 300 million year time gap between the two rocks.

The dales are a classic example of what geologists call an 'unconformity'. And the varied and spectacular landscapes of the Yorkshire Dales certainly do not conform to the preconceived ideas that many people have about the North of England.

There are none of Blake's 'dark, Satanic mills' here, instead you will find a fascinating and ever-changing landscape which graduates between high and bleak gritstone moors, splendidly isolated mountains, wide pastoral dales and dramatic limestone gorges with waterfall-filled ravines.

The oldest rocks are those multi-coloured slates of the Doe and Twiss glens above Ingleton, which are variously estimated to be between 500 and 600 million years old, from the Cambrian or Ordovician eras.

The majority of the dales' structure, however, was laid down, like the rest of the Pennines, in the warm, tropical seas of the Carboniferous period, about 300 million years ago. The limestones formed in these peaceful conditions are today known as the Great Scar or mountain limestones, and give us the distinctive landscape features of the many 'scars' or steep outcrops of naked white rock which culminate in the impressive amphitheatres of Malham Cove and Gordale Scar, revealed by the line of the Mid-Craven fault.

Above the scars are broad areas of a landscape so foreign to our eyes that it could almost be called lunar. These are the so-called limestone pavements; but despite their name, great care should be taken when walking across them.

The white-grey limestone is split into deep crevices called 'grikes' which shelter shade-loving ferns and flowers, leaving blocks called 'clints' which themselves are often weathered into curious water-filled grooves.

Carboniferous limestone is soluble in the weak carbonic acid formed by rainwater and in the humic acid of the soil, and over thousands of years these two acids have eaten into the joints of the rocks, leaving the strange pavements of today.

The best examples of these pavements can be seen above Malham Cove, which once had a waterfall higher than Niagara pouring over its 300 ft (91 m) cliff, and on the broad limestone plateau on which Ingleborough rises.

The whole of the limestone region is a country made hollow through the action of water on rock. Miles of underground caverns have been traced by intrepid pot-holers who follow the swallow holes and sinks where the water suddenly disappears.

The best known pot is the fearsome, 365 ft (111 m) deep fern-fringed hole of Gaping Gill on the slopes of Ingleborough above Clapham. The huge cavern excavated by the waters of Fell Beck is said to be large enough to swallow St Paul's Cathedral, and miles of passages lead off under the hillside.

But the best way for the tourist to explore underground Yorkshire is through one of the many show caverns open to the public, like Ingleborough Cave, or the White Scar Cave on the Ingleton-Hawes road. For the more adventurous, caving holidays are run from the Whernside Cave and Fell Centre, near Dent.

Sylvan Wensleydale, formed by the River Ure, was formerly known as Yoredale. As such it gave its name to the other important series of rock types in the National Park – the Yoredale series.

These are a succession of repeated but often irregular cycles of limestones, shales and sandstones which give us the stepped profile of many dale sides and hills, created when the more easily-eroded shales left projecting ledges of harder sandstones or limestones.

The proud outlines of Ingleborough and Pen-y-Ghent, often and accurately likened to crouching lions, result from this uneven erosion, and they are capped by a resistant layer of millstone grit from the same era.

The small, conical hills around Thorpe and Malham are the ancient remains of coral reefs – just like those found in the modern Pacific Ocean – which built up in the shallow waters of that Carboniferous sea. Strangely, similar 'reef knolls', as they are known, are also to be found round the village of Thorpe in the Derbyshire Peak District.

Nowhere in England will you find better evidence of the effects of glaciation than here in the Yorkshire Dales. The great, overhanging scar of Kilnsey Crag in Wharfedale marks the height of the top of the glacier when the rock face was eroded and the broad U-shaped valley was created.

At Norber Brow, above Austwick on the western edge of the Park, the enormous power of the retreating ice is graphically illustrated. The Norber erratics are a collection of dark-coloured, Silurian rocks perched incongruously on limestone pedestals after being carried some 400 ft (122 m) uphill by the ice, perhaps 20,000 years ago.

There are not many lakes in this fast-draining lime-

Left: Gordale Scar.

Right: Drystone walls, Horton-in-Ribblesdale.

stone country, but both Semerwater near Bainbridge and Malham Tarn were created by the terminal moraines left by the melting glaciers.

Malham Tarn Field Centre, at Tarn House on the shores of the 153 acre (62 ha) lake is a nationally respected field studies centre for those wishing to learn more about the fascinating natural history of the dales. Charles Kingsley stayed here while he wrote *The Water Babies*, and it's hard to imagine a more idyllic setting.

The brilliant gold lanterns of the globe flower are a feature of the approach to the tarn from Longcliffe; and elsewhere on the limestone, the scarlet stars of herb robert and the delicate fronds of hart's-tongue fern peep out from the grikes of the serrated pavements. Quite extensive patches of rare native orchids are also found on the high limestone pastures, with scented carpets of wild thyme – but please leave them all for others to enjoy.

The native tree cover has long since been removed in most places, but here and there stands of dark green stunted yews hang on, in the sparse soil of the ledges of the scars, along with ash and hawthorn. The same trees, with the addition of the opportunist sycamore, provide shelter for stock in the more lush pastures of the dale bottoms.

All the most common species of British mammals – the fox, badger, rabbit, hare, stoat and weasel – inhabit the valleys, but there are few deer.

Bird life is dominated on the heather moorland by red grouse, golden plover, skylarks and meadow pipits, but perhaps the most typical sound is the one all fell walkers love to hear, the bubbling call of the curlew.

Dippers are common in the river valleys, and woodcock and snipe can be seen 'roding' along the rides of the woodlands.

Two dozen 'Sites of Special Scientific Interest' are listed by the Nature Conservancy Council covering 10 per cent of the National Park, and there are National Nature Reserves at Colt Park (an ash wood) and Ling Gill (a limestone gorge) in Ribblesdale.

The Yorkshire Dales have, so far, escaped the large-scale attentions of the Forestry Commission, but nevertheless more than half the Park's acreage of woodland is filled with soft-wood conifers planted since 1966. These are most noticeable in Langstrothdale, where, ironically, a place named Green Fields on the OS map is now completely submerged under uniform forestry plantations.

Left: Lead mining remains, Gunnerside Gill.

Right: Ingleborough, from Twistleton Scar End.

MAN'S INFLUENCE: A SENSE OF PLACE

It is said that a practised listener can tell, just by hearing a dalesman speak, not only which dale he comes from, but what part of that dale.

A glance at the Ordnance Survey map shows a distinct pattern of settlement along each valley, with place names of villages and natural features giving tell-tale clues as to who first named them. Successive invasions by Anglian, Danish and Norse settlers occupied those parts of the dales which best suited their own farming systems.

Thus, as Dr Arthur Raistrick has shown, place names which end in the suffix 'ley' from the Anglian *leah* meaning a clearing (for example, Wensley) or the suffix 'ton' from *tun* meaning an enclosed settlement, as in Horton-in-Ribblesdale, Bolton, Grinton or Grassington, indicate early settlements by these pirates from the Saxon coast. Generally speaking, they settled in lower valleys where the pastures suited their arable or cattle-breeding systems.

Further up the dales, there is a belt of Danish-sounding names – typically ending in 'by' and 'thorpe'; for example, Kirkby Malham, or Thorpe – which show how far the 9th century Danish invasions reached.

The final invasion came over the fells from the west, when the Norsemen or Vikings flooded into the

dales from Ireland and the Lake District to settle on the land which was most like their homeland in Norway.

They preferred the steep, dale heads and fells where they could run their sheep in peace; for the bleak country had been left largely uninhabited by the Angles and Danes.

Limestone pavement, Malham.

You can see the evidence of their settlement everywhere, because they were the first to put a name to many natural features. Examples are, *fell, beck, gill, mere, moss, tarn, foss* (waterfall) and *rigg* (ridge), all of which are pure Norse names which would be recognised just as easily by a farmer from Bergen or Buckden. Even the word *dale* (valley) comes from those Norse settlers of ten centuries ago.

Thwaite is another typically Norse name, for example, Yockenthwaite in Langstrothdale, or simply, Thwaite in Swaledale; and 'seat' or 'side' which comes from the Norse *saetr* for a spring shieling or pasture, can be seen in Gunnerside (Gunnar's saetr), and Rogan's Seat and Lovely Seat, above Keld – also in the far north of the National Park.

Although these Vikings, Angles and Danes were the first people to put recorded names to the parts of the dales they knew, the history of Man's settlement goes back much further.

Scattered, isolated finds of tiny flint or chert implements, known as 'microliths', have been made high on the peaty moorlands above the dales. These provide conclusive proof that Middle Stone Age (Mesolithic) man used these then heavily wooded uplands

to scrape a living, by hunting wild beasts or gathering fruit or nuts.

The dales do not have the large numbers of hill-top burial mounds or tumuli found further south in the Pennines, but in the pleasant, dry and warm climate of the Bronze and Iron Ages, the people of the dales flourished, as is shown by the profusion of so-called 'Celtic Fields' marked on the Ordnance Survey map.

Around Grassington, Malham and Ingleborough there are extensive remains of the small, usually rectangular fields and hut sites of the Bronze Age, Iron Age and the Romano-British period. They are best seen from aerial photographs, but, in the right conditions of a low sun in the early morning or late afternoon, the slightly raised embankments of the walls can be picked out by their shadows on the ground. Lynchets, long, stepped fields on the dale sides formed by constant ploughing by teams of oxen, are also commonly visible.

The Romans passed this way, but made surprisingly little impression on the life of the dales. The Roman fort at Brough Hill in Bainbridge in Wensleydale is one of the few tangible remains, although their road across Dodd Fell to Ingleton can still be traced.

The lead deposits around Greenhow Hill in the south-east corner of the Park, and in Swaledale in the far north, were the major attraction for the Romans, and pigs of lead have been found inscribed with the names of the emperors Trajan and Hadrian.

One pig of lead also carried the abbreviation 'Brig', thought to represent the tribal name of the Brigantes, who occupied the area at the time. The great Brigantian leader, Venutius, is thought to have used the great Iron Age hillfort, on the 2,373 ft (723 m) summit of Ingleborough, as his headquarters at the time of his unsuccessful revolt against the Romans in 74 AD.

About 20 circular hut sites can still be traced on the summit plateau, along with the remains of a stout military wall defending them.

The departure of the Roman legions left the area clear for the Vikings, Angles and Danes who, as already said, were the first people to 'civilise' the region.

The iron hand of the Norman invader was felt, and left its mark in the splendid ruins of Bolton Castle in Wensleydale, where Mary Queen of Scots was imprisoned for a time, and in Barden Tower in Wharfedale.

Most of the present area of the dales was used for hunting by the mediaeval landlords, and it is interesting to see that the Ordnance Survey still persists with

Muker, Swaledale.

the ancient name of Langstrothdale Chase for the area at the heart of the National Park around Buckden in Upper Wharfedale.

The most important monastic remains are the ruins of the Augustian priory at Bolton, now known as Bolton Abbey and still used, in part, as the parish church. The name Fountains Fell in Littondale, gives a clue to the power exercised by the white-robed Cistercian monks of Fountains Abbey in far-off Nidderdale, who used vast areas of the fells as sheep ranches.

Sheep are still the biggest money-spinners in the Park, and the hardy hill breed known as the Swaledale, after the valley of its origin, still grazes the pastures that were walled so many years ago.

The other major industries were lead mining,

probably started by the Romans, a small amount of local coal-mining in shallow pits, and those water mills, used successively for corn, textiles, cotton and woollens or worsteds, whose presence can be seen in most valleys, now either as private houses or in place-names alone.

For those interested in the increasingly popular hobby of industrial archaeology, the area around

An erratic boulder, Norber Brow.

Gunnerside in Swaledale is a fascinating centre for the exploration of the old lead mines.

The walk up Gunnerside Gill will reveal many remains of the days of the 17th and 18th century 'lead boom' in the area. The ruins of the smelt mills, and the levels and shafts of the old miners can still be seen, and the deep ravines in the now quiet hillsides are known as 'hushes', after an old method of reaching the lead veins by damming a stream and then releasing the water, which effectively excavated the hillside.

Other famous and impressive remains are at the Old Gang Mines, in Hard Level Gill near Healaugh, lower down the dale. At one time there were 20 smelt mills in Swaledale, and you can still pick up oddly-heavy stones from the old miners' waste tips which indicate the presence of the precious galena or lead ore.

Perhaps the best centres for exploring Swaledale and the wild north of the Park are the villages of Reeth (the market town for the dale) and Grinton which has the mainly-Perpendicular mother church of the dale. Gunnerside is also convenient for exploring the lead-mining remains, the wild side-valley of Arkengarthdale and the famous pot-holed pass which links Swaledale with Wensleydale – the 1,726 ft (526 m) Buttertubs.

Wensleydale, the valley of the River Ure, is probably best known for giving its name to a pale, mild cheese. The dale is threaded by the A684, and includes the honeypots of the Aysgarth Falls, Castle

Thornton Force, Ingleton.

Bolton and Hardraw Force waterfall, the longest single-drop fall in the country.

Hawes is the main centre for Upper Wensleydale and is now the main market place for dales sheep, with up to 100,000 a year bought and sold. Bainbridge, with its Roman fort and 17th century Yorebridge Grammar School, retains the custom of a nightly curfew horn.

Many people's favourite dale is Wharfedale, including its charming subsidiary of Littondale. From Bolton Abbey, with the famous Strid rapids in its grounds, up to Grassington, Kilnsey, Kettlewell and Buckden, the dale offers everything that is best about this part of England. Arncliffe in Littondale, is said to get its name from 'eagles cliff', but the modern eagles are hang gliders who soar just as effortlessly from Knipe Scar over the appropriately named High Wind Bank.

The fascinating geology and history around Upper Airedale is best explored from Malham, where the

youth hostel is named after John Dower, who lived here when he produced his historic report to Parliament which led to the establishment of our National Parks.

Wild Ribblesdale, with its dramatic though threatened 24-arch Batty Moss viaduct on the spectacular Settle-Carlisle line, was once proposed as a separate wilderness area at the heart of the National Park. This is the centre of Three Peak country, with the market town of Settle or Horton-in-Ribblesdale as the most convenient centres.

Sedbergh is the best centre for exploring the remote and almost forgotten dales of Dentdale and Garsdale on the western edge of the Park, or the smooth slopes of the Howgill Fells which give a gentle introduction to the drama of the Lakeland Peaks.

A line of lovely, stone-built villages runs along the A65 which forms the southern boundary of the Park – including Ingleton (with its justly famous Waterfalls Walk and ease of access to the pot-holes and crags of Ingleborough), Clapham, Settle and finally Skipton, just outside the Park but the famous castle-crowned 'Gateway to the Dales'.

Left: Pen-y-Ghent from Horton-in-Ribblesdale.

Below: Limestone columns, Buttertubs Pass.

What to do

HOW TO GET THERE

BY ROAD From the south, the motorist has the choice of either the M1–M6 or the M1–A1. Choice will depend on what part of the Park a driver wishes to visit, but as most dales run west-east, the most direct route from the A1 will take the motorist on the A59 from Harrogate to Bolton Abbey and Wharfedale, the A684 from Ripon for Wensleydale, or the A6136 for Richmond and Swaledale.

The A65 for the centres of Ribblesdale and Malham can best be reached from the west from Junction 31 (Preston) or 34 (Lancaster) off the M6.

BY RAIL Inter-City services go to Settle and Skipton and there are paytrain services to Gargrave, Hellifield, Long Preston, Giggleswick, Clapham and Bentham. In addition the National Park authority has pioneered a special service along the celebrated Settle-Carlisle line called Dalesrail. It serves the double purpose of getting visitors from the towns to the dales for sightseeing and walking, and getting dales people to the towns for shopping. Linked with guided walks and special connecting bus services, it shows that public transport *can* be made to work in isolated rural areas.

WHERE TO STAY

The National Park authority produces its annually updated, comprehensive *Accommodation Guide* (including camping and caravan sites), in conjunction

Pennine Way walkers, Pen-y-Ghent.

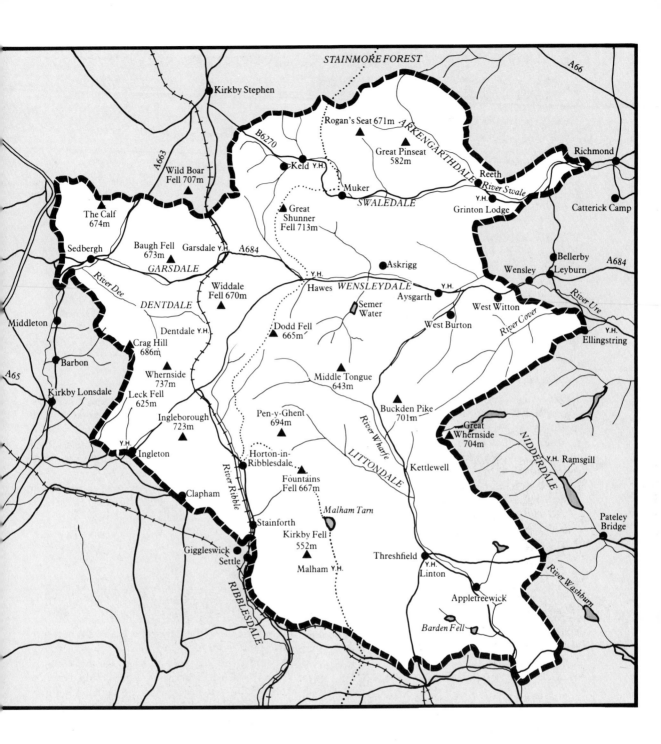

STAINMORE FOREST

A66

Kirkby Stephen

Rogan's Seat 671m

ARKENGARTHDALE

Great Pinseat 582m

Richmond

B6270

Keld Y.H.

Reeth

Muker

River Swale

Catterick Camp

Wild Boar Fell 707m

A663

SWALEDALE

The Calf 674m

Great Shunner Fell 713m

Grinton Lodge

Sedbergh

Baugh Fell 673m

Garsdale Y.H.

A684

Askrigg

Wensley

Bellerby

Leyburn

A684

Widdale Fell 670m

GARSDALE

River Dee

DENTDALE

Hawes Y.H.

WENSLEYDALE

Y.H.

Aysgarth

West Witton

River Ure

Middleton

Dentdale Y.H.

Semer Water

West Burton

River Cover

Y.H.

Ellingstring

Barbon

Crag Hill 686m

Dodd Fell 665m

A65

Kirkby Lonsdale

Whernside 737m

Leck Fell 625m

Middle Tongue 643m

Buckden Pike 701m

Great Whernside 704m

NIDDERDALE

Ingleborough 723m

Pen-y-Ghent 694m

River Wharfe

LITTONDALE

Y.H. Ramsgill

Y.H.

Ingleton

Horton-in-Ribblesdale

Kettlewell

Clapham

River Ribble

Fountains Fell 667m

Pateley Bridge

Stainforth

Malham Tarn

Kirkby Fell 552m

Threshfield

Y.H.

Linton

River Washburn

Giggleswick

Settle

Malham Y.H.

Appletreewick

RIBBLESDALE

Barden Fell

National Park Boundary
▲ Spot Heights

Road

Pennine Way

Railway

Motorway

Y.H. Youth Hostel

with the Yorkshire Dales Tourist Association. It includes self-catering units, bunkhouses, hotels, guest houses and a list of activity centres in the Park.

YOUTH HOSTELS There are hostels at Aysgarth, Dentdale, Garsdale, Grinton, Hawes, Ingleton, Keld, Kettlewell, Linton, Malham and Stainforth.

CAMPING AND CARAVAN SITES Camping and caravanning information is provided in a Dales Park/Tourist authorities' joint accommodation booklet, available from information centres.

PLACES OPEN TO THE PUBLIC

BOLTON ABBEY Really a priory of the Augustinian Order, founded in 1151, it occupies picturesque grounds in the wooden valley of the Wharfe, with walks to the famous narrow rock channel of the Strid.

CASTLE BOLTON Sir Nikolaus Pevsner called this massive ruin 'a climax of English military architecture', and it certainly still dominates the lower reaches of Wensleydale, as it was intended to do when first built in the late 14th century. Mary Queen of Scots was held here in 1568.

Other castles worth visiting on the edge of the Park are at Middleham further down Wensleydale near Leyburn, and Skipton at the southern 'gateway'.

There are show caves open to the public showing the underground splendours of the limestone at Ingleborough Cave near Clapham, White Scar Caves, Ingleton and at Stump Cross Caverns on top of the moors between Wharfedale and Nidderdale.

ANCIENT MONUMENTS

	Grid reference
Yockenthwaite Stone Circle, Buckden	(SD 899794)
Grassington Enclosure	(SE 004650/7)
Ingleborough Hill Fort	(SD 742746)
Maiden Castle Hill Fort, Grinton	(SE 022981)
Bainbridge Roman Camp	(SD 938901)
Ellerton Priory, Swaledale	(SE 078974)
Bolton Castle, Castle Bolton	(SE 034918)
Barden Tower, Wharfedale	(SE 051572)

MAPS

Two excellent Ordnance Survey Outdoor Leisure maps, based on the 1 : 25,000 scale ($2\frac{1}{2}$ in to the mile) and showing all the detail anyone could reasonably require, cover most of the Park. They are *The Three*

Peaks and *Malham and Upper Wharfedale*. In addition, Landranger maps (1 : 50,000 scale – $1\frac{1}{4}$ in to the mile), nos 92, 97, 98, 99, 103 and 104 also cover the area.

FURTHER READING

Brumhead, Derek, *Geology Explained in the Yorkshire Dales*, David & Charles, 1979.

Dalesman Guide to the Yorkshire Dales, The, Dalesman, 1980.

Hartley, M, & Inglby, J, *The Yorkshire Dales*, Dent, 1963.

Raistrick, Arthur, *The Pennine Dales*, Eyre Methuen, 1968.

Raistrick, Arthur, *Old Yorkshire Dales*, David & Charles, 1968.

Scott, Harry, *Portrait of Yorkshire*, Hale, 1965.

Simmons, I G (ed), *Yorkshire Dales National Park*, HMSO, 1971.

Wainwright, A, *Walks in Limestone Country*, Westmorland Gazette, 1970.

Yorkshire's Three Peaks, Dalesman, 1969.

The Yorkshire Dales National Park authority also publishes a fine range of walking and specialist subject leaflets. Also recommended are the fine series of Dalesman booklets by Dr Raistrick, including *Ice Age in Yorkshire*, *Lead Mining in the Yorkshire Dales*, *Prehistoric Yorkshire*, *The Romans in Yorkshire* and *Vikings, Angles and Danes in Yorkshire*, together with his *Monks and Shepherds in the Yorkshire Dales*, published by the National Park authority.

DRIVING

Most visitors come to the dales by car, and too few ever leave them, as any fine weekend at Malham on the B6160 through Wharfedale, or the B6479 through Ribblesdale will show. Because most roads, by necessity, must follow the dales, and many are narrowly hemmed in by drystone walls, they get congested in the summer holiday period. Even so, the B6255 or B6479 – which will take you to the desolate heart of Ribblesdale – or the run up or down the B6270 through Swaledale, or the A684 through Wensleydale are fine routes.

WALKING

Anyone wishing to walk in Three Peaks country should not go without Wainwright's *Walks in*

Clints and grikes, Twistleton Scar End, near Ingleton.

Malham Cove.

Limestone Country. Based on the A65 route from his beloved Lake District, its list of more than 30 walks is the best possible introduction to these parts.

Wainwright believes the 9 mile (14.5 km) return route from Clapham, through the Reginald Farrer Nature Trail (4 miles/6.4 km for the less energetic) via Ingleborough Cave, Trow Gill and past Gaping Gill to Ingleborough is the finest of the lot, and for continuous interest, it does take some beating. The Ingleton Glens walk (4.25 miles/6.8 km) has the advantage that it can be done in most weathers because much of it is over made paths and stairways, and the range of waterfalls seen in the twin valleys of the Doe and Twiss is unrivalled, with Thornton Force as the reward at the top.

The National Park's excellent OS-based walks leaflets with informative maps are highly recommended for short walks based in each of the major dales.

For the more ambitious, the Pennine Way which

snakes through the Park, and the Dalesman Hike between Kettlewell and Settle both offer sterner challenges.

CLIMBING, TREKKING AND CANOEING

Severe climbing routes on the vertical and overhanging limestone cliffs of Malham, Gordale and Kilnsey are strictly for the experts, but there are a number of less serious crags to tempt the scrambler. Permission should be sought from landowners first.

There are an increasing number of pony-trekking centres, and some canoeing takes place on the Wharfe and Ure. In addition, you can enjoy a casual holiday on the Leeds & Liverpool Canal, which runs through part of the dales.

USEFUL ADDRESSES

Yorkshire Dales National Park Office
'Colvend'
Hebden Road
Grassington
Skipton BD23 5LB.

(tel. Grassington 752748)

Yorebridge House
Bainbridge
Leyburn, NL8 5BP.

(tel. Wenslydale 50456)

The Yorkshire Dales Tourist Association
2 Raines Meadows
Grassington
Skipton BD23 5NB.

(tel. Grassington 752388)

Whernside Centre
Dent
Sedbergh
Cumbria LA10 5RF.

(tel. Dent 213)

Malham Tarn Field Studies Centre
Malham
Settle
North Yorkshire.

(tel. Airton 331)

NATIONAL PARK INFORMATION CENTRES

These can be found at Aysgarth
(tel. Aysgarth 424), Hawes (tel. Hawes 450),
Clapham (tel. Clapham 419), Malham (tel. Airton 363)
Sedbergh (tel. Sedbergh 20125) and Grassington 752748

TOURIST INFORMATION CENTRES

These can be found at Bentham
(tel. Bentham 61043), Ingleton (tel. Ingleton 41049),
Leyburn (tel. Wensleydale 23069),
Ripon (tel. Ripon 4625),
Settle (tel. Settle 3617)
and Skipton (tel. Skipton 2809).

Richmond (tel. Richmond 3525),
Harrogate (tel. Harrogate 65912),
Horton-in-Ribblesdale (tel. H-in-R 333),
Reeth (tel. Richmond 84373 – evenings only).

Lake District National Park

A NATIONAL PROPERTY

To the Tourist Board of today, it is quite simply 'the most beautiful corner of England', but to Daniel Defoe, the cynical 18th century journalist and writer, it was 'a country eminent only for being the wildest, most barren and frightful of any that I have passed over in England.'

For Defoe – writing in his *Tour Through the Whole Island of Great Britain* – the Lakeland hills 'had an inhospitable terror in them', and Dr John Brown, describing the lake and vale of Keswick in 1769, saw 'rocks and cliffs of stupendous heights, hanging broken over the lake in horrible grandeur.'

Thomas Gray, author of the famous *Elegy*, dared go no further into the jaws of Borrowdale than Grange in the same year, explaining 'all farther access is here barred to prying mortals.'

It is easy to scoff at the fears and opinions of these 18th century romantics and travellers. After all, these paths are now trodden by infants and pensioners alike, thrilled to come into contact with the most superb mountain scenery in England.

But we should not forget that landscape appreciation is a relatively modern phenomenon, and that 200 years ago if an area did not yield commercial wealth or possibilities it was not considered important enough to merit comment.

Holidays and leisure pursuits for the mass of the people were unheard of in those days, and there was little demand for the kind of 'Picturesque Beauty' which travellers like Brown, Gray and later William Gilpin so admired.

It was in the Lake District that the popularisation of natural beauty began, through William Wordsworth, the Cumbrian poet who not only first described its beauties to a wider audience in his famous *Guide Through the District of the Lakes*, but also foresaw the problems such popularity would bring.

The 1835 Wordsworth guide is still one of the finest there is to the district, but it highlights the quandary every sensitive guidebook author faces

Fairfield from Loughrigg Fell.

when writing about beautiful unspoiled country. A good description will inevitably lead to an increased number of visitors. When the extension of the London-Carlisle line from Oxenholme to Kendal and Windermere opened, Wordsworth thundered in one of his most famous outbursts, 'Is then no nook of English ground secure from rash assault?'

Today, with the Lake District a mere five hours from London and only two from Manchester on the M6, tourists swarm to the 'honeypots' of Windermere, Grasmere and Hawkshead, and the villages are beginning to suffer from the sheer weight of car-borne visitors.

Visitor management is the most pressing of the problems facing the Lake District National Park, which was designated in August, 1951 and covers 880 square miles (2,280 sq km). It is the largest of our National Parks and is administered, like the Peak District, by an autonomous planning board, within Cumbria County Council.

People throng to the Lake District today for the same reasons as Wordsworth, who wrote in his 1822 *Description of the Scenery*, 'I do not know any tract of country in which, in so narrow a compass, may be found an equal variety in the influences of light and shadow upon the substance and beautiful features of the landscape.'

It is not a large area and the hardy walker – which must include Wordsworth, who was estimated by his friend Thomas de Quincey to have covered between 175,000 and 180,000 miles (282,000–290,000 km) on foot – can cross it in a day. But other visitors have often compared its modest hills and mountains with the best of the Alps.

When you enter the impressive valley of Wasdale, with the distinctive crag-bound triangle of Great Gable (2,949 ft/899 m) at its head, flanked on one side by Lingmell, and by Yewbarrow on the other, with the whole group reflected in the sinister surface of Wastwater, it is indeed easy to add a thousand feet or more to their height in your imagination.

The secret of the Lake District lies in its *scale*. Nowhere else in Britain is there found such a mixture of broad expanses of water, noble fells, craggy and challenging mountains, and lush green valleys. But the scale is always intimate, and never as vast or immense, to our modern tastes at least, as say the Torridon Highlands or the Cairngorms of Scotland.

It is a place where Man has come to terms with nature without actually taming it. The farms or statesmen's houses seem to blend naturally into the fellside, and the mountains, although the highest that England has to offer, always seem attainable, as does the stone-walled network of the valley floor when seen from the tops.

It is an odd fact that although the area has always been known as 'the Lakes', only one lake is shown on the 1 in Ordnance Survey map. Bassenthwaite Lake in the north west is the only lake to carry that suffix, the rest all being 'meres', 'waters', or, if one of the smaller reed-fringed pools high in the hills, 'tarns' (from the Old Norse *tjorn*). So it is as incorrect to refer to *Lake* Windermere, or *Lake* Coniston Water as it is to talk about the High Street Road or Mount Snowdon Hill.

Each lake has its special and distinct character, from the busy, commercial bustle of popular Windermere, at 10.5 miles (17 km) the largest lake in England, to the sombre scree-fringed shores of Wastwater, the deepest. Ullswater, with its three distinct reaches, is many people's favourite, winding in a serpentine fashion from the high fells of Patterdale to the gentler pastures of Pooley Bridge at its northern end. The banning of motor boats here was a godsend and has restored the peace of these still, reflective waters.

The hand of Man is evident in other lakes, however, with Thirlmere (formerly Leathswater) and Haweswater (formerly a small lake in Mardale) both acting as reservoirs for the thirsty people of far-off Manchester. Both lakes are periodically subject to the unsightly scum of a shoreline of pale exposed rocks when the reservoirs are 'drawn down' in times of drought. This is a phenomenon not seen in natural lakes, and lovers of the district were greatly heartened when plans by British Nuclear Fuels to use both Wastwater and Ennerdale Water as reservoirs for the pure water needed at Windscale, were turned down after a public enquiry in 1980.

Ennerdale, in the west of the National Park, has already suffered enough from another, insensitive kind of eyesore left by Forestry Commission plantations, which superimpose their alien, geometric forms high up the valley as far as Black Sail. Thankfully, new planting is more imaginative, and the Commission's huge Grizedale Forest in the south with its splendid visitor centre and 'theatre in the forest' is an object les-

son in wildlife interpretation and visitor management.

The sport of rock climbing was born here a century ago, in the highest hills centred round Scafell Pike which, at 3,206 ft (977 m) is the summit of England. But Helvellyn (3,116 ft/950 m) and the Langdale Pikes, (Harrison Stickle, 2,403 ft/732 m and Pike of Stickle, 2,323 ft/708 m) are also popular hill climbs for fell walkers. There is such a richness of fell wandering to be done here that a lifetime would not be enough to explore the area properly.

Lakeland people, who are a rich mix of Celtic, Anglo-Saxon and Norse-Viking influences, may seem blunt to the point of brusqueness to the southern visitor. But it should be remembered that their ancient insular existence, perhaps never straying more than a few miles from their native valley, has given them a proud independence.

The Lake District National Park has done much to smooth over the impact of the millions of visitors through its hard-working Ranger Service and the excellent National Park Visitor Centre at Brockhole on the Windermere shore between Windermere village and Ambleside. Changing exhibitions, audio-visual presentations, films and lectures give the day visitor a comprehensive grounding in the appreciation of Britain's premier National Park. You can even try your hand at building a drystone wall in the 30 acre grounds, which were recently used by local farmers for their sheep sales and sheep-dog trials.

The largest single landowner in the National Park is the National Trust, one of whose founders was the early Cumbrian conservationist Canon Hardwicke Rawnsley, vicar of Crosthwaite near Keswick and also founder of the Lake District Defence Society, a forerunner of today's pressure group, the Friends of the Lake District.

It is appropriate that the Trust, whose 86,000 acres (34,803 ha) of land is held in inalienable trust and which has such a fine record of conservation and freedom of access to its properties, should be the major landlord in Wordsworth's 'national property'.

THE NATURAL LANDSCAPE: THE ICE-CARVED WHEEL

It was William Wordsworth who first compared the map of the Lake District to the radiating spokes of a wheel. It is a long-lasting analogy which has illustrated many geography lessons over the years, and still holds good today.

The ridges and dales, some containing the lakes

Evening on Derwent Water.

themselves, seem to spread out from a central point somewhere near Dunmail Raise, the ancient boundary marker between the kingdoms of Cumberland and Strathclyde, now on the much-improved road between Grasmere and Keswick.

Actually, as Norman Nicholson has pointed out, the shape, especially on the western sector, is more like that of a lemon squeezer, with the dales gouged out of a dome and sloping out to the rim.

The pass of Dunmail Raise, between Seat Sandal and Steel Fell is a good place to start if you want to understand the underlying geology which has shaped the National Park. Those odd, round, grassy hillocks by the roadside are 'drumlins' or moraines left by the retreating glaciers of the last Ice Age, perhaps 10,000 years ago. And looking either way from the head of the pass, towards Grasmere or Thirlmere, you will notice the distinct U-shape of the valleys – another sure sign of the passing of a glacier.

Just beyond the broad bulk of Helvellyn, which towers above the conifers of Wythburn on the shores of Thirlmere, there is a classic ice-carved corrie – or 'cove' as they are known locally.

A walker approaching Helvellyn from Glenridding at the head of Ullswater could not have a better object lesson in the formation of these features. As you approach the famous 'Hole in the Wall' on Grisedale Brow, the whole majestic east face of the mountain is revealed, with the clear sparkling waters of Red Tarn nestling beneath the summit.

The arm of the spectacular knife-edge ridge of Striding Edge beckons the walker to the broad, almost flat summit, and the other arm of the equally sharp ridge of Swirral Edge encloses the northern aspect to Catstycam, one of the most shapely peaks in Lakeland.

You can easily imagine the corrie that you see filled with the serrated surface of the Red Tarn Glacier, while other glaciers born in the snowy recesses of neighbouring Nethermost Cove and Brown Cove were chiselling out the other sides of the Striding Edge and Swirral Edge ridges.

It is evident to anyone who has walked these ridges – another classic example is the appropriately-named Sharp Edge on Blencathra – that it was the gouging, grinding power of the glaciers which shaped the Lake District we know today.

And it was the huge ice cap, perhaps centred on the high points of Scafell, Esk Hause or Helvellyn, which gave us that cartwheel effect of radiating ridges and dales, making valleys which were once a V in cross-

Kirkstone Pass.

158

section, into a U. The glaciers also left us the 'hanging valleys' with their waterfalls, like Aira Force, Scale Force and Dalegarth Force. And the ice gave us 'erratic' misplaced boulders – like the massive Bowder Stone in Borrowdale – which were carried and then unceremoniously dumped far from the fellside of their origin.

But, most importantly, the ice carved out the basins in which the lakes were formed, damming their outlets by a ridge of glacial moraine. The enormous excavating power of the ice can be realised by looking at the great depth of the lake beds. Ullswater, Windermere and Wastwater all exceed 200 ft (61 m); and in the case of Wastwater, the bottom is 58 ft (17.6 m) below the level of the Irish Sea, which can be glimpsed from above the shores of the lake.

The base rocks of the Lake District constitute three main types, each of which dictates its own distinctive landscape.

The oldest rocks are the Skiddaw slates, formed perhaps 500 million years ago in the Ordovician era. These are among the oldest rocks in Europe, and give us the steep but generally smooth profiles of the northern fells like Skiddaw itself (the great backcloth to the town of Keswick), Blencathra – or Saddleback – and Grisedale Pike.

The scenery of the central section of the district, around Borrowdale, Langdale, the Helvellyn Range and Wasdale, is more dramatic, with jutting crags, rocky scree slopes and jagged ridges. These landscapes were formed from volcanic rocks thrown up through the older slates at the end of the Ordovician period and are known collectively as the Borrowdale volcanics.

These rocks are more resistant to erosion, which explains the knobbly, rugged outlines of the central fells, typified by those great crags of Pillar, Scafell, Dow Crag (on Coniston Old Man) and Honister. Fine volcanic dust deposited at this time was compressed to form the distinctive green Lake District slate quarried at Honister and Coniston, and still used to clad modern buildings like Coventry Cathedral.

The third rock type, found south of a line crossing the heads of Coniston Water and Windermere, is from the Silurian period, laid down beneath the sea perhaps 440 million years ago. This gives us the softer, well-wooded landscapes of Windermere and Coniston, with few peaks above 1,000 ft (305 m). A ring of Carboniferous limestone encircles the borders of the National Park, and the whole top of the Lake District

Aira Force, Ullswater.

dome has been sliced off by ice, wind, rain and rivers to form the landscape we see today.

The natural vegetation cover of the district is broad-leaved woodland such as that seen around the Borrowdale village of Grange and along the shores of Windermere and Coniston. But the woods of sessile oak, birch, holly and Scots pine are becoming rare and are being replaced by fast-growing softwood plantations.

There is no comparison between the two, as anyone who has seen the glory of a Lakeland autumn will testify. The vivid splashes of colour, the reds, browns and yellows which paint the glorious mixed woodlands along the western shore of Windermere are spectacular in contrast with the drab bottle-green firs or anaemic yellow spruces of nearby Grizedale Forest.

But the conifers are not entirely a desert for wild life. Those same forests support a large population of Britain's biggest wild animal, the red deer, and there are also herds of the more delicate roe deer. The Lake District also has the distinction of being the last stronghold of the native red squirrel, which likes a mixture of hazel and pine.

One of the greatest success stories of modern Lake District natural history has been the return of the majestic golden eagle to nesting sites which had been abandoned for over 200 years. Place names like Heron Crag (from the Celtic *irein* for eagle) show us that this magnificent bird was once common. The nesting sites are kept secret, because of the mindless activities of nest robbers.

The lakes themselves hold two rare species of whitefish, the schelly, found only in Haweswater and Ullswater where Skelly Nab reminds us of the narrow point in the lake where they were once netted, and the vendace, found only in Derwent Water and Bassenthwaite Lake.

A speciality of Windermere is a member of the trout family, known as the char, which cannot exist in water with a temperature above 15°C (59°F).

It could be that all three of these piscatorial rarities are throwbacks to earlier occupants of these icy cold lakes left by those great landscape sculptors, the Ice Age glaciers.

MAN'S INFLUENCE: HIGHLY INDUSTRIAL

Walkers approaching the rocky, 2,323 ft (708 m) summit of Pike of Stickle – the thimble-like peak so prominent in the sweeping view of the head of Langdale when seen from Wall End – can be excused

Lingmell Beck and Wastwater from Great Gable.

for believing that they have escaped from the industrial society.

Not so, for on the precipitous scree and rock slopes below their bird's-eye viewpoint of Mickleden (with Great End and Great Gable beyond) have been found remains of the Lake District's, and probably Britain's, oldest industry.

A glance at the Ordnance Survey map will reveal the words 'Stone Axe Factory' printed in the Gothic lettering used to mark antiquities. Other factories have also been discovered a few yards from the busy Mickledore track to Scafell Pike, and on the rocky little peak of Glaramara, making the Central Fells of the Lake District a veritable hive of Stone Age industry.

Perhaps 'factory' is too modern a word to use for these exposed Neolithic (New Stone Age) workshops which were in business between 3,000 and 5,000 years ago. But 'business' is certainly accurate, for the finished axes were exported as far away as Ireland, the Isle of Man, Scotland and the south of England, as far as Hampshire and the Thames basin.

Those Neolithic settlers knew their geology, for they discovered that the fine-grained, greenish-grey volcanic tuff found in veins at between 1,500–3,000 ft (457–914 m) was ideally suited for chipping to those sharp cutting edges which were to clear much of

The Langdale Pikes from Loughrigg Fell.

Britain of its virgin forest. The shape of the axes was roughed out high on these bleak fellside workshops, then the axes were transported to the more densely populated coastal sites, where they were polished with softer sandstone to produce artefacts of great precision and beauty.

So the mineral wealth of the Lakeland hills was exploited by the earliest settlers. It was the beginning of a mining economy which was to extend to the important copper mines of Coniston (whose considerable remains are still to be seen in the Coppermines Valley on Coniston Old Man), the iron-ore mines in the same area, the workings of plumbago or graphite – locally known as wad – from Seathwaite (which founded the famous Lakeland and Cumberland pencil industry of Keswick) and the green Lakeland slate quarries of Honister, Langdale and Coniston.

But the most striking and obvious reminders of the earliest settlers are the mysterious and still powerful stone circles which stand, mute yet expressive, on the fellsides.

The best known of these is the Castlerigg stone circle, standing on a little knoll just outside Keswick and surrounded by an encircling ring of mountains. Looking north west, the impressive, humped backcloth to the Castlerigg stones is Blencathra, and it provides a much-photographed viewpoint. Less well

163

known and even more evocative is the smaller circle of Swinside, standing on a green moorland shoulder of Black Combe, the southernmost outlier of the Lakeland hills.

Long Meg and her Daughters, outside the National Park boundary at Little Salkeld, near Penrith, gave Wordsworth 'a weight of awe not easily to be borne' when he first saw 'that sisterhood forlorn', and they can certainly still excite the imagination.

Tucked away in a backwater of north-west England, the Lake District was slower to develop than the south. It is believed, for example, that when the Iron Age culture was building the great hill forts of Maiden Castle and Uffington on the chalk downs of Dorset and Berkshire, the Lake District was still languishing in the Bronze Age. The only definite sign of the distinctive hill forts so common during the Iron Age period is the five acre site surrounded by a single fallen stone rampart on Carrock Fell on the Caldbeck Fells, 'Back o' Skiddaw' in the far north of the Park.

The Romans stamped their authority and left their mark in forts such as the one that commands Eskdale and the route to Ravenglass and the sea at Hardknott. The round-cornered shape of the foundations is still visible in this splendid fort from Hadrian's time, whose preservation is probably due in no small measure to its isolation.

When today's adventurous motorist follows the winding route over the Wrynose and Hardknott passes, from Ambleside to Ravenglass, he or she follows in the footsteps of the Roman legions, who had forts at each end of the route. Another traceable Roman road between Brougham and Ambleside crosses the 2,000 ft (610 m) High Street range.

When the Romans left, with their 400-year presence hardly noticed among the hills, invaders from the north and south, Vikings and Anglians, filled the vacuum and left vigorously carved crosses at Irton and Gosforth, and a possible Viking meeting place or 'Thingmound' at Fell Foot in Little Langdale.

The major legacy of the Vikings is evident almost everywhere, in the names they gave to the settlements and natural features of the landscape. Tenth century Norse Vikings gave us the many 'thwaites' (clearings), for example, Esthwaite, Braithwaite and Bassenthwaite, while fell (*fjall*) is a mountain with open grazing, tarn (*tjorn*) is a small mountain lake, and beck (*bekkr*) a brook or stream. Ravines are still called gills or ghylls, from the Norse *gil* and waterfalls are forces (*foss*).

Langdale Pikes from Elterwater.

Many Norse settlers are still remembered by their personal names, immortalised in placenames like Ennerdale (Einarr's dale). Thirlmere (Thorhallr's lake) or Windermere (Vinnunder's lake).

Like the Romans before them, the Normans made little impact on the Lake District and their castles, like Carlisle and Kendal, are mainly on the fringes of the hills. There is even one valley, as recorded in Nicholas Size's novel *The Secret Valley*, which escaped the *Domesday Book* surveyors. The monasteries, like Furness, Cartmel and Calder, also kept to the more civilised edges of the mountain mass and by medi-aeval times, farming, particularly of sheep, was the major industry.

The hardy, rough-fleeced Herdwick is the district's own rare breed, and the wool from these white-faced animals is highly prized. Don't be surprised if you see a black lamb on the fells, for all Herdwicks are born that colour and their fleece whitens with age. So, for a Herdwick, it's no disgrace to have a black sheep in the family!

The multi-coloured wool was spun on the farms in spinning galleries, like the one seen at the farm beyond High Yewdale Bridge on the Coniston-Ambleside road, and the golden fleece of the Herdwicks brought prosperity to market towns like Kendal, Ambleside and Hawkshead in the 16th and 17th centuries.

Kendal, famous for its high energy delicacy, Kendal Mint Cake – a must for Himalayan moun-taineering expeditions – is the southern gateway to the National Park. It is a busy, bustling town, badly affected by traffic but with an exceptionally good Museum of Lakeland Life and Industry. The ruins of a castle in which Catherine Parr, sixth wife of Henry VIII, was born are in the Park.

Next stop on the main A591 is Windermere, for-merly known as Birthwaite before the coming of the railway in 1847. This is an out-and-out tourist town, now merged with Bowness-on-Windermere, which is the part actually on the lake. It becomes very crowded during the holiday period, but visitors heading west can avoid the congestion by travelling on the B5284 from Kendal through Crook to reach the chain-operated ferry across the lake south of Belle Isle.

North of Windermere, the A591 takes you to Ambleside, one of the most popular tourist resorts. The Bridge House, literally one up and one down, is built across the River Rothay and is now in the care of the National Trust.

The next village is Grasmere, where Wordsworth's

Little Langdale from the Wrynose Pass.

home of Dove Cottage is the major attraction. It could well be called the centre of the Wordsworth industry, with Rydal Mount, where the poet died, a short walk away back along the road from Windermere.

Wordsworth was a student at Hawkshead Grammar School, founded in 1585, and in the well preserved school room visitors can still see the desk on which he carved his name (as generations of schoolboys have done before and since). Hawkshead, with narrow streets and cobbled courtyards, has the air of a West Country holiday village, but its intimacy has been spoiled by the enormous car and coach park on its outskirts.

Just down the road towards Windermere is Far Sawrey, and Hill Top where Beatrix Potter wrote her books about Peter Rabbit and the others. She later became a noted breeder of Herdwick sheep.

The natural centre for the exploration of the northern fells is Keswick, which commands the northern end of Derwentwater, the broadest and shallowest of the major lakes and second only in popularity to Windermere. The view from pine-clad Friar's Crag is famous, and is backed by the nobbly outline of Catbells (where Mrs Tiggywinkle lived) and Maiden Moor across the broad, sail-splashed lake. Keswick is a good starting place to explore rugged Borrowdale and to cross the Honister Pass to the twin lakes of Buttermere and Crummock Water, or go north to gentle, little-frequented Bassenthwaite Lake.

Coniston, with its fascinating reminders of the copper industry and associations with Ruskin, is as dominated by the Old Man (2635 ft/801 m) as Fort William is by Ben Nevis or Zermatt by the Matterhorn. The long (5 miles/8 km) lake of Coniston Water was the scene of the ill-fated attempt on the world water-speed record by Donald Campbell in 1967.

Today's visitors can enjoy a more leisurely sail on the lake, on the National Trust's beautifully restored steam yacht *Gondola*, as far down as Peel Island, (the Wild Cat Island of Arthur Ransome's famous children's book, *Swallows and Amazons*).

Ravenglass, a one street estuary village on the Irish Sea coast and site of the Roman fort of Glannaventa, is a good centre for the wild, western fells, giving easy access to the splendid valley of Wasdale. It is also the southern terminus of the miniature Ravenglass and Eskdale Railway, affectionately known as 'Ratty'. This is a splendid way to explore upper Eskdale, and the indefatigable Wainwright has even produced a charming little booklet of walks centred on the railway stations.

Windermere from Brockhole Pier.

Above: Old Grammar School, Hawkshead.

Above: The grave of William and Dorothy Wordsworth in Grasmere churchyard.

Overleaf, left: Tarns Hows in winter.

Overleaf, right: Causey Pike from Friar's Crag, Derwent Water.

What to do

HOW TO GET THERE

BY ROAD The Lake District is well served by the motorway system, with the M6 bringing the carborne visitor to within easy reach from most parts of the country. If you are visiting the southern, central or western lakes, you need to leave the M6 at Junction 35 or 36 for the A591 to Kendal, or if your destination is the northern fells of Skiddaw and Blencathra, then Junction 40 (Penrith) is more suitable, using the A66 to Keswick.

Once in the district it is a good idea to avoid congested roads and enjoy the scenery by leaving the car behind. You can do this by taking advantage of the Mountain Goat mini-bus service. These 12-seater, white-painted buses are a familiar sight, and they offer tours or even complete holidays based on the popular centres of Windermere and Keswick. They also allow walkers the opportunity of extending the distance walked away from their cars, returning to them by mini-bus.

BY RAIL The London (Euston) – Glasgow line skirts along the eastern edge of the Lake District, and Oxenholme, near Kendal, is the station for the Lakes. There are also connecting paytrains to Windermere from here.

If you wish to travel further north, Penrith is the next stop, and is a convenient starting point for the northern fells.

WHERE TO STAY

A comprehensive accommodation guide covering the whole of the National Park is *Where to Stay in English Lakeland-Cumbria* published by the Cumbria Tourist Board. Also, most Tourist Board information centres run an accommodation booking service.

In addition, the Tourist Board has collaborated with the National Park authority to produce *Freedom of Cumbria*, a praiseworthy booklet which describes the accommodation and recreational opportunities for the disabled visitor. (Other Parks please note!)

YOUTH HOSTELS As might be expected of one of Britain's premier holiday areas, the Lake District is well served by youth hostels, from the former shepherd's hut at Black Sail at the summit of Ennerdale, to the 240-bed 'special' grade unit at Ambleside.

There are other hostels at Buttermere, Cockermouth, Coniston (Coppermines and Holly How), Derwent Water, Duddon, Elterwater, Ennerdale, Eskdale, Grasmere (Butharlyp How and Thorney How), Hawkshead, Helvellyn (Greenside), High Close (Loughrigg), Honister Hause, Kendal, Keswick, Longthwaite (Borrowdale), Patterdale, Thirlmere, Wastwater and Windermere.

CAMPING AND CARAVAN SITES All you need to know is provided in the joint Tourist Board/National Park publication, *Sites for Caravans and Tents in Cumbria, including the Lake District National Park*. In addition, a Caravan Advisory Service for touring caravanners operates during the peak period from Easter to September on Windermere 5555 or 5515.

PLACES OPEN TO THE PUBLIC

These are far too numerous to list in full, but this is a selected list of the more interesting among the many.

BRANTWOOD, CONISTON Home of John Ruskin for his last 28 years, when his mental condition was slowly deteriorating. The house contains an extensive collection of his paintings and possessions, and there is a nature trail down to the shores of Coniston Water in the grounds.

BELLE ISLE, WINDERMERE A circular Georgian house sited on the largest and only inhabited island on Windermere. Many intimate family possessions and a small, formal garden. The house is reached by boat from Bowness.

DOVE COTTAGE, GRASMERE Where William and Dorothy Wordsworth lived from 1799 to 1808. The small cottage at Town End, Grasmere is almost a time capsule of their period and despite the thousands of visitors, looks today much as it must have done then.

HILL TOP, SAWREY Another house with strong literary associations, this typical, small 17th century Lakeland farmhouse was the home of Beatrix Potter when she wrote and illustrated her famous *Tale of Peter Rabbit* and other books for children. It suffers today from over-popularity and visitor numbers are often restricted at peak times. Go early, because there is no electric light in the house and it closes at dusk.

HOLKER HALL A large deer park surrounds this beautiful, 16th century country house near Grange-

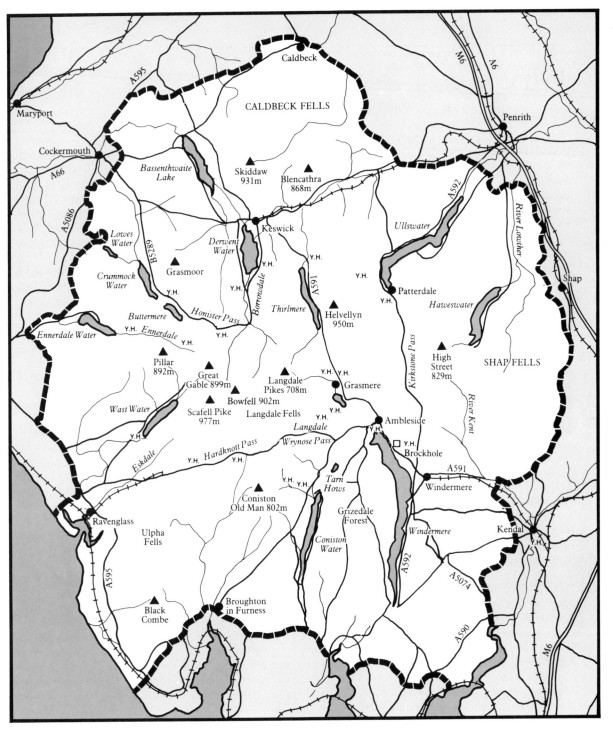

Maryport

Cockermouth

A595

A66

A5086

A5289

CALDBECK FELLS

Caldbeck

Skiddaw
931m ▲

Blencathra
868m ▲

Penrith

M6

A6

Bassenthwaite
Lake

Lowes
Water

Crummock
Water

Grasmoor ▲

Derwent
Water

Keswick

Thirlmere

A591

Ullswater

A592

Patterdale

Haweswater

Shap

River Lowther

Y.H.

Y.H.

Borrowdale

Y.H.

Helvellyn
950m ▲

Y.H.

Y.H.

SHAP FELLS

Buttermere

Honister Pass

Ennerdale Water

Y.H. Ennerdale

Y.H.

Pillar
892m ▲

Great
Gable 899m ▲

Wast Water

Scafell Pike
977m ▲

Bowfell 902m ▲

Langdale
Pikes 708m ▲

Langdale Fells

Grasmere

Kirkstone Pass

River Kent

High
Street
829m ▲

Y.H. Y.H.

Y.H.

Ambleside

Brockhole

Y.H.

A591

Windermere

Eskdale

Y.H.

Hardknott Pass

Y.H.

Wrynose Pass

Langdale

Y.H. Y.H.

Tarn
Hows

Grizedale
Forest

Windermere

A592

Kendal

A5074

Y.H.

Ravenglass

Ulpha
Fells

Coniston
Old Man 802m ▲

Coniston
Water

A595

Black
Combe ▲

Broughton
in Furness

A590

M6

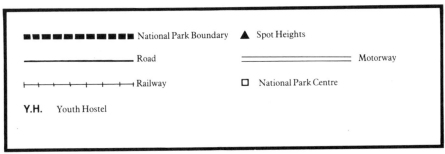

▬ ▬ ▬ ▬ ▬ National Park Boundary   ▲ Spot Heights

──────── Road   ════════ Motorway

╁─╁─╁─╁─╁─╁ Railway   ☐ National Park Centre

Y.H.   Youth Hostel

over-Sands. There are numerous other attractions for children and a countryside museum.

LEVENS HALL A Norman pele tower, converted to an Elizabethan house with notable panelling, plaster-work, furniture and paintings. There is a famous steam collection and the gardens are renowned for their topiary (ornate shrubs, shaped by trimming).

RYDAL MOUNT, RYDAL Another former Wordsworth home, originally a 16th century farmhouse. Pleasant gardens.

SIZERGH CASTLE Another house which started life as a pele tower to give protection from border raiders. Sizergh, near Kendal boasts a splendid Great Hall dating from the 15th century, some fine furniture and colourful gardens.

TOWNEND, TROUTBECK A superb Lakeland house built about 1626 and lived in by a small yeoman family – the Brownes – for over three centuries. The National Trust is to be congratulated for its sensitive policy of leaving things as they were, and thus giving the visitor such a complete picture.

CARLISLE CASTLE On the edge of the National Park, the castle is an impressive border stronghold dating back to the 12th century and is well worth a visit.

KENDAL CASTLE The ruins of this 12th century castle and former home of Catherine Parr are now in a public park with free access.

HARDKNOTT ROMAN FORT (MEDIOBOGDUM) One of the most dramatically-sited of all Roman forts, on a 1,200 ft (365 m) shoulder of the fells overlooking Eskdale. These impressive remains, including a still discernible parade ground, are as evocative in their way as Northumberland's Roman Wall.

In addition to these houses and castles, there are a large number of interesting museums on all aspects of Lakeland life in centres such as Ambleside, Hawks-head, Kendal, Keswick, Grasmere and Windermere.

ANCIENT MONUMENTS

	Grid reference
Long Meg and her Daughters Stone Circle	(NY 571372)
Castlerigg Stone Circle, Keswick	(NY 291236)
Swinside Stone Circle, Millom	(SD 172882)
Carrock Fell Hill Fort	(NY 342336)
Ambleside Roman Fort	(NY 372034)
Hardknott Roman Fort	(NY 218015)
Ravenglass Roman Fort, Muncaster	(SD 088958)
Shap Abbey	(NY 548152)
Penrith Castle	(NY 513298)
Kendal Castle	(SD 522924)
Irton Cross	(NY 091004)

MAPS

Indispensible for a proper exploration of the Lake District are four Ordnance Survey Outdoor Leisure maps (1 : 25,000 scale) covering the Park in great detail in North East (Ullswater and Haweswater), North West (Ennerdale and Derwent), South West (Wastwater and Coniston) and South East (Windermere and Kendal) sections.

Also excellent value is the OS 1 in to the mile, Tourist map, covering the whole of the Park in one sheet. Landranger maps (1 : 50,000 scale) nos 85, 89, 90, 96 and 97 also cover the National Park.

FURTHER READING

Davies, Hunter, *A Walk around the Lakes*, Weidenfeld & Nicolson, 1979.

Griffin, A Harry, *Inside the Real Lakeland*, Preston, 1961.

Griffin, A Harry, *The Roof of England*, Hale, 1968.

Lake District National Park, The, HMSO, 1969.

Millward, Roy, & Robinson, Adrian, *The Lake District*, Eyre Methuen, 1974.

Nicholson, Norman, *Portrait of the Lakes*, Hale, 1963.

Parker, John, *The Observer's Book of the Lake District*, Warne, 1978.

Poucher, W A, *The Lakeland Peaks*, Constable, 1960.

Spencer, Brian, *A Visitor's Guide to the Lake District*, Moorland, 1981.

Wainwright, A, *A Pictorial Guide to the Lakeland Fells* (7 vols), Westmorland Gazette, 1955–1966.

Wyatt, John, *Reflections on the Lakes*, W H Allen, 1980.

An extensive range of inexpensive information leaflets is published by the National Park authority, including walking guides based on popular centres and many aspects of natural history and the country-side.

DRIVING

The brunt of visitor traffic through the Lake District is taken by the A66 Penrith to Keswick road, the A592 Windermere-Penrith or the A591 Kendal/

The Screes, Wastwater.

Windermere/Ambleside/Keswick routes. These are good, fast arterial roads with dual carriageways for much of their length and get you from A to B quickly and safely, but they do not show you the real Lake District.

If you really want to get a taste of the fells and cannot leave your car, then the unclassified narrow road between Langdale and Eskdale, traversing both the Wrynose and Hardknott passes is unmatched. But with inclines of up to 1 : 3, steep drops on either side and a series of hair-raising hairpin bends, this road is not for the nervous or inexperienced driver, and is *not* recommended for caravans. The 1,291 ft (393 m) summit of Hardknott, close by the Roman fort, is often littered with broken down vehicles, radiators steaming, proving that they should not have been subjected to the route.

Less adventurous but equally rewarding runs can be made into Borrowdale via the B5289 and Honister Pass under frowning Honister Crag to the less visited lakes of Buttermere and Crummock Water; and the reward after crossing Hardknott and Wrynose is the incomparable route to the head of Wasdale in the heart of England's highest hills.

WALKING

Wordsworth first realised it, and Wainwright made it possible for millions of others to capitalise on the fact. The best way of getting to know the Lake District is to don walking boots and take to the hills!

It is impossible to give anything but a taste of the tremendous variety of walks in the district, many of them now signposted and maintained under the Park authority's Upland Management Experiment (UMEX). Many people will not be able to resist the well-trodden paths to the popular summits, but whenever you leave the valley floors, please remember that each year ill-equipped people are killed in these deceptively beautiful mountains, and you should be prepared for the worst weather in every season. If you are not, there is no shame in turning back. Daily weather forecasts can be obtained by telephoning Windermere 5151.

Your best guide is Wainwright, whose meticulous pen and ink drawings and hand-scripted text will take you safely to whichever top you desire. But if you want to experience the real wilderness try to avoid the Brown Tongue route to Scafell Pike from Wasdale (about 7 miles/11 km), the badly-eroded route to the Pikes from Langdale, the White Stones route to Helvellyn from Thirlspot or the bridleway from Keswick to Skiddaw on Bank Holiday weekends.

Swaledale tup, Watendlath.

A delightful low level route for the less energetic, or for a day when cloud obscures the tops, is the easy, 9 mile (14.5 km) stroll from Windermere to Grasmere, taking in the yeoman house of Townend, and Rydal Mount and Dove Cottage (homes of Wordsworth) ending at St Oswald's Church, Grasmere, where the poet is buried.

The National Park authority runs an extensive programme of guided walks; there are town trails in many centres and the Tourist Board issues a list of nature and forest trails.

CLIMBING, TREKKING AND CYCLING

It is no exaggeration to say that the sport of rock climbing was born in the Lake District, and the actual birthplace was in the noble group of fells which crowd round the head of Wasdale. The 'father' of the sport was Walter Parry Haskett Smith, whose 1886 lone ascent of Napes Needle on Great Gable, when he felt 'as small as a mouse climbing a milestone,' was the genesis of the sport. Today there are at least 3,000 separate routes in the district, of varying grades of difficulty – some would say impossibility.

Pony trekking is as popular in the Lake District as it is elsewhere, and the best guide to what's available is the joint Tourist Board/National Park leaflet *Riding and Pony Trekking*.

The same two bodies produce joint leaflets on cycling, swimming, golf, fishing and boating, all available from information centres.

Useful Addresses

Lake District National Park Office
Busher Walk
Kendal
Cumbria LA9 4RH.

(tel. Kendal 24555).

National Park Information
and Ranger Service
Barclays Bank Chambers
Crescent Road
Windermere
Cumbria LA23 1AF.

(tel. Windermere 2498 – ranger / 5555 – information)

National Park Visitor Centre
Brockhole
Windermere
Cumbria LA23 1LJ.

(tel. Windermere 2231)

Cumbria Tourist Board
Ashleigh
Holly Road
Windermere
Cumbria LA23 2AQ.

(tel. Windermere 4444)

The Friends of the Lake District
Gowan Knott
Kendal Road
Staveley
Kendal
Cumbria LA8 9LP.

(tel. Staveley 821201)

National Park Information Centres
(open Easter–October) These can be found at Ambleside (tel. Ambleside 32582), Bowness-on-Windermere (tel. Windermere 5602), Coniston (tel. Coniston 41533), Glenridding (tel. Glenridding 414), Hawkshead (tel. Hawkshead 525), Keswick (tel. Keswick 72645), Pooley Bridge (tel. Pooley Bridge 530), Seatoller (tel. Borrowdale 294) and Waterhead (tel. Ambleside 2729).

There are tourist information centres in most villages and settlements, the majority of which provide a tourist accommodation booking service.

The National Trust has information centres at Ambleside, Hawkshead, Grasmere, Keswick and Newby Bridge (tel. Newby Bridge 31273), and there are Forestry Commission visitor centres at Grizedale (tel. Satterthwaite 373) and at Whinlatter (tel. Braithwaite 469).

North York Moors National Park

A MARVELLOUS FREEDOM

You first catch sight of them as a blue misty outline looking impossibly high, away to the east as you travel north on the A1 – the Great North Road.

The North York Moors have always stood apart, perhaps the most self-contained and physically best defined of all our National Parks. Geology and history have seen to that and it remains the only Park to touch the North Sea coast or cross the geographer's Tees-Exe line.

That remoteness is perhaps the North York Moor's greatest advantage. It is among the least-visited and quietest of our National Parks, despite its situation on the doorsteps of Middlesborough and the teeming towns of Teeside.

It is also, perhaps significantly, the Park with the lowest average altitude and the one which enjoys the lowest annual rainfall of them all, a fact which should influence holidaymakers.

As you explore the fascinating mixture of rolling heather moors, gentler southward-running dales and the spectacular sea-coast you will often find you have the place surprisingly to yourself – a rare enough happening these days.

This isolation has attracted lovers of solitude for centuries – from the Bronze Age chieftains who were buried on the moorland heights, to the monks and friars of the Middle Ages who searched far and wide to find the quiet life needed for their devotions.

One such in the 12th century, was St Ailred, the third abbot of Rievaulx Abbey in Ryedale on the edge of the moors. He wrote that he found in the moors and dales surrounding his secluded community of monks and lay brethren, 'peace, everywhere serenity and a marvellous freedom from the tumult of the world.'

Eight centuries later, those attributes served as one of the qualifications which made the North York Moors a National Park. They are the very qualities which modern visitors come to find, and can still find, thanks to the vigilance and careful planning of the Park authority.

The North York Moors National Park was designated in 1952 – the sixth to be confirmed – and covers an area of 533 square miles (1,432 sq km).

The isolated upland block formed by the Cleveland Hills in the north overlooking the valley of Eskdale, and the limestone Tabular Hills in the south, is dissected by gentle dales, each with its own distinctive character. But the serenity which St Ailred so admired is best found up on those high, rolling moors, known anciently as 'Blackamor'.

They are, in the words of the National Park authority, 'the central attraction'. And certainly if you are lucky enough to visit them in late summer they present an expanse of unbroken colour which is unmatched in England.

Left: Wild daffodils, Farndale.

Right: The Bridestones, above Stain Dale.

Detail, Rievaulx Abbey.

In late August and September, the central moors are ablaze with the royal-hued massed flowers of ling, bell heather and cross-leaved heath.

Despite recent and regrettable agricultural reclamation and afforestation which the Park authority is virtually powerless to stop, some 40 per cent of the Park remains open moorland.

It is still the largest area of heather-covered moorland in England, but it is a fragile resource. In the last 30 years about a quarter of the open moorland has been lost to agriculture and forestry.

Visitors should also always remember that without the landowners who use these vast expanses of heather for one major enterprise – grouse rearing – all would have been converted to improved pasture for sheep long ago.

The heather is regularly burned under careful supervision, to provide the special patchwork of old and young plants that give red grouse their ideal feeding and roosting conditions. The burned areas, an operation always done in winter, are known locally as 'swiddens'. But like any peat-based moorland area, the North York Moors are *not* the place to play with fire during the dry, summer season, as the many disastrous blazes have proved.

The North York Moors National Park is the only one to compete with the Pembrokeshire Coast in the magnificence of its coastal scenery. Some of the finest clifftop scenery in Britain occurs where the moors meet the sea, and Boulby Head at 690 ft (210 m) on the northern extremity of the Park is the highest point on the east coast of England. Charming fishing villages like Robin Hood's Bay and Staithes give the coastal fringe a flavour of the West Country.

It is in this area that another, even more destructive threat faces the Park. The area around Whitby contains Britain's only reserves of potash, an important agricultural fertiliser. Such is its national importance that planning permission was given for its extraction near Boulby. But an application for a second site, which would have involved a chimney 262 ft (80 m) high, was thankfully turned down by the Secretary of State.

The North York Moors is one of the most underrated of our ten National Parks. Those who have learned to love its intimate charms hope it long remains so.

THE NATURAL LANDSCAPE: OLDER THAN THE HILLS

As if modern pressures were not enough, the North York Moors National Park is slowly being worn away by an agency which is literally older than the hills.

An average of 3 in (7.5 cm) a year – in some places as much as 3 ft (.9 m) – is taken from the magnificent Heritage Coast, which forms the north-eastern boundary of the Park, by that oldest and most powerful of eroders – the sea.

And the sea, over the vastness of geological time, has been the prime architect of what we now know as the North York Moors.

Most of the bedrock of this isolated upland, which stands out like a shoulder halfway up England's east coast, was laid down in the shallow seas and deltas of the Jurassic period about 150 million years ago. The area was submerged under this warm, quiet ocean for hundreds of millions of years until, about 70 million years ago, it was slowly lifted to form what we call the Cleveland Dome.

This structure dominates the high sandstone northern and western moorlands of the National Park, but even a cursory look at the moors above Osmotherley and Stokesley will soon show that the dome has long since been planed smooth to create the even, tabletop horizons of today.

Further marine erosion, after another period of

Rievaulx Abbey, from Rievaulx Terrace.

submersion under that restless ocean, sliced off the top of the dome, and the highest point on the moors today, at Botton Head, 1,490 ft (454 m) on Urra Moor at the head of Ingleby Beck, is several hundred feet below what was the original summit of the region.

The North York Moors were not high or cold enough to merit their own ice cap during the Ice Age, but the action of frost and snow, on this ice-free island above the glaciers of the rest of Yorkshire, still left its mark.

The glaciers which lapped its shores left gravel ridges with stones known as 'erratics' carried by the ice from the other side of the country, and the sticky boulder clay common along the coast.

When the ice and snow finally melted, the newly formed rivers drained from the hills, carving out the many deep dales which are so characteristic of the region.

To the south and west of the National Park, the dominant rock is limestone, creating the softer, more gentle landscape of the Hambleton and Tabular Hills, in sharp contrast to the heather-capped sandstone moors of the north, and strongly reminiscent of the Cotswolds.

The steep western escarpment provides, at places like Sutton Bank where there is a thriving gliding club, an unparalleled view towards the Pennine dales. And you'll soon see why the Tabular Hills get their name if you travel along the Helmsley to Scarborough road, where the vale of Pickering rises gently northwards to the broad, flat-topped heights.

One of the most impressive scenic features of the National Park is the sequence of 'surprise views' which delight the motorist who travels across the grain of the landscape between Rievaulx and Scarborough. The waters of becks like the Rye, Riccal, Hodge and Dove cut deep valleys through the limestone and leave the tabular blocks, still and silent as sphinxes, gazing stonily northward.

Above the valley of the Dovedale Griff, the Bridestones are a fantastic collection of wind-eroded limestone rocks as eccentric as their more famous counterparts at Brimham in Nidderdale.

To the north, a series of delightful dales – which rival, on a smaller scale, any of those which flow into the Humber – bite deep into the moorland heart. In sequence, they are Bilsdale, Bransdale, Farndale, Rosedale and Newtondale; and while each has its special charms, they all exhibit the gradual transition from valley pastures and tree-lined banks through a network of drystone walls to the bracken and heather of the tops.

All these dales drain into the Derwent, while the shorter, northern series of dales, Baysdale, Westerdale, Danby Dale, Great Fryup Dale and Glaisdale flow into the broad pastoral valley of the Esk, which enters the sea at Whitby.

If water has shaped the land, then the land shapes the region's natural history.

Walkers attempting that most arduous of long-distance time-trials – the 40 mile (64 km) Lyke Wake Walk which traverses the highest and wildest moorland tops between Osmotherley and Ravenscar – may not have much time to appreciate the wildlife of the moors.

But it is there nevertheless, and the broad banks of heather support a wide range of wildlife quite apart from the red grouse for which it is managed. The heather itself is divided into three distinct types; the dominant Scottish heather or ling which bursts into bloom in early August to late September; the earlier deep purple of bell heather; and the large, rose pink flowers of the cross-leaved heath, which usually occupies the wetter sites.

Birdwatchers are most likely to see that uniquely British game bird, the plump, croaking red grouse, but the meadow pipit, lapwing, curlew and golden plover are also common residents of the high moors.

Adders, Britain's only poisonous snake, are also common here, but they are such shy, timid creatures that you are most unlikely to see one. Despite its unfortunate reputation, a sun-basking adder is more than likely to have disappeared into the heather

Left: Spring blossom, Beck Hole.

Right: Early morning, Robin Hood's Bay.

Mallyan Spout, near Goathland.

before any unsuspecting visitor has the chance or misfortune to step on it.

The broadleaved woodlands of the dale sides are rich in plant and animal life, and if the moors are famed for their heather, then it is the carpet of miniature wild daffodils which annually carpet the floor of Farndale which are the great glory of the North York dales.

The nodding pale yellow trumpets of the daffodils along the River Dove are the first heralds of spring, and the Farndale area was made a local nature reserve as early as 1955, just three years after the creation of the National Park.

Bluebells and the white stars of wood anemones also cover the denser woodland floor in spring, and if you are really lucky and exceptionally quiet, you may just glimpse a sight of one of the Park's three species of native deer, the roe, red or fallow.

About 15 per cent of the National Park is now covered with the blanket coniferous plantations of the Forestry Commission, especially in the south-facing valleys running down to the Derwent. The

forests of Cropton, Pickering, Wykeham and Dalby have added a new dimension to the landscape, echoing the days when the moors themselves were forested – in those days with native deciduous trees. The range of wildlife which can be supported in the spruce and fir plantations cannot compare with that of the native woodlands of oak, birch, ash and pine.

The springtime flowers of the coastal belt are primroses, which flourish on the boulder clay left by the glaciers. Birdwatchers will be fascinated by the majestic aerobatics of the graceful fulmars or the raucous calls of the herring gulls which nest on the rocky North Sea cliffs.

MAN'S INFLUENCE: TAMING THE MOORS

The stark, simple emblem of the North York Moors National Park shows the imposing, 9 ft (2.7 m) high Ralph Cross which stands at the very centre of the Park on Westerdale Moor.

It is a fitting badge, for it shows that even here, at over 1,400 ft (426 m) on the highest and wildest part of the ancient Blackamor, man's influence is still felt as a tangible part of the landscape.

The first settlers on these now wild moorland heights came to a landscape very different from that which we see today. Then, in the New Stone Age (3,000–1,800 BC), the climate was much kinder, and in those warmer and drier conditions the fur-clad hunter-gatherers made temporary shelters in clearings, in what peat-pollen analysis has shown to be a heavily forested landscape.

They made their homes high on the ridges (locally known as 'riggs') because that was where they felt the safest. And it was here that they chose to bury their dead, leaving monuments which we can still see today. A glance at the OS Tourist map will show an abundance of Gothic-lettered 'antiquity' sites, such as howes or tumuli.

These mark the burial mounds of the long-forgotten dalesmen, and the place name 'howe' from the Scandinavian *haugr* is equivalent to the 'low' of the Peak District.

There are reckoned to be over 3,000 of these howes, mainly dating from the Bronze Age (1,800–500 BC), dotted across the moors, and many of them carry the names of the people buried there, such as Lilla Howe on Fylingdales Moor, which commemorates a loyal henchman of King Edwin of Northumberland who died stopping an assassin's dagger meant for his master.

Not a mile from this lonely and evocative spot,

where the Lyke Wake walker gets his first tantalising glimpse of the sea, is revealed what is surely the most intrusive evidence of Man's presence in a National Park. The huge white radomes of Fylingdales Ballistic Missile Early Warning Station will probably give the West its first warning of approaching Armageddon, just as Lilla did for Edwin. The radomes stand like so many gigantic golf balls waiting to be teed off into the North Sea.

But, away from this 'deeply regretted incursion', as Dr Arthur Rastrick has called it, the other most common evidence of Man on the moors is the frequency of the moorland crosses, which turn up at vital meeting places of tracks or at lonely crossing points.

There are more than 30 of these crosses, most erected in mediaeval times as waymarks for travellers crossing the inhospitable moors. And many of them carry the names of the dalespeople who erected them or on whose land they stood. Ralph Cross has already been mentioned, and there are other crosses named

Hutton-le-Hole.

after Percy, John, Ana, Redman, Anna and Job, to name a few. Some show the sense of humour of these hard but fair people, like Fat Betty and Blue Man-i'-th'-Moss, other standing stones which are vital landmarks on the open moors.

The Romans had passed this way too, and on Wheeldale Moor the line of Wade's Causeway represents one of the best preserved Roman roads in Britain. It is an undeniable thrill to walk along the restored section near the Wheeldale Lodge Youth Hostel, and perhaps catch your boot on the same stone as did a Roman legionary 2,000 years before. The Romans also built signal stations on the coast at Ravenscar, (now the site of the Raven Hall Hotel), and at Goldsborough and Huntcliffe, east of Saltburn.

After the Romans, the Danish influence, which was strongly felt, left a rich legacy of Scandinavian place names, such as the many 'howes' and the village names which end in the tell-tale suffix of 'by'.

Although thinly settled during the Norman period, the invader left his mark in the now-ruined castle sites of Helmsley, Pickering and Scarborough. But the white-robed Cistercian monks of Rievaulx and Byland were the great influence of mediaeval times. They were said to 'glory in their poverty' and always chose wild country in which to settle.

Above: Space Age geometry, Fylingdales.

Left: Lilla Cross, Fylingdales Moor.

The influence of these men of God was enormous. They were the first large-scale sheep farmers in Britain, and the present-day appearance of the moors round Ryedale and Bilsdale owes as much to their influence eight centuries ago as to anything which has happened since.

At one time, Rievaulx alone had more than 14,000 sheep on these moors, and merchants came from as far away as Flanders, France and Italy to buy their wool.

Rievaulx was the first house of the Cistercian Order in Britain, founded in 1131 on land on the east bank of the Rye given by Walter L'Espec, Lord of the Manor of Helmsley. In St Ailred's day, it supported 140 monks and over 500 lay brothers.

Many people believe that the ruins of Rievaulx, dissolved by Henry VIII after 1536, are the most beautiful in England. And when you approach the site on the footpath from Helmsley via Whinney Bank and see it first from the 18th century grassy terrace, it is difficult to argue with that assessment.

Close at hand, the three-storied ruined nave and chancel, growing almost organically from the hillside, speak volumes of the power and faith of these dedicated men.

Byland Abbey, 5 miles (8 km) away across the heights of Scawton Moor, was 'transplanted' from the nearby village of Old Byland when it was considered that two abbeys less than a mile apart were too much of a good thing. The ruins, which include some fine decorated tile floors and a larger church and cloister than even Fountains or Rievaulx, are impressive in a quieter way than either of the other better-known abbeys.

Monastic sheep ranches were among the first large-scale industries in the area. But like other places where rocks break the surface of the land, they were soon to be exploited by Man. The oldest buildings, like the abbeys of Rievaulx and Byland, were constructed from the native stone, as are the best of modern buildings today. Each village had its own building-stone quarry, and the limestone of the south was also extensively used as a fertiliser, after burning in the many lime kilns still to be found round the outskirts of the farming settlements. And indeed, sandstone from the North York Moors was used to build Barry's mock-Gothic masterpiece of the Houses of Parliament.

Those mediaeval monks of Rievaulx and Byland were also among the first to use the extensive reserves of ironstone found on the northern moors, and at one time the dales rang with the sounds of heavy industry from forges and bloomeries for iron making.

Most extraction was carried on in the Cleveland area, near Teeside north of the Park boundary, but there are also extensive remains in Rosedale of this industry, which was still active in the latter years of this century.

The enquiring visitor can still see the sandstone arches of the kilns at Rosedale Bank Top, and can follow the line of the former ironstone railway track which runs for about 20 miles (32 km) around the head of the valley and Farndale, to drop off the moors at Greenhow Bank above Battersby. But sadly the prominent landmark of Rosedale Chimney was demolished in 1972.

Alum shale, used for dyeing and tanning leather, was also mined near Sandsend, and Whitby jet, actually a type of fossilised wood, has been prized as an ornament since Bronze Age and Roman times. The small amount still used today in jewellery is usually gleaned from the sea shore.

As in other British National Parks, the biggest and oldest single industry today is farming, with livestock predominating. The sheep industry started by the Cistercians continues to occupy the most important role; and the National Park authority estimates that there are at least 50,000 sheep on 125,000 acres (50,000 ha) of moorland. Dairy farming is also important in

Left: Farndale.

Below: The village green, Goathland.

Roseberry Topping.

the lower dale bottoms, and store cattle are raised for fattening on lowland farms.

A traditional 16th century cruck-framed farm house and former inn at Spout House, in Bilsdale, has been carefully restored by the National Park authority and is open to visitors, to show them what life was like in the old days.

The settlements in the National Park are chiefly confined to the dales where villages are generally formed by small and scattered groups of farm houses.

One of the show places is Hutton-le-Hole, at the foot of glorious Farndale. Set round a large green, with the Hutton Beck running through it, Hutton's apparently random scatter of cottages with their foot-bridges looks surprisingly like a Cotswold village transplanted to the north. Other villages have snug thatched and whitewashed cottages more fitting to the South Downs than the North York Moors.

Goathland is a popular holiday centre, idyllically set round a large sheep-cropped village green, but this time high on the moor. It is the first stop on the 18 mile (29 km) Grosmont to Pickering North York

Moors Railway. Osmotherley, western terminus of the Lyke Wake Walk, is an ancient market town complete with market cross and stone table, and is a good centre for exploring the ancient Hambleton Drove Road over the Hambleton Hills. Thousands of sheep and cattle were driven along this ancient route between Scotland and the lucrative markets in the south during the Middle Ages, but the route was probably first used by prehistoric Man as a ridgeway above the thickly forested valley floors.

Helmsley is the southern gateway to the Park, a pleasantly situated market town with a large square and the imposing keep of a 13th century castle, mostly ruined.

Among the many pretty dale villages, mention should be made of Lastingham, lying in a fold of the hills between Rosedale and Farndale. The church was built on the site of St Cedd's monastery, and an 11th century crypt remains.

Danby is a good centre for exploring upper Esk-dale and Danby Lodge, a former shooting lodge, is now the National Park's visitor centre, an ideal place to plan your visit and to learn more about this fascinating area.

Of the delightful coastal villages perhaps Staithes, with its jumble of cottages spilling down the headland to meet the sea, is best known. Here it was that the young James Cook was apprenticed to a local grocer before finding his destiny as a round-the-world explorer, sailing from Whitby. Some women still wear the traditional fishwives' bonnets here.

Hutton-le-Hole.

Robin Hood's Bay, said to be named after one of the legendary outlaw's many hiding places, has a Cornish smuggling-village feel about it, as pantile-roofed cottages tumble down the steeply-sloping ginnels to the sea.

The cliffs here are rich in fossils and at low tide you may be treated to one of the great geological sights of Britain, as the sweeping curved scars of the bedrock of the bay are exposed.

What to do

HOW TO GET THERE

BY ROAD Most motorists will approach the Park by the A1, leaving on the A64 through York, the A168 to Sowerby or the A684 from Northallerton. The roads A170, 171 and 172 form a neat ring round the Park borders.

BY RAIL There are Inter-City rail services to York from King's Cross with connections to Scarborough. And the historic steam-driven North York Moors Railway threads 18 miles (29 km) through the moors via the spectacular scenery of Newtondale, from Grosmont on the Esk valley, Whitby-Middlesborough line, to Pickering.

WHERE TO STAY

The National Park produces an annual accommodation guide and a caravan and camping site leaflet, obtainable from the National Park Office or any information centre.

YOUTH HOSTELS

There are hostels at Osmotherley, Helmsley, Saltbury, Whitby, Boggle Hole, Westerdale Hall, Wheeldale Lodge, Lockton, Scarborough and Malton.

CAMPING AND CARAVAN SITES

A regularly up-dated leaflet is produced by the National Park authority, and a list of camp sites along the 100 mile (160 km) route of the Cleveland Way is also available from the National Park Office.

PLACES OPEN TO THE PUBLIC

RIEVAULX ABBEY (terrace and temples) Perhaps the finest of the ruined abbeys of the area, Rievaulx is a must for lovers of romantic ruins. The terrace, a beautiful piece of landscape gardening, was laid out in 1758 on the crest of the valley, giving superb views of the abbey.

BYLAND ABBEY Another abbey in the care of the Department of the Environment, less dramatic than Rievaulx, but impressive none the less.

MOUNT GRACE PRIORY near Osmotherley, represents the Carthusian order and was founded in 1398.

HELMSLEY CASTLE Built between 1186 and 1227, it has an imposing keep and a better-preserved 16th-century addition which was once the home of the disgraced Duke of Buckingham.

RYEDALE FOLK MUSEUM, HUTTON-LE-HOLE Situated in old farm buildings, this splendid little museum shows the visitor what life was like on the moors in days gone by. There are reconstructions of a forge, a wagon park and an Elizabethan glass furnace.

There are other museums reflecting the life of the moors at Scarborough, Whitby and the Beck Isle Museum at Pickering.

ANCIENT MONUMENTS

	Grid reference
Blakey Topping Stone Circle, near Pickering	(SE 873934)
High Bride Stones Stone Circles near Whitby	(NZ 855044)
Loose Howe Barrow, Danby High Moor	(NZ 703008)
Western Howes Barrows, Danby High Moor	(NZ 682023)
Boltby Scar, Iron Age Hill Fort	(SE 506857)
Wade's Causeway Roman Road, near Goathland	(SE 806979)
Ravenscar Roman Signal Station	(NZ 980019)

MAPS

Two new Outdoor Leisure maps from the Ordnance Survey cover the North York Moors in east and west sheets to the scale of 1 : 25,000 or $2\frac{1}{2}$ in to the mile. These marvellously-detailed maps show places of interest and rights of way. The covers feature that typical bird of the moors, the red grouse.

The Ordnance Survey 1 in to the mile (1 : 63,360 scale) Tourist map of the North York Moors also covers the whole of the Park in great detail.

Sheets 93, 94, 99, 100 and 101 of the $1\frac{1}{4}$ in to the mile (1 : 50,000 scale) Landranger maps also cover the

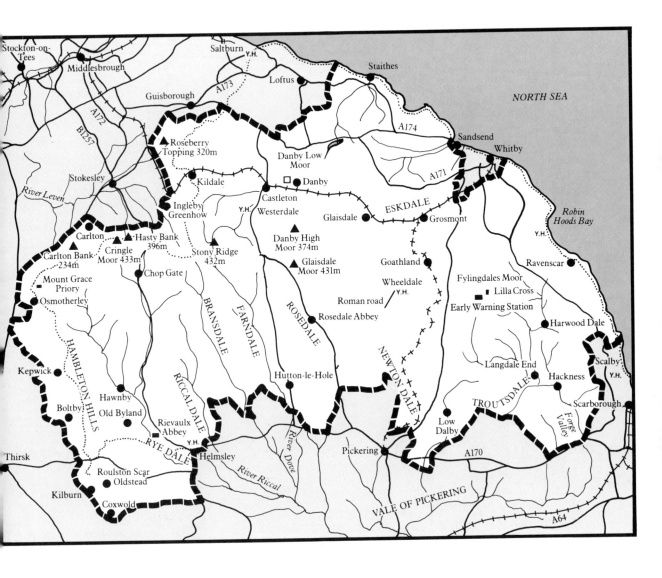

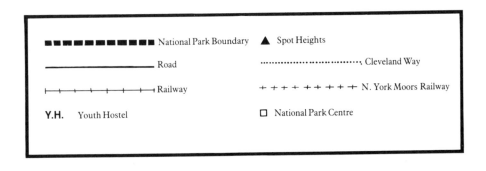

▪▪▪▪▪ National Park Boundary	▲ Spot Heights	
——— Road	·············· Cleveland Way	
+—+—+—+ Railway	+ + + + + + + N. York Moors Railway	
Y.H. Youth Hostel	☐ National Park Centre	

area, and a useful addition is the North sheet of the 1 in to 10 mile specialist map of Monastic Britain. The Forestry Commission also produces a useful map of the Dalby Forest area.

FURTHER READING

Boyes, M, *Exploring the North York Moors*, Dalesman, 1976.

Brumhead, Derek, *Geology Explained in the Yorkshire Dales and on the Yorkshire Coast*, David & Charles, 1979.

Cowley, Bill, *Lyke Wake Walk*, Dalesman, 1959.

Falconer, Alan, *The Cleveland Way*, HMSO, 1977.

Harland, O, *Yorkshire – North Riding*, Hale, 1951.

Mead, Harry, *Inside the North York Moors*, David & Charles, 1978.

North York Moors – a guide, The, North York Moors N P Authority, 1981.

Raistrick, Arthur (ed), *North York Moors National Park*, HMSO, 1966.

Titchmarsh, P A, *North York Moors by Car*, Jarrold.

Wainwright, A, *A Coast to Coast Walk*, Westmorland Gazette, 1973.

In addition, the National Park authority produces a range of informative leaflets on the area.

DRIVING

Of all our National Parks, the North York Moors is probably the most suited to the car-borne tourist. Several roads cross the highest points of the moors, for example the A169 Pickering-Whitby road, or the B1257 Helmsley-Stokesley road or the unclassified routes between Westerdale and Castleton to Hutton-le-Hole, and from Glaisdale or Egton Bridge to Rosedale. All the routes give the motorist that 'top of the world' feeling, but these routes should not be attempted in bad conditions or by drivers of a nervous disposition who are unused to steep climbs and sudden drops. The A170 which skirts the southern edge of the Park has a famous climb and hairpin at Sutton Bank, with many surprise views.

WALKING

The North York Moors has two famous long distance footpaths which are well-trodden and can be joined or left at many convenient points. The Cleveland Way is a 100 mile (160 km) horseshoe-shaped

The fishing village of Staithes.

route which goes north from Helmsley via Sutton Bank over the Hambleton Hills, to turn east along the northern moors, taking in the volcano-shaped Roseberry Topping before hugging the cliff tops of the coast to end at Filey.

The Lyke Wake Walk is an unofficial 40 mile (64 km) trek across the watershed of the moors from Osmotherley to Ravenscar. It was initiated by a local farmer, Bill Cowley, and follows in the footprints of the earliest settlers who buried their dead on the moorland tops. It takes its name from the *Lyke Wake* (corpse watch) *Dirge* – one of the oldest of dialect verses; and the funereal connection is sustained by the members of the Lyke Wake Club, who, if they complete the route in 24 hours, become entitled to a 'Card of Condolence'.

But so many people now use the Lyke Wake Walk that erosion problems are becoming serious, and the

Roman Road, Wheeldale Moor.

National Park authority actively discourages its use.

Shorter walks include the 3 mile (4.8 km) route from Helmsley to Rievaulx and back (already described) and the Bridestones Moor nature walk, east of the Pickering-Whitby road on the edge of the conifers of Dalby Forest.

Another fascinating short walk can be taken to St Gregory's Minster in Kirkdale, where a rare Saxon sundial is carved on the outside and the 'Hyena's Cave' yielded evidence of the moor's oldest archaeological site. The walk runs for 4 miles (6.4 km) up the valley to Mell Bank Wood.

CLIMBING

There are a limited number of short climbing routes on the craggy rims of the upper reaches of some of the dales, for example, at the head of Fryup Dale, but this is superlative walking country and not for the rock 'tigers'.

USEFUL ADDRESSES

The North York Moors National Park Office
The Old Vicarage
Bondgate
Helmsley
York.

(tel. Helmsley 70657)

The North York Moors National Park Centre
Danby Lodge
Danby
Whitby
N Yorkshire.

(tel. Castleton 60654)

NATIONAL PARK INFORMATION CENTRES

Sutton Bank Information Centre
Sutton Bank
Thirsk
N Yorkshire YO7 2EK.

(tel. Thirsk 597426)

Pickering Station Information Centre
Pickering
N Yorkshire.

(tel. Pickering 73791)

Helmsley Information Centre
Claridges Book Shop
Church Street
Helmsley.

(tel. Helmsley 70401)

TOURIST INFORMATION CENTRES

Yorkshire and Humberside Tourist Board
Tadcaster Road
York YO2 2HF.

(tel. York 707961)

Whitby Information Centre
New Quay Road, Whitby
N Yorkshire.

(tel. Whitby 602674)

Scarborough Information Centre
St Nicholas Cliff, Scarborough
N Yorkshire.

(tel. Scarborough 372261)

Ryedale Folk Museum
Hutton-le-Hole
York.

(tel. Lastingham 367)

Northumberland National Park

THE EMPTY QUARTER

Northumberland has been described as England's empty quarter. Nowhere else in this overcrowded little country can you feel quite so completely, sometimes so frighteningly, alone.

Statistically, Northumberland is our most thinly populated county; but there's more to that chilling solitude than mere statistics.

As the motorist drives north from Hadrian's Wall, up the A68 or the A696 from Newcastle through Redesdale, the feeling of disquiet can even permeate the heated comfort of a car.

Maybe it is the presence of the military, who still occupy 90 square miles (233 sq km) at the heart of the Park; or perhaps it is a sense of the region's bloody history. Whatever it is, you are never in any doubt that this is frontier country. You begin to believe that you are on the edge of civilisation; in a no-man's land where you could disappear with no-one being any the wiser. It is an honest motorist who is not afraid to admit that he or she hasn't wondered what might happen if the car broke down on one of these long, wild, moorland routes.

If the safely-cocooned motorist can feel something of the power of these places, then the Pennine Way walker pounding out the last gruelling miles of a 250 mile (400 km) marathon is certainly not immune from an overwhelming sense of history.

Tom Stephenson's classic route up England's backbone threads through the 50 mile (80 km) length of the National Park from Thirlwall, eventually crossing the border at Yirk Yetholm.

The bald and boggy Cheviots round Windy Gyle (2,036 ft/620 m), are Tom's favourite walking country, and many ramblers who know these broad, rolling summits and open grassy ridges will agree. The actual 2,676 ft (815 m) summit of the Cheviot is, in many ways, a fitting finale to the Pennine Way, echoing as it does the tussock-strewn slime and peat hags of Kinder Scout and Black Hill where the Way began in Derbyshire.

River Coquet and Simonside Hills.

The Cheviots were one of the major reasons for the creation of the Northumberland National Park in 1956. But it had always been envisaged that the Roman Wall should be similarly protected, so the two were lumped together in an elongated 398 square mile (1,030 sq km) area. It is 50 miles (80 km) long and averages only 10 miles (16 km) across, with that mysterious no-man's land in between.

This was the land of the moss-troopers and border-reivers, cattle and horse rustlers in the best traditions of the Wild West. They took no heed of national boundaries and swept back and forth across these lonely hills leaving a trail of blood and fire behind them.

Five hundred years later, the area between the Wall and the Cheviots is still a battleground; as if these summits have not suffered enough. The Ministry of Defence who, like the Forestry Commission own almost one fifth of the National Park, still use the area between Redesdale and the valley of the Coquet for military training.

Even knowing all this it still comes as something of a shock to be confronted with the unwelcoming notice:

Danger
Military Target Area
Do not touch anything
It may explode and Kill you

This is at the heart of a National Park dedicated and set aside by an Act of Parliament, 'for public open-air enjoyment.' There is obviously much work still to be done.

In fact, you *are* allowed to drive across the range on days when the red flag is not flying. But when the flags are up, the ranges are active and access is barred. The Pennine Way skirts the western edge of the firing area, and most rights of way leave it severely alone.

The other intrusion into this great northern wilderness has been made by the Forestry Commission with their regimented rows of ugly, alien conifers.

The largest man-made forest in Europe impinges on the western border of the Park and is centred on Kielder, where a huge new reservoir has also been constructed. The Commission, mindful of their recreational role, now call Kielder Forest 'the Border Forest Park', and to their credit provide many way-marked paths through the blank conifers as well as car parks and picnic sites. A forest drive takes visitors from Kielder to Byrness in Redesdale, and caravan and camping sites are also provided, at Stonehaugh and Byrness.

Wark Forest spreads across the south of the Park, cloaking the once-bold summits of hills like Black Fell and Round Top under the uniform evergreens.

The Simonside Hills, occupying a small, eastern enclave of the Park south of Rothbury, are similarly affected, with their craggy summits just pushing clear of the trees.

The southernmost base of the National Park is Hadrian's Wall – unquestionably the most impressive Roman remain in Northern Europe and a superb reminder of the might of that once all-powerful empire.

It does not take much imagination to realise the feelings of a Roman auxiliary 'posted to the Wall'. They must have been similar to those experienced by German soldiers sent to the Russian front during World War 2. It must have seemed like the edge of the world to soldiers recruited from the hot shores of the Mediterranean. And looking north, to the lough-spattered emptiness of the Northumberland interior from their outpost on the Whin Sill at Housesteads, it is easy to put yourself in their place.

The same biting wind as today would have swept across the moors, driving the stinging rain into their faces. And all the time, there would have been the constant, nagging threat of invasion.

The Wall itself was a miracle of civil engineering, constructed in eight short years between 122 and 130 AD. The fact that so much of it still remains is, in part, due to the region's isolation and, in part, to its effectiveness as a barrier. Today's visitor sees as much of the wall as anyone has seen for hundreds of years, thanks to the constant and careful reconstruction carried out by the Department of the Environment.

The Wall, as it is simply known, provides an ideal introduction to the Northumberland National Park – still the last frontier of England and one of the last true wildernesses of our island.

Yet even this final frontier is not inviolate, for there was a recent proposal to store nuclear waste in the granite masses of the Cheviots – a move so far successfully opposed by the National Park authority.

THE NATURAL LANDSCAPE: THE RESTLESS EARTH

Three hundred million years ago, a vast volcano centred just west of the present summit of the Cheviot, spewed out molten lava and fire over much of what we now know as the Northumberland National Park.

The restless earth heaved and contorted under this violent onslaught for uncounted years, and at the end the land was covered with lava flows several thousands of feet thick.

These pinkish old red sandstone lavas are the oldest rocks in the National Park and still centre on the old volcanic hot bed of the Cheviots.

The central area – around Cheviot itself (2,676 ft/815 m), conical Hedgehope Hill (2,348 ft/714 m) and Combe Fell (2,132 ft/650 m) – was later to be transformed into the distinctive grey granite of the highest summits.

At the time, most of the rest of Northumberland was under the sea, and as the ancient volcanoes began to succumb to the relentless forces of erosion by wind and rain, this shallow sea started to fill with the sediments washed down from the still-smoking summits.

A succession of alternating layers of sandstone and shale were laid down, and at times when the sea became clear enough to support tiny sea creatures, their fossilised remains formed what we now know as limestone. In swampy areas, lush vegetation grew and decayed to give us the thin seams of coal found around Bellingham.

Further earth movements caused these horizontal layers to be tilted, generally to the east away from the highest granite hills. But the unquiet earth had not finished sculpting the landscape, and further rumblings deep beneath the earth's crust forced up walls of molten basalt through the fault lines created by previous movements.

This produced the spectacular north-facing wall of the Great Whin Sill (*sill* is the local term for basalt) – along which the Roman engineers constructed much of their frontier wall – on the southern edge of the National Park. It outcrops again on the coast in the spectacular fortress site of Bamborough and the Farne Islands.

The finishing touches to this great natural masterpiece were given by the crushing power of the Ice Age glaciers, a mere 20,000 years ago. These great rivers of ice ground the hills into the shapes we see today; and the rushing rivers of the Cheviot, which largely drain north into the River Tweed, and

The Empty Quarter – on the Pennine Way in the Cheviots.

Hen Hole, from the head of the College Valley.

the broader valleys of the North Tyne and Rede, which flow south east into Newcastle's Tyne, finally smoothed the edges.

The series of deep lakes (or 'loughs') at the foot of the Whin Sill – Greenlee, Broomlee and Crag – occupy basins gouged out by the same retreating glaciers.

The dalesmen of Northumberland have long dis-tinguished 'the Black Country', the dark, heather-clad sandstone slopes of the Harbottle and Simon-side Hills from the lighter, bent-grass covered slopes of the granite Cheviots, known as 'the White Country'.

So whether they realised the geological reasons for

it or not, those old countrymen certainly knew the difference in vegetation.

On the broad, grassy ridges of the Cheviots (once heavily afforested like the whole of the National Park) coarse grasses predominate – and you may be lucky enough to spot the dashing flight of one of our rarer birds of prey, the merlin.

But the most typical bird of this area, and indeed of the whole Park, is the curved-beaked curlew, the elegant wader chosen as the National Park's own emblem. For many people, the curlew's piquant piping call epitomises the spirit of these lonely heights, sending a chill up the spine of the listener.

Buzzards and ravens also hunt here and adders and common lizards are often among their victims. Even one or two of our rarest but surely most charming mammals, the much-persecuted otter, might be seen on some of the remote mountain burns.

Most of the Park's heather moorland is found in the Simonside and Coquetdale areas, south of the Cheviot. Here the white-bibbed ring ouzel, or mountain blackbird, can be seen and more often heard, chattering away above the noise of the mountain streams running in rocky valleys, known locally as 'cleughs'. That perky underwater swimmer, the dipper, is another common sight, curtsying to all on a convenient mid-stream rock.

In the relict oak woodlands of the river valleys, a wide range of birds can be identified, along with ancient colonies of badgers and foxes.

The dense, dark conifer plantations of the Wark Forest and Harwood are the home of the Park's only native species of deer, the roe. Usually, however, the only glimpse the visitor has of these shy creatures is the flash of white on their rumps as they bolt into the undergrowth when disturbed.

Northumberland is one of those shrinking areas inhabited by our only truly native squirrel, the rare and industrious red. The red squirrels face no competition here from the ubiquitous greys which have invaded so much of Lowland Britain. And while walking in the Cheviots, you might be lucky enough to see some of those feral goats, whose ancestors were abandoned by long-dead shepherds.

Redesdale and the valley of the North Tyne is the best area for wetland enthusiasts. The bogs stand out as islands of white in a sea of green on the Ordnance Survey maps, and perhaps the best example is to be found at the National Nature Reserve of Coom Rigg Moss, near Muckle Samuel's Crags at the head of the Chirdon Burn.

Bright green sphagnum moss grows here, along with the insectivorous long-leaved and round-leaved

Linhope Spout.

sundew. The local, highly descriptive names for these raised bogs are 'flow' or 'flothers', while the many frequently-flooded water meadows are known as 'haughs'.

Place names like these, when spoken in the lilting, Northumbrian dialect, are music to the ears of the returning visitor, and they tell us much about the area's history. And that overpowering sense of history, in a land fought over for so many centuries, is also reflected in words like the Scottish *burn* for beck, and *law* for hill, as in Cold Law and Cushat Law, which have somehow been left stranded on the English side of the modern border.

MAN'S INFLUENCE: LEGIONARIES AND OUTLAWS

It is an odd fact that the loneliest spots in our countryside are often those which were once densely populated.

The same melancholy chill that can be felt in the abandoned crofts of the Highlands of Scotland or in the deserted mediaeval villages of the Midland shires, can also be sensed in the wild, seemingly abandoned landscape of the Northumberland border country.

For despite their huge expanses of open fellside – where the only sound is the mournful cry of the curlew, or the pitiful bleating of the white-faced Cheviot sheep – these hillsides were once over-populated by hundreds of small farms.

As in many other isolated mountain communities in the 16th century, it was the custom for a father to divide his property equally among his sons on his death. The result was an explosion of small farms, none of which was really big enough to support a family. This was a major reason behind the border preoccupation with cattle stealing, which reached the status of an honourable profession during the wild and lawless days recorded so vividly in the Border ballads.

What with this sporadic skirmishing and the regular wars between England and Scotland – the last battle took place at the pass of Carter Bar as late as 1575 (although some claim they continue on the

Hadrian's Wall between Steel Rigg and Housesteads.

fields of Wembley and Hampden!) – it is small wonder that the area has been the setting for so many Walter Scott novels. Or that briefly, the word 'ritstall' (for Redesdale) passed into the language as a synonym for wild or thieving.

Villagers defended themselves against the regular incursions of the raiding Scots by sticking together in communities like the perfect border village of Elsdon. Here, the large village green served a double purpose, acting as a communal cattle pound which could be defended in times of trouble, and as a market place in times of peace.

The classic building of this troubled frontier is the Northumbrian pele house, a defensible farm or dwelling on the same principle as the much earlier Scottish brochs.

Elsdon has a fine 14th century example of what is

known locally as a vicar's pele, because it was used by wealthy local priests, but there are more than a score of these part-house, part-castles in the area. Bastles, like that at Gatehouse, north of Greenhaugh, were a smaller form of fortified dwelling in which the ground floor was windowless for better defence against the raiders.

Defence was always a key word in these bleak, sweeping hills, where the inhabitants never knew when the next attack would come.

The Romans certainly realised it during their 300 years of occupation, for they built their magnificent last outpost of the empire – Hadrian's Wall. But even their immediate predecessors on the hills knew that unity meant strength, as is witnessed by the huge and impressive Iron Age hill fort of Yeavering Bell, standing at over 1,100 ft (335 m) on the northernmost

extremity of the Park above Kirknewton, and almost overlooking the fateful Flodden Field.

This is the largest and best preserved of a number of Iron Age hill forts in the Park, with 13 acres (5.2 ha) contained within a solid stone wall defending at least 130 circular hut sites, still discernible as shallow depressions in the coarse grass. The windswept height may have been one of the last strongholds of the native Votadini whose territory, in Roman times, stretched from the Tyne to the Forth.

Apart from a few enigmatic 'cup and ring' inscriptions on moorland rocks and some burial cairns and cists, there is little evidence of earlier occupation in the Park.

Even the proud Votadini eventually succumbed to

Roe deer in the regimented conifers of the College Valley.

the might of Imperial Rome; and Northumberland today is probably best known for its awe-inspiring Roman remains.

Fifteen miles (24 km) of what most people agree is the best stretch of the 73 miles (117 km) of Hadrian's Wall form the southern boundary of the National Park, while to the south runs the 20 ft (6 m) wide *vallum*, a sort of military 'no-go' area between the wall garrison and the civilian population.

With milecastles every mile – an essential communications link – plus larger, playing-card-plan forts like Housesteads (at one of the highest and wildest points along the natural defence line of the Whin Sill), the wall still marches with Roman precision across the neck of England.

In the 17th century, 1,200 years after the last auxiliaries left to defend their own homelands, a corner of Housesteads fort was still being used by a gang of horse-stealers and plunderers.

In the mysterious hiatus of the Dark Ages, after the legions had gone, Northumberland (or Bernicia as it was known) became an outpost of Christianity.

Excavations have shown that Yeavering Bell may have enjoyed a new lease of life as a royal palace under the Northumbrian King Edwin; and the influence of the Venerable Bede from nearby Jarrow was felt at the many early Christian sites such as the Lady Well at Holystone.

The Norman Conquest left the legacies of the green motte-and-bailey castle mounds at Elsdon and Harbottle, but most of the area fell under the independent liberties of Redesdale and Tynedale and apparently did not merit supervision by the crown. This may have been one reason for the later lawlessness of the 14th, 15th and 16th centuries.

Farming and, to an increasing extent, forestry remain the biggest industries in the Park today, and the hills are farmed in large units of up to 2,000 acres (810 ha), using either the hardy Cheviot or Scotch Blackface sheep. Galloway or 'blue-grey' suckler cows with calves are also kept on the hills.

Most of the major settlements in this sparsely populated wilderness (in the mid-1970s the total population of the Park was estimated at only 2,400) are to be found around the perimeter or in the broad river valleys of the North Tyne, Rede or Coquet.

Elsdon has already been mentioned as a classic border village. It was the ancient capital of Redesdale and today it is a good base for exploring the craggy-topped Simonside or Tosson range of hills, which reach 1,447 ft (440 m) at Tosson Hill.

Reconstructed Roman fort, Vindolanda.

The other great mediaeval centre was Harbottle in Coquetdale, once the headquarters of the Lord Warden of the Middle Marches. A favourite walk from here is to the Drake Stone, a huge boulder set high in the rugged hills to the west, while the castle mounds dominate the village from a grassy knoll.

Alwinton, a short step up the valley of the Coquet is an excellent starting point for the exploration of the Cheviots and is the terminus of the mediaeval trade route known at Clennell Street, which still makes a fine ridge-route to Yirk Yetholm across the border. It is also the venue for the annual Border Shepherds' show in October.

Bellingham (pronounced Bellin-jam) is a well-known stopping-off place for the Pennine Way traveller. It has a well-appointed youth hostel and many of its houses were constructed for the families of forestry workers in the vast nearby forests of Kielder and Wark.

Holystone is a delightful stone-built village on the Coquet surrounded by evidence of the past. Nearby are an Iron Age hill fort at Campville, an alignment of five Bronze Age barrows and stones (known as the Five Kings) on Beacon Hill, and the Roman road between Rochester and Bridge of Aln also passes this way.

Holystone takes its name from the tree-sheltered Lady Well, which once supplied water to a nearby mediaeval nunnery, and a local legend has it that St Ninian baptised no fewer than 3,000 Northumbrians at this sacred spot.

The name of Kirknewton, the tiny village on the northern edge of the Park, also indicates its religious connections. The church (Scottish *kirk*) has a splendid vaulted chancel and transept. But it is perhaps best known for its mediaeval sculptured relief of the Adoration of the Magi.

A strange feature of the Park, which may hark back to the violence and barbarism of its past, is the vigorous survival of most forms of field sports.

The College Valley pack of foxhounds is, perhaps, the best known of some nine packs which regularly hunt here. Hare coursing is another popular, if controversial, pastime and packs of beagles regularly use the Park for hunting.

Grouse and pheasant shooting also take place and there is even some controlled shooting of the attractive roe deer.

But the custom which catches the spirit of this wild and beautiful place best of all is the making and playing of the Northumbrian small-pipes.

The North Gate at Housesteads on Hadrian's Wall.

Live firing warning sign and flag.

These North-Country bagpipes are smaller and less ostentatious than their counterparts from across the border. And their sweeter, more intimate piping is as evocative of Northumberland's empty moors as is the haunting call of the curlew.

What to do

HOW TO GET THERE

BY ROAD The much-improved A1 or Great North Road, is the best route from the south. Turn off at Newcastle on to the A69 for the southern and central parts of the Park, or the A68 or A696 for Elsdon and Redesdale.

BY RAIL Inter-City trains from King's Cross reach Newcastle in three hours en route for Edinburgh and Aberdeen. From Newcastle local services will take you west along the Tyne valley to Haltwhistle, which is a few miles from the Wall.

WHERE TO STAY

With so few settlements inside the Park boundary, the staying visitor will probably have to settle for a village on the outskirts. However, the traditionally warm Northumbrian welcome will be found at many farms which provide bed and breakfast accommodation. The English Tourist Board produces its annual *Where to Stay* guide for Northumbria, and this is obtainable at most information centres.

YOUTH HOSTELS Hostels of varying grades are situated at Once Brewed (on the Wall near Haltwhistle), Greenhead (also on the Wall), Bellingham, Acomb (near Hexham), Byrness, Wooler and Yirk Yetholm.

CAMPING AND CARAVAN SITES Unfortunately these are also fairly limited, although the National Park authority does own a modern, well-equipped site on the River Breamish near Powburn, managed by the Caravan Club. Enquiries should be made through the Warden on Powburn 320.

The Forestry Commission runs caravan and camp sites at Stonehaugh, Byrness and Kielder Water.

National Park or Tourist Board information centres will supply details of the sites.

PLACES OPEN TO THE PUBLIC

HADRIAN'S WALL Easily the most heavily-visited site in the Park, the Wall has a number of well-interpreted sites along the 15 mile (24 km) stretch within the Park. Chesters, near Chollerford on the North Tyne crossing, just outside the Park limits, was the headquarters of a 500-strong cavalry regiment and you can see the impressive remains of the bath house used by those elite troops. Below the bath house, in the river bed, can be seen the remains of the original bridge abutments.

Brocolitia, further west along the Wall near Carrawburgh, is a fort not yet completely excavated but well worth a visit for its Mithraic temple.

Housesteads, however, is *the* showplace of the Wall, and its fine situation on the Whin Sill ridge overlooking the sparkling loughs of Greenlee (where there is some sailing) and Broomlee is worth the visit, if only for the view. There is an interesting museum in an adjacent barn showing some of the finds made here.

For the true 'feel' of the Wall, walk west from Housesteads through the pine-clad heights above Crag Lough towards Winshields, then look back at the sinuous line of the 1,800 year old boundary.

Due south from here is Vindolanda, a fort on the ancient Stanegate road, which actually pre-dates the Wall. This fort has been imaginatively excavated

Northumbrian farmhouses are often lonely and isolated, like this one near Cawfields.

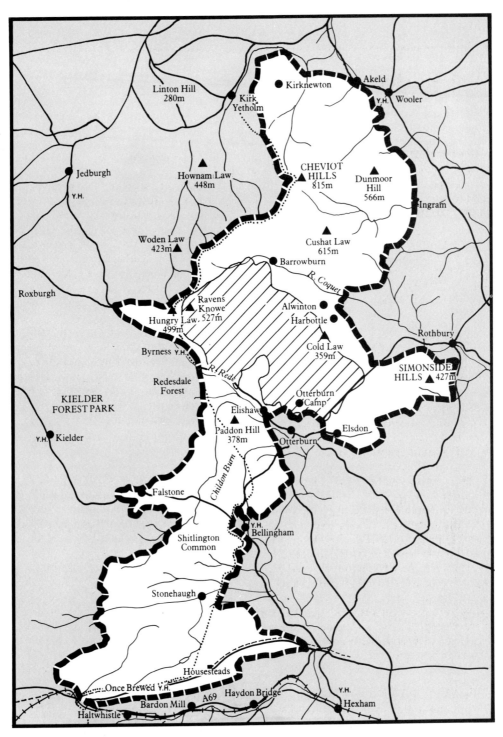

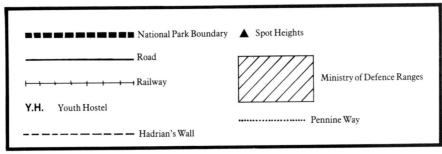

National Park Boundary ▲ Spot Heights

Road

Railway

Y.H. Youth Hostel

Hadrian's Wall

Ministry of Defence Ranges

Pennine Way

and reconstructed by a private trust, and brings the Roman period to life – for children especially – in a way that mere foundations can never do.

A useful summer bus-service links sites along the Wall between Hexham and Haltwhistle via the military road (B6318).

There are other interesting museums with finds from the Wall at Corbridge and Newcastle-upon-Tyne.

ANCIENT MONUMENTS

Grid reference

Five Stones, Standing Stones, near Holystone	(NT 958001)
Campville Iron Age Camp, Holystone	(NT 949027)
Holystone Priory (site of), Holystone	(NT 955026)
Elsdon Mote Hills, Castle Site	(NY 939935)
Harbottle Castle	(NT 932048)
Harecleugh Pele Tower	(NT 966003)

MAPS

Unfortunately there is no Ordnance Survey $2\frac{1}{2}$ in to the mile Outdoor Leisure map covering the area. But the $1\frac{1}{4}$ in to the mile Landranger maps, sheets 74, 75, 80, 81, 86 and 87 cover the Park. In addition, the OS's excellent Hadrian's Wall strip map (scale 1 : 31,680/ 2 in to the mile) is the perfect companion for anyone wishing to follow the footsteps of the legions and tramp all, or part, of the 73 miles (117 km) of the Wall.

FURTHER READING

Birley, A R, *Hadrian's Wall – an illustrated guide*, HMSO, 1963.

Davies, Hunter, *A Walk Along the Wall*, Weidenfeld & Nicolson, 1974.

Look Around ... Hadrian's Wall, Northumberland N P Authority, 1982.

McDonald Frazer, G, *The Steel Bonnets*, 1974.

Philipson, John (ed), *Northumberland National Park*, HMSO, 1969.

Ridley, Nancy, *Portrait of Northumberland*, Hale, 1965.

Robson, D A, *A Guide to the Geology of the Cheviot Hills*, Natural History Society of Northumberland, 1976.

Talbot White, J, *The Scottish Border and Northumberland*, Eyre Methuen, 1973.

Walks and Trails in Northumbria, Northumbria Tourist Board, n.d.

Walks in the Cheviot Hills, Northumberland N P Authority, 1981.

Walks in the Hadrian's Wall Area, Northumberland N P Authority, 1982.

The Northumberland National Park authority also produces a range of information papers on various topics, and an annual *Walks, Trails and Events* leaflet which is invaluable if you wish to get the most from your visit.

DRIVING

The roads most suitable for leisure motoring are to be found in the central section of the Park, where picnic sites and parking facilities have been provided along the popular routes.

These will take the visitor through the North Tyne valley to Kielder, on the A68 through Redesdale to Byrness, or through Coquetdale via Holystone and Harbottle to Alwinton.

But you must always beware of those red flags when driving near the military training area between Redesdale, Coquetdale and the Grasslees Burn between the Simonside Hills and Rushy Knowe, to the east.

The Forestry Commission have also provided a forest drive on plantation roads to link Kielder and Byrness, with parking and picnic facilities en route. But as this route is along private roads, a charge is made.

WALKING

As usual, walking is the finest way to appreciate the beauty of the National Park.

For a real 'walk on the wild side' try the section of the Pennine Way between Byrness via Windy Crag and Raven's Knowe to Coquet Head and the Border Fence, returning via Spithope Burn (about 9 miles/14.5 km). You should be well-shod and equipped before attempting this walk.

Also worth investigating is the beautiful Harthope Valley, with the 4.5 miles (7 km) walk up the Harthope Burn to Langlee, returning via the deserted mediaeval village of Old Middleton.

Another pleasant short walk (4 miles/6.4 km) will

Coniferous gloom, Wark Forest.

Vicar's Pele, Elsdon.

take you to see one of the finest of the few waterfalls in the Park, Hareshaw Linn, above Bellingham. Take the West Woodburn road out of the village and turn left along the lane by the Hareshaw Burn. The route runs through delightful woodland to reach the ravine through which the falls tumble.

But perhaps the finest walk is along the Wall, between Steel Rigg and Housesteads, along Hotbank Crags and above Crag Lough. If you don't want to risk the speeding traffic along the Military Road then use the summer bus service to get you back to your starting point.

In addition, the National Park authority and the Forestry Commission organise special trails and guided walks for those who prefer to be guided. Details are given in the Park's *Walks, Trails and Events* leaflet, and they cover a wide variety of themes so that the interested visitor can learn something as well as enjoying the superlative scenery.

CLIMBING

Routes of various stages of severity are found at three main rock outcrops – on the basaltic Whin Sill around Crag Lough on the Wall, on the fell sandstone outcrops of the Simonside Hills and on the firm granite of the Cheviots, particularly in the precipitous valley of the Henhole.

Riding, angling and canoeing facilities are also provided to cater for these increasingly popular sports.

Details from the National Park office or information centres.

USEFUL ADDRESSES

The Northumberland National Park Office
Eastburn, South Park, Hexham.

(tel. Hexham 605555)

Forestry Commission
Walby House, Rothbury.

(tel. Rothbury 20569)

Northumbria Tourist Board
9 Osborne Terrace, Jesmond
Newcastle-upon-Tyne NE2 1NT.

(tel. Newcastle 817744)

NATIONAL PARK INFORMATION CENTRES
(usually open only during the summer months, April – September.)
Ingram, Cheviot Hills (tel. Powburn 248),
Rothbury, Coquetdale and Simonside
(tel. Rothbury 20887), Once Brewed,
Hadrian's Wall (tel. Bardon Mill 396).

Other information centres are at
Housesteads (tel. Bardon Mill 525),
Harbottle and a seasonal information
van based at Cawfields.

TOURIST INFORMATION CENTRES
Tynedale District Council
The Manor House
Hallgate
Hexham.

(tel. Hexham 605225)

Alnwick District Council
The Shambles
Alnwick.

(tel. Alnwick 603129)

Berwick Borough Council
Environment Department
Wallace Green
Berwick TD15 1ED.

(tel. Berwick 6332)

Conclusion

NATIONAL PARKS ON THE CHEAP

For less than the price of a first-class postage stamp, each of us can enjoy the finest scenery this country can offer. The amazing fact is that spending on our National Parks in 1986/87 cost every man, woman and child in the country a mere 16p.

A pitiful £8.6 million was all that was granted by the Exchequer to manage that 10 per cent of this country which contains what has been officially designated and set aside as the cream of our scenic heritage.

Millions of people from all walks of life visit and enjoy our ten National Parks every year. These people value the Parks as an escape from everyday urban environment, and as a welcome chance to re-charge their physical and mental batteries with the clean, fresh air of the moors and the mountains.

Whether it is the highly-esoteric pleasure of 'bog-trotting' across the groughs of Kinder Scout and Bleaklow in the Peak District when the 'clag' is down; or strolling through fragrant meadows ablaze with wild flowers on the Pembrokeshire Coast Path on a scorching summer's day when the wind comes off the azure Atlantic like a breath of heaven – these are experiences to treasure. And they become increasingly precious and valuable as more and more of our 'green and pleasant land' disappears under concrete or tarmac. The problem is an old one, for it is difficult, if not impossible, to put a price on the intangible benefits of natural beauty.

In sharp contrast, the budget of the Arts Council, which looks after the interests of such things as the theatre, art galleries, ballet and opera, is more than ten times that allocated to National Parks. However laudable or necessary such support is, it must be admitted that it benefits only those who can afford what, after all, are still minority interests. That Arts Council budget, which could be used in part to support a flagging opera company or theatre group which might be enjoyed by hundreds, is obviously important. But how much more important are the gems of our shrinking countryside, which are enjoyed by millions every year?

Even urban parks and open spaces receive 30 times the amount spent on National Parks, and the total spent on all sports and recreation by local authorities is 55 times higher. Yet walking in the countryside is easily the most popular participant sport or hobby in Britain, with eight million regular devotees, and the number is growing every year.

In fact, one of the biggest problems facing our National Parks, as their use increases, is the sheer weight and pressure of visitor numbers. It is estimated that some 20 million people make day trips to the Peak District every year, which makes it the second most heavily visited National Park *in the world*.

So bad is the erosion on the first section of the Pennine Way through Grindsbook Meadows, in Edale, that no fewer than six 'lanes' have been worn in the grass, and sections have had to be experimentally paved.

Snowdon summit, which receives up to half a million walkers every year, is in danger of being physically worn away, and a team of people is employed full-time on restoration work. Similar footpath erosion has resulted in the 40 mile (64 km) Lyke Wake Walk, across the highest and wildest part of the North York Moors, resembling a vast elephant trod.

These hardy walkers, who often leave an unpleasant trail of litter in their wake, are in danger of destroying the very solitude and beauty they come to find. Pembrokeshire's rash of caravan sites and the interminable traffic queues streaming off the M6 into the Lake District every summer weekend are other examples of our Parks being too beautiful for their own good.

These are national problems which should be resolved by co-ordinated national action, backed by adequate financial resources.

In the end, it is really a question of balancing our resources, for they do seem sadly out of balance at the moment.

When it comes to financial support, the artistry of nature has come a very poor second to the artistry of Man in the eyes of successive governments.

Apart from the shamefully inadequate funding of our National Parks, their very existence is being eroded, much more subtly, by policies which seem designed to bring about their eventual destruction.

Lip service is still paid regularly by various ministers of the Crown to the need for conservation of our countryside. Yet, at the same time, they give tacit support for policies which do exactly the opposite. Huge sums of money are given in capital grants which enable farmers and landowners to destroy landscapes which have taken 4,000 years or more to evolve. An ancient natural or semi-natural woodland, which may well have been mentioned in the *Domesday Book*, can be grubbed out overnight by some ruthlessly 'efficient' and grant-aided farmer – and there's nothing that can be done to stop him.

Ancient buildings usually enjoy slightly better protection (if they are listed) but many still collapse and eventually disappear from deliberate neglect.

The Wildlife and Countryside Act, on which such high hopes were pinned, was not given the teeth it so urgently required; and it operates on the already-tried system of consultation, compromise and compensation. But no further money was made available to the conservation agencies of the National Parks and Nature Conservancy Council to pay for things like a landowner's theoretical loss of profit caused by the refusal of permission to improve or develop.

Ann and Malcolm MacEwen made a reasoned and eloquent plea for the radical restructuring of farming and forestry policies in National Parks in their book *National Parks: Conservation or Cosmetics?* They showed how government policies were actually contributing towards the decline of the upland communities so essential to the lived-in and living landscapes of our National Parks.

Far from assisting hill farmers, the present agricultural support system may actually be creating a wide range of social and environmental problems, aggravated by an acute shortage of labour on farms. As the MacEwens point out, block 'headage' payments for livestock are a crude and inefficient form of support which, in fact, contribute towards rural depopulation, declining rural services and the erosion of the environment.

Their book called for a restructuring of the system of payments for upland farmers to benefit small-scale labour-intensive units, and for the principles of conservation to become of prime importance in *all* government policies affecting the protected landscapes of our National Parks.

It is not only insensitive agricultural policies which are threatening our Parks. The preceding chapters have highlighted several other recurring problems which affect all our National Parks to a greater or lesser degree.

The insidiously creeping, bottle-green tide of Forestry Commission spruce and fir plantations continues to spread across many of our most glorious open fellsides, sterilising the soil and landscape under a blanket of pine needles and masking the noble shapes of the hills. Ennerdale in the western Lake District is a case which springs to mind, where the ruler-straight lines of the Commission's forest march up the slopes of High Stile and Pillar in uncompromising dark battalions. Northumberland, the North York Moors and Snowdonia are also badly affected by vast coniferous plantations, put in for no other reason than they grow quickly and produce a fast profit. Anyone who has walked through these dark green corridors, which deaden sound and wildlife alike, will know how depressing it can be.

The deep, glaciated valleys of our National Parks are ideal for another kind of exploitation, which also effectively bars them from the walker. Many have been de-populated, dammed and flooded to provide water for the thirsty industry and populations of nearby cities. Not everyone objects to reservoirs, of course, certainly not yachtsman or anglers, when they are allowed to use them. And it is true that when a reservoir has been built for a long time, it can blend quite well into the landscape (apart from the obtrusive masonry of the dam). Examples of this are the small dam of Llyn-y-Fan Fach in Brecon's Black Mountain, and the Fernilee and Errwood reservoirs in the Goyt valley in the western Peak District.

But at times, when the reservoirs are 'drawn down' and the ugly pale scum of the exposed rock is revealed all round the shoreline – something which never happens in a naturally-regulated lake – then one wishes the clock could be turned back, and the dale restored. The drowned villages of Derwent in the Peak District and Mardale, now under Haweswater in the Lakes, were surely better than this, and the final poignant reminder is when the stone walls and foundations of these sacrificed houses are revealed.

The one absolutely finite resource we must look after on this small island is our land, and surely there must be a better way of obtaining water than by drowning large areas of our most precious upland scenery.

Still on the subject of water – something our upland National Parks are better at attracting than money – the question of hydro-electricity and pumped storage schemes should also be mentioned.

The giant £500 million Dinorwic pumped storage scheme in Snowdonia would seem to indicate the way ahead. The power station has been sunk underground in the largest man-made cavern in the world, and is virtually invisible under the already scarred hillside of Elidir Fach.

But a similar pumped storage scheme planned for

Pentre Ifan Cromlech, Pembrokeshire Coast.

Longdendale in the northern Peak District would involve the construction of a reservoir on wild Robinson's Moss. The Peak authority has been told that if the scheme went ahead, its coveted Council of Europe Diploma for Nature Conservation, first awarded in 1966, would probably be withdrawn.

Nor must we forget the two literally explosive threats to our National Parks – mineral extraction and military use. Both, figuratively and literally, have rocked the peace and serenity of most of our National Parks ever since they were designated 30 years ago.

To the lover of fine scenery, and to the holiday-maker, National Parks represent the very best of our scenic beauty, and a vital component of this is the exposures of rock on mountain, moor or dale. But to the industrialist, those same rocks represent an easily-accessible mineral field, ripe for development.

In the Yorkshire Dales, North York Moors, Peak District, Dartmoor and Snowdonia, the scars of a still highly active mineral-extraction industry are glaringly evident. And in the absence of any national co-ordinated mineral policy, it looks as if it will always be so.

What really annoys conservationists is not only the extraction but also the use to which some of these minerals are put. For example, the very pure lime-

217

stone taken from the Horton-in-Ribblesdale area of the Yorkshire Dales or the Tunstead quarries, near Buxton on the edge of the Peak District, should surely be used for chemical processes where purity is important. But no, all too often the majority goes for use as hardcore or aggregate for road making.

Surely, there is a case here for an investigation into why such high-grade material is being put to such low-grade use. On the other hand, the waste produced from Dartmoor's china clay workings or Snowdonia's slate is low-grade rock, which creates eyesores by its disposal. It does not take a genius to realise that there might be a correlation between these two problems; and a national minerals policy might just find the answer.

Dartmoor, Northumberland, the Brecon Beacons and the Pembrokeshire Coast are, as we have seen, National Parks under fire, not only from the developers and industrialists, but also from the howitzers and tanks of the military.

Few things are more jarring to a visitor seeking peace and quiet in a National Park than to be told that large areas, often the wildest and most remote sections, are closed for live-firing exercises by the Army. Some people will point out that our forces have to train somewhere, in the interests of national defence. But does it seem fair to use these most beautiful places, which after all have been designated for 'public enjoyment'?

Ninety-one per cent of the Ministry of Defence's land holdings are in England and Wales and only nine per cent are in the more extensive wildernesses of Scotland, so it does seem that there may be scope for spreading the load a little more evenly.

All these threats and problems may put our Parks in peril, but every now and again a small victory is won. One of the most heartening was the recent decision of the Secretary of State for the Environment to turn down two schemes which would have turned two of the Lake District's most remote and beautiful valleys into reservoirs.

British Nuclear Fuels and the North West Water Authority wanted to use Wastwater and Ennerdale Water for 'pure-water extraction', which would have involved the construction of sluices and embankments, and the raising of water levels with the subsequent, inevitable draw-downs in times of heaviest use. Opposition to the twin schemes, led by the Lake District National Park authority and the Friends of the Lake District, came from all over Britain and within weeks £10,000 had been raised by the cam-

Harbottle, in the Coquet valley, Northumberland.

218

paign committee to fight the plans.

Another encouraging event was the help given to the Exmoor National Park authority by the National Heritage Memorial Fund, when the authority wanted to buy 2,200 acres (810 ha) of the Fortescue estate in the Park threatened with agricultural reclamation and ploughing.

Since then, the Fund has been used to help the Peak National Park with its purchase of the 6,400 acre Eastern Moors estate, but only after Ministerial intervention had delayed the sale and forced the price up by £140,000 to £665,000. Ownership is always the surest form of protection, but the Peak still only owns about four per cent of its area, including the dramatic scenery of the 975-acre Roaches estate near Leek.

In recent years, all the parks have been developing a radically different approach to reconciling the potentially-conflicting demands of conservation, recreation and the maintenance of the local economy. Management agreements with landowners, although a crippling drain on limited budgets, have at least meant that a dialogue has begun with farmers, and mutual problems are beginning to be understood.

The Brecon Beacons National Park now has 450 woodland management schemes with landowners, and in the North York Moors, the National Park has helped farmers clear encroaching bracken, resulting in mutual benefits in terms of scenic and pasture improvement.

The 'greening-up' of politics in the mid-eighties has seen a welcome more-enlightened and sympathetic attitude by farming and forestry interests in the parks, and new EEC initiatives are likely to mean grant aid for conservation, as opposed to the pointless and wasteful over-production of food we do not need.

One of the problems faced by rural communities in the parks is the plethora of often-conflicting grant aid which is available. Farmers can receive Ministry of Agriculture grants to install post and wire fences to replace broken-down drystone walls, or to spray and re-seed traditional herb-rich hay meadows: but that just creates alien landscapes in our uplands, and results in the gradual destruction of the scenery people know and love, and the disappearance of ancient skills.

Other grants are available for new buildings for commercial or tourist enterprises, while traditional vernacular buildings are allowed to crumble and decay. Young local people are forced to move away from their villages by rocketing house prices or lack of employment; the schools eventually close, and the villages start to die.

The Integrated Rural Development (IRD) experiment in the Peak National Park aims to reverse this trend. With the initial help of a grant from the European Commission, it has set up over 50 schemes in Longnor and Monyash in which grants from most of the different agencies which operate in the countryside were pooled for conservation and social ends.

Instead of being paid for fencing and spraying, farmers were paid on the maintenance of their walls, and on the number of wild flowers in their hay meadows. A radical approach, but it worked and has won widespread acclaim.

Schemes like this have given our National Parks a well-earned reputation for ingenious solutions to sticky rural problems, and all the parks were praised for their overall efficiency in a recent Government study. As a result of that study, all now produce concise 'functional strategies' based on their needs, to help the Government decide their annual level of support.

Despite recent increases, the amount of that support is still less, in real terms, than it was ten years ago, and important planning decisions still seem to go the wrong way when they reach Whitehall.

One of the latest examples was the shameful affair of the Okehampton By-pass in Dartmoor. In spite of stated Government policy against new major roads in National Parks, despite a perfectly-acceptable alternative being available and the ruling of an all-party Parliamentary Committee, the Department of Transport opted for a route which will take the motorway-standard road through the National Park. The £22 million cost of the road would, incidentally, run our ten National Parks for two years on current levels!

With Government attitudes like that, the future of our National Parks may seem to be less than assured, and far removed from the heady idealism and enthusiasm experienced in the immediate post-war period when they were set up.

In an effort to increase public and political awareness of the threats faced and achievements made by our National Parks, the Countryside Commission launched a two-year campaign in 1985 under the slogan 'Watch over the National Parks'. Greater national and local support are key objectives, and after its public welcome for the campaign, the Government will be judged on its reaction to current threats, such as the limestone quarry extensions at Coolscar in the Yorkshire Dales, and Topley Pike and Eldon Hill in the Peak.

One thing I hope this book will show, through its words and pictures, is that despite all the problems there are still large areas of magnificent and unique natural countryside to be enjoyed in our ten National Parks. This countryside must be fought for jealously, and without compromise, if it is to survive for the benefit of future, unborn generations.

General Reading List

Bell, Mervyn (ed), *Britain's National Parks*, David & Charles 1975

Berry, Geoffrey, *A Tale of Two Lakes, Friends of the Lake District*, 1982

Boyes, Malcolm & Chester, Hazel, *Great Walks of the North York Moors*, Ward Lock, 1988

Bush, Roger, *The National Parks of England and Wales*, Dent 1973

Defoe, Daniel, *A Tour through the Whole Island of Great Britain*, reprinted Penguin, 1971

Duncan, Andrew, (ed), *Walkers' Britain*, Pan/Ordnance Survey, 1982

Duerden, Frank, *Great Walks of the Yorkshire Dales*, Ward Lock, 1988

Duerden, Frank, *Great Walks of North Wales*, Ward Lock, 1986

Economy of Rural Communities in the National Parks of England and Wales, The, Tourism and Recreation Unit, University of Edinburgh, 1981

Hill, Howard, *Freedom to Roam*, Moorland, 1980

Hoskins, W G, *The Making of the English Landscape*, Hodder & Stoughton, 1955

Hoskins, W G, *English Landscapes*, BBC, 1973

Hoskins, W G, *One Man's England*, BBC, 1978

MacEwen, Ann & Malcolm, *National Parks: Conservation or Cosmetics?* Allen & Unwin, 1982

MacEwen, Malcolm & Sinclair, Geoffrey, *New Life for the Hills*, Council for National Parks, 1983

Mattingly, Alan, *Walking in the National Parks*, David & Charles, 1982

Millward, Roy & Robinson, Adrian, *Landscapes of Britain*, David & Charles, 1977

Millward, Roy & Robinson, Adrian, *Upland Britain*, David & Charles, 1980

Nuttall, Ann & John, *Great Walks of the Peak District*, Ward Lock, 1987

Redfern, Roger, *Walking in England*, Hale, 1976

Shelbourn, Colin, *Great Walks of the Lake District*, Ward Lock, 1987

Shoard, Marion, *The Theft of the Countryside*, Temple Smith, 1980

Thomas, Roger, *Great Walks of the Brecon Beacons and Pembrokeshire Coast*, Ward Lock, 1989

Wordsworth, William, *A Guide through the District of the Lakes*, reprinted Rupert Hart-Davies, 1951

Weir, John & Le Messurier, Brian, *Great Walks of Dartmoor and Exmoor*, Ward Lock, 1988

USEFUL ADDRESSES

The Countryside Commission
John Dower House
Crescent Place
Cheltenham
Gloucestershire GL50 3RA
(Tel. 0242 521381)

Nature Conservancy Council
Northminster House
Peterborough PE1 1UA
(Tel. 0733 40345)

The National Trust
36 Queen Anne's Gate
London SW1H 9AS
(Tel. 071-222 9251)

Council for the Protection of
Rural England
Warwick House
25 Buckingham Palace Road
London SW1W 0PP
(Tel. 071-235 9481)

Council for the Protection of
Rural Wales
Ty Gwyn
31 High Street
Welshpool
Powys SY21 7JP
(Tel. 0938 552525)

English Tourist Board
Thames Tower
Blacks Road
Hammersmith
London W6 9EL
(Tel. 081-846 9000)

Wales Tourist Board
2 Fitzalan Road
Cardiff CF2 1UY
(Tel. 0222 499909)

The Ramblers' Association
1/5 Wandsworth Road
London SW8 2XX
(Tel. 071-582 6826)

The Council for National
Parks
45 Shelton Street
London WC2H 9HJ
(Tel. 071-240 3603/4)

Index

References in *italics* are to illustrations.

Aberdyfi 106
Abergavenny 67, 72, 73
Aberglaslyn *112*
Abermawr 78
Afon Twrch 67
Ailred, Saint 179, 187
Aira Force *160*, 161
Airedale 147
Alan 78
Alderman's Barrow 50
Alfred, King of Wessex 24
Allerford 45–6, 48, *50*
Alport 132
Alwinton 209, 212
Ambleside 156, 164, 167, 174
Amroth 78
Arans 97, 102, 112
Arbor Low 121, *124*, 130, 132
Arennigs 97, 102
Arkengarthdale 145
Arlington Court 48
Arncliffe 147
Arthur 95–6, 105
Arthur's Seat 73
Ashbourne 124, 132
Ashburton 25, 26, 28, 30, 32
Aysgarth Falls 145

Badgworthy Water 38, *51*, 52
Bagshaw Cavern 128
Bailea 73
Bainbridge 142, 147, 150
Bakewell 124, 128, *132*
Bala Lake 102, 105, 113
Bala Lake Railway 111
Bamborough 200
Barden Moor and Fell 136
Barden Tower 142, 150
Barle River 38, 41, 44, 45, 53
Barmouth 96, 106
Bassenthwaite Lake 156, 161, 164, 168
Bat's Castle 50
Batty Moss Viaduct 147
Baysdale 182
Beacon, The 43
Beacon Hill 209
Beck Hole *182*
Becka Brook 32
Becky Falls *16*, 26, 28, 32
Beddgelert 106, 112
Bede, the Venerable 206
Belle Isle 172
Bellingham 200, 209, 214
Belstone 32
Berry, Geoffrey 220
Berwyns 97, 102
Betws-y-Coed 106, 111, 112
Bigland, John 135
Bilsdale 182, 187, 190
Black Combe 164
Black Fell 200
Black Hill 199
Black Mountain 56, 62, 72
Black Mountains 57, 72
Black Sail 156
Black Tor Beare 17, 18
Blackmore, Richard Doddridge 35
Blaenau Ffestiniog *97, 98*, 106,

111, 112
Blakey Topping Stone Circle 192
Bleaklow 115, 215
Blencathra 158, 161, 163
Blorenge 67
Blue John Cavern 120, 124, 128
Boevey, James 36, 44
Boltby Scar Hill Fort 192
Bolton 141
Bolton Abbey 136, 144, 147, 150
Bolton Castle 142, 147, 150
Bolton Head 182
Booth, Richard 67
Borrow, George 67, 97
Borrowdale 161, 168, 176
Boulby Head 180
Bovey Tracey 32
Bovey River 18
Bowder Stone 161
Bowerman's Nose 18, 26
Bowness-on-Windermere 167
Braich-y-Dinas 105
Braithwaite 164
Bransdale 182
Brecon 67, 68, 70, 72, 73
Brecon Beacons 38, 55–73, *57, 62, 63*, 105, 218
Brecon-Pontypool Canal 73
Brendon 45
Brendon Hills 37, 43, *45*
Brentor *25*, 26
Bridestones *179*, 182
Bridge of Aln 209
Brimham 182
Broadun Ring Settlement 30
Brockhole 156
Brocolitia 210
Broomlee 202, 210
Brough Hill 142
Brougham 164
Brown Cove 158
Browne family 174
Bryberian 75
Bryn Teg 55, 73
Bryn-y-Gefeiliau 105, 111
Brynaman 72
Buckden 144, 147
Buckfast Abbey 28
Buckfastleigh 26, 28
Buckland-in-the-Moor 26, 32
Bush Down 30
Buttertubs Pass 145, *147*
Buttermere 168, 176
Buxton 125, 132
Bwlch Glas 100
Bwlch Llyn Bach 112
Bwlch-y-Saethau 93, *104*
Byland Abbey 187, 192
Byrness 200, 212

Cadair Idris 97, 98, 102, *107*, 112, 113
Caernarfon 104, 105
Caffin Cross 43
Caldbeck Fells 164
Calder 167
Caldey Island 86, 91
Campbell, Donald 168
Campville 209, 212

Cantilever Stone 102
Capel Curig 106, 112, 113
Capel Garmon 104, 111
Capel-y-Ffin 70
Caratacus 65; stone 43, 50
Carew 82, *84*, 88, 91
Carew River 75
Carl Wark 121, 130
Carlisle 167, 174
Carn Goch 65, 70
Carn Ingli 84, 91
Carn Llidi 78
Carn Meini 76
Carnedds 97, 102, 106, 112
Carreg Cennen Castle *60*, 67, 70
Carreg Sampson 84, 91
Carreg Wastad 82, 113
Carrock Fell 164, 174
Carter Bar 204
Cartmel 167
Castell Dinas 65
Castell-y-Bere 106, 110, 111
Castle Bolton 150
Castle Drogo 28
Castlemartin 77
Castlerigg Stone Circle 163, 174
Castleton 118, 120, 121, 124, 133
Castleton (NYMs) 195
Cat Rock *76*
Catbells 168
Catstycam 158
Causey Pike *171*
Cave Dale 118
Cawfields *211*
Cawsand Beacon 32
Cefn Cwm Llwch 73
Cemaes Head 91
Chagford 25, 26, 28, 32
Challacombe (Dartmoor) 25, 26, 30, 32
Challacombe (Exmoor) 41, 43, 50, 52
Chapman Barrows 50
Chatsworth 124, *127*, 128
Chelmorton *126*
Chesters 210
Cheviots 199, 200, *201*, 202–3, 214
Chirdon Burn 203
Chrome Hill 118
Cilgerran 82, 84, 91
Clapham 147, 152
Cleddau Rivers (West and East) 75, 86
Cleeve Abbey 48
Clennell Street 209
Cleveland 189
Cleveland Hills *179*
Cleveland Way 195, 197
Clogwyn Du'r Arddu 113
Clogwyn-y-Garnedd 100
Clogwyn-y-Grochan 113
Clydach Gorge 67, *70*
Cnicht *99*
Cold Law 203
College Valley *202, 205*
Colt Park 141
Combe Fell 200

Combe Martin 38, 48, 53
Coniston 161, 163, 168, 172
Coniston Water 168
Conwy 104, 105, 112
Conwy River 97, 104
Cook, James 191
Coom Rigg Moss 203
Coquet River *198*
Coquetdale 203, 212
Corbridge 212
Corn Du 55, 58, 73
Countisbury 43, 53
Cowley, Bill 197
Crag 202
Crag Lough 210, 214
Craig Cerrig Gleisiad 57, 62
Craig Ddu 113
Craig-y-Nos Country Park 57, 62, 68
Craig-yr-Aderyn 102, 111
Cranbrook Castle Hill Fort, 30
Cranmere Pool 16, 32
Cresswell River 75
Crib Goch *94*, 100, 102, *105*
Crib-y-Ddysgl 100, *105*
Cribyn 55, *72*, 73
Criccieth 104
Crickhowell 67, 70, *72*
Crockern Tor 25
Cromford 132
Crook 167
Crowfield 73
Crugiau Cemais 84, 91
Crummock Water 168, 176
Culbone 46, 53
Cushat Law 203
Cwm Bwchel 73
Cwm Clydach Nature Reserve 64
Cwm Glas 102
Cwm Idwal 102, 113
Cwm Twrch 67
Cwm-y-Cau 102, 113
Cymer Abbey 111

Dale peninsula 91
Dalegarth Force 161
Dalesman Hike 153
Dan-yr-Ogof Caves 57, 62, 68
Danby 190, 192
Danby Dale 182
Dart Rivers (East and West) 18, 30, 32
Dart Valley Steam Railway 28
Dartington 28
Dartmeet 32
Daugleddau 75
Deepdale *134*
Defoe, Daniel 58, 115, 155
Dentdale 135, 147
de Quincey, Thomas 155
Derwent 216
Derwent River 115, 118, 121, 125, 182
Derwentwater *157*, 161, 168
Devil's Quoit 91
Dinas Cromlech 113
Dinas Head *76*
Dinas Island 78, 91, *92*
Dinas Mawddwy 112

Dinorwic 106, 111, 216
Ditsworthy Warren 20, 30
Doccombe 30
Dodd Fell 142
Doe Valley 137, 152
Dolbadarn Castle 108, 110, 111
Dolgellau 106, 112, 113
Dolwyddelan Castle 110, 111
Doone family 35, 44
Doone Valley 45, 52
Dove River 182, 184
Dove Valley 124
Dovedale 118
Dovedale Griff 182
Dow Crag 161
Dower, John 147
Dowlow 132
Down Tor 20
Doyle, Sir Arthur Conan 15, 22
Drake Stone 209
Drewsteignton 28, 30
Druid's Circle 105
Dulverton 38, 43, 45, 52
Dunkery Beacon 36, 52
Dunmail Rise 158
Dunsford 28, 30
Dunster 43, 45, 47, 48, 50, 52
Duty Point 37

Edale 133
Edwin, King of Northumbria 206
Egton Bridge 195
Elegug Stacks 78, 80–1
Ellerton Priory 150
Elsdon 204–5, 206, 212
Elterwater 164–5
Ennerdale Water 156, 167; 216, 218
Errwood Hall 115
Esk Hause 158
Esk River 182
Eskdale 164, 168, 176, 179
Esthwaite 164
Exe River 38, 45, 53
Exeter 28
Exford 43, 46, 52
Exton 46

Fairfield 154
Fairholmes 132
Far Sawrey 168
Farley Water 38, 41
Farndale 178, 182, 184, 188–9
Fechan River 57
Fell Beck 138
Fell Foot 164
Ffestiniog 111
Ffestiniog Railway 111, 111
Fforest Fawr 57, 64, 67, 72
Ffostyll Long Barrows 70
Filey 197
Fin Cop 121, 130
Fingle Bridge 30
Fishguard 77, 86, 91
Five Barrows 50
Five Kings 209
Five Stones 212
Fleming's Way 84
Foel Cwm Cerwyn 75, 92
Foel Drygarn 84, 91
Foreland Point 37, 53
Fountains Abbey 136, 144
Freshwater 78
Friar's Crag 168, 171
Furness 167
Fylingdales Moor 184, 185, 187

Gaping Gill 138, 152
Garsdale 135, 147
Garwnant Forest Centre 70
Gateholm 79, 84
Gatehouse 205
Gelliswick 86
Gib Hill Round Barrow 130
Gidleigh 32
Gilpin, William 155

Giraldus Cambrensis 75, 88
Glaisdale 182, 185
Glaramara 163
Glaslyn 104, 106
Glenthorne Estate 36
Glossop 132
Glyders 97, 102, 112, 113
Goathland 189, 190
Goldsborough 187
Goodwick 82, 86
Gordale 135, 153
Gordale Scar 138, 138
Gosforth 164
Goultrop 78
Goyt Valley 115
Graig Lwyd 105
Grange 155, 161
Grasmere 117, 155, 167–8, 172, 174
Grassholm 78, 84
Grassington 141, 142, 147, 150
Grasslees Burn 212
Gray, Thomas 155
Great Fryup Dale 182, 197
Great Gable 155, 177
Great Mis Tor 18
Great Whin Sill 200, 214
Green Bridge of Wales 78
Greenhow Bank 189
Greenhow Hill 142
Greenlee 202, 210
Grey Wethers Stone Circles 24, 30
Grimspound 22, 23, 26, 30, 32
Grindslow Knoll 133
Grinton 141, 145
Grisedale Brow 158
Grisedale Pike 161
Grizedale Forest 156, 161
Grosmont 190
Gunnerside 137, 142
Gunnerside Gill 140, 145
Gwaun Valley 78
Gwydyr Forest 106, 113

Haddon 124
Haddon Hall 128
Hadrian's Wall 199, 200, 204–5, 205, 206, 210, 214
Hambleton Hills 182, 190, 197
Hames, Rev. Hayter 26
Hamps River 120
Hangingstone Hill 16
Hangman Hill 37
Harbottle 206, 209, 212, 218–19
Harbottle Hills 202
Hard Level Gill 145
Hardknott 164, 174, 176
Hardraw Force 147
Hardraw River 135
Harecleugh Pele Tower 212
Hareshaw Linn 214
Harlech 100, 104, 106, 110
Harrison Stickle 156
Harthope Valley 212
Hartington 124, 125, 132
Harwood 203
Hathersage 124
Haverfordwest 82, 86, 91
Hawes 136, 147
Haweswater 156, 161
Hawkridge 44
Hawkshead 155, 167, 168, 168, 174
Hay-on-Wye 57, 66, 67, 70, 73
Hay Tor 17, 18, 21, 26
Heddon River 38
Heddon's Mouth 37, 53
Hedgehope Hill 212
Helmsley 187, 190, 192, 195, 197
Helvellyn 156, 158, 161
Hen Cloud 116
Hen Hole 202, 214
Hen Tor 18
Henry VII 104
Hepste River 61
Heron Crag 161
High Bride Stones 192
High Peak Trail 115, 132

High Stile 216
High Willhays 16
High Wind Bank 147
Hill Top, Sawrey 168, 172
Hoaroak Hill 36
Hoaroak Water 37, 37, 38, 41
Hoccombe Combe 52
Hodge Beck 182
Holker Hall 172
Holwell Castle 43, 50
Holystone 206, 209, 212
Honister 161, 163, 168, 176
Hooker, John 15
Hookney Tor 32
Hope Valley 129
Horton-in-Ribblesdale 136, 139, 141, 147, 218
Hotbank Crags 214
Hound Tor 17, 18, 19, 24, 26, 32
Housesteads 200, 206, 208, 210, 214
Howgill Fells 147
Huccaby Tor 32
Huntcliffe 187
Hutton-le-Hole 185, 190, 191, 192, 195

Ingleborough 135, 138, 141, 142, 147
Ingleborough Cave 138, 150, 152
Ingleby Beck 182
Ingleton 137, 142, 147, 152
Irton Cross 164, 174
Ivybridge 26, 28

Jacob's Ladder 133
Jarrow 206
Jervaulx Abbey 136

Keld 136
Kendal 167, 174
Keswick 155, 168, 174
Kettlewell 147, 153
Kielder Forest 200, 209, 212
Kilnsey 135, 136, 147, 153
Kilnsey Crag 138
Kinder Low 133
Kinder Scout 114, 115, 133, 199, 215, 220
Kingsdale Beck 137
Kingsley, Charles 141
Kinsford Gate 53
Kirkby Malham 141
Kirkdale 197
Kirknewton 205, 209
Kirkstone Pass 158–9
Knight, John 35, 45; family 44–5, 52
Knipe Scar 147

Laddow 133
Ladybower Reservoir 131, 132
Landacre 44
Langdale 161, 163, 176
Langdale Pikes 152, 162, 164–5
Langlee 212
Langstrothdale 141, 144
Lastingham 190
Lathkill Dale 118, 119, 132
Lathkill River 120
Laugharne 82
Lee Moor 26
Leeds & Liverpool Canal 153
Levens Hall 174
Lhuyd, Edward 102
Libanus 72
see also Mountain Centre
Lilla How 184, 187
Ling Gill 141
Lingmell 155
Lingmell Beck 163
Linhope Spout 203
Linney Head 91
Little Langdale 166–7
Little Salkeld 164
Littondale 135, 147
Llanberis 102, 106

Llanberis Lake Railway 111
Llanberis Pass 100–1, 112
Llandovery 67, 72
Llaneleu 70
Llangadog 65, 70, 72
Llangasty 71
Llangorse Lake 57, 58, 59, 62, 64, 73
Llanhamlach 70
Llanrwst 110
Llanstephan 82
Llanthony Priory 58, 67, 70, 72
Llawhaden 82
Lliwedd 93, 102, 105
Llyn Cwm Bychan 113
Llyn Cwm Llwch 62, 73
Llyn Idwal 98
Llyn-y-Fan Fach 56, 62, 64, 216
Llyn Padarn 110
Llywelyn the Great 96, 106
Llywelyn the Last 96, 106
Long Meg and her Daughters 164, 174
Long Stone 41, 43, 50
Longcliffe 141
Longdendale 217
Longford Tor 18
Longnor 124
Loose Howe Barrow 192
Losehill Hall 115, 118
Loughrigg Fell 154
Lovely Seat 142
Lower Tor 26
Lydford 24, 26, 28, 30, 32
Lyke Wake Walk 182, 190, 197, 215
Lyme Park, Disley 128, 132
Lyn Rivers (West and East) 37, 38, 41
Lynmouth 34, 37, 38, 46, 52, 53
Lynnau Cregennen 103
Lynton 37, 46, 48, 52, 53

Macclesfield Forest Chapel 117
MacEwen, Ann 216; Malcolm 17, 216
Machynlleth 112
Maen Madoc Standing Stone 70
Maen-y-Bardd 104, 111
Magpie Mine 121
Maiden Castle Hill Fort 150
Maiden Moor 168
Malham 135, 136, 138, 142, 142, 147, 153
Malham Cove 138, 152
Malham Tarn 141
Mallyan Spout 184
Malmsmead 45, 52
Mam Tor 121, 130
Manaton 26, 30
Manifold River 118, 120, 124
Manorbier Castle 75, 78, 82, 88
Mardale 216
Mardon Down 30
Marloes 77, 78, 79, 91
Martinhoe 43
Mastiles Lane 136
Matlock 124–5
Matlock Bath 124–5
Mawddach 97, 113
Melchett, Lord Peter 220
Mell Bank Wood 197
Mellte River 61
Merrivale 32
Mickleden 163
Middleham Castle 150
Middleton Top 132
Migneint 97
Milford Haven 78, 86, 92
Miller's Dale 118
Minehead 37, 52, 53
Moelwyn Mawr 98
Moelwyns 97
Monmouthshire & Brecon Canal 67
Monsal Dale 118
Monyash 132

Moretonhampstead 26, 28, 30, 32
Mount Grace Priory 192
Mountain Centre, Brecon Beacons 57, 68, 72
Muckle Samuel's Crags 203
Muker *143*
Musselwick 86
Mynydd Du 64, 67

Nab Head 84
Nant Ffrancon 102, 106, 112
Nant Gwynant 102, 112
Nantlle 102
Narberth 82
Navio Roman Fort 121, 130
Nethermost Cove 158
Nevern 78, 91
Newcastle upon Tyne 212
Newgale 78, 82
Newport 78, 82, 84
Newtondale 182
Nicholson, Norman 158
Nidderdale 182
Norber Brow 138, *145*
North Bovey 32
North Hessary Tor 32
North Lees Hall 124
North Molton 50
North Tyne River 202, 203, 212
North York Moors 179–97, 215, 216, 217
North York Moors Railway 190

Oare 45, 59, *52*
Offa's Dyke 57, 72
Okehampton 26, 28, 30
Okement Rivers (West and East) 18
Old Barrow 43, 50
Old Gang Mines 145
Old Middleton 212
Oldbury Castle Hill Fort 50
Osmotherley 180, 182, 190, 197
Over Haddon 132
Owain Glyndwr 67

Pan-yr-Afr 78
Parkhouse Hill 118
Parr, Catherine 167
Parracombe 50, 52
Peak Cavern 120, 128
Peek Hill 30
Peel Island 168
Pembroke 82, 86, 91
Pen Cerrig Calch 67
Pen-y-Fan 55, 72, 73
Pen-y-Gaer 111
Pen-y-Ghent 135, 138, *146, 148*
Pen-y-Pass 106, 112
Pencaer 78
Penmaenmawr 96, 104
Pennine Way 153, 199, *201*, 212, 215
Penrith Castle 174
Pentre Ifan 84, 91
Perrot, James 26, 32
Peter Tavy 32
Peveril Castle *120*, 121, 128, 130
Pickering 182, 187, 190, 192, 195
Pickering Forest 184
Picton Castle 82, 88
Pike of Stickle 156, 161
Pile's Copse 18
Piles Mill 48
Pillar 161, 216
Pilsbury Castle Mounds 130
Pinkworthy Pond 38
Plas-y-Brenin 113
Plymouth 28
Plympton 25
Pontneddfechan 61
Poole's Cavern 128
Poppit Sands 77
Porlock 37, *39*, 46, 50, 52, 53
Porth Clais 86
Porth-yr-Ogof 61, *65*
Porthmadog 111, 112

Postbridge 28, 30
Potter, Beatrix 168, 172
Presely Hills 75, 78, 82, 84, 91, *93*
Prestonbury Hill Fort 30
Princetown 26, 30, 32, *33*

Raistrick, Dr Arthur 137, 141, 185
Raleigh, Sir Walter 15
Ralph Cross 184
Ramsay, Andrew 102
Ramsey Island 78, 81, 86, 91–2
Ravenglass 164, 168, 174
Ravenglass & Eskdale Railway 168
Raven's Knowe 212
Ravenscar 182, 187, 192, 197
Rawnsley, Canon Hardwicke 156
Red Tarn 158
Rede River 202
Redesdale 199, 203, 204, 206, 212
Reeth 145
Rhinogs 97, 102, 106, 113
Rhys ap Meredydd 104
Ribblehead 135
Ribblesdale 135, 147, 150
Riccal Beck 182
Ridgeway 84
Rievaulx Abbey 179, *180*, *181*, 187, 192, 197
Roaches *116*, 133
Robin Hood's Bay 180, *183*, 191
Robin How 52
Robinson's Moss 217
Roborough Down 32
Roch 78, 82
Rochester 209
Rogan's Seat 142
Roseberry Topping *190*, 197
Rosebush 92
Rosedale 182, 189, 195
Rothay River 167
Rothbury 200
Round Top 200
Rowbarrows 52
Rundlestone 32
Rushy Knowe 212
Ruskin, John 168, 172
Rydal Mount 168, 174
Rye Beck 182
Ryedale 187

Saddle Gate 53
Saddleback 161
St Cedd's Monastery 190
St David's 77, 78, 82, *85*, 86, 88, 91
St David's Head *83*
St Govan's 77, 84, 88
St Govan's Head 91
St Gregory's Minster 197
St Justinian's Chapel 84
St Non's Chapel 84
St Patrick's Chapel 84
Sandsend 189
Sarn Helen 105
Saundersfoot 77, 78, 86
Sawrey 168, 172
Scafell 158, 161
Scafell Pike 156, 163
Scale Force 161
Scarborough 187, 192
Scorhill 24, 30
Screes, The *175*
Seat Sandal 158
Seathwaite 163
Sedbergh 147
Selworthy *42*
Selworthy Beacon 53
Semerwater 141
Sennybridge 72, 73
Setta Barrow 50
Settle 147, 153
Sgwd Clun Gwyn *54*, 61
Sgwd Isaf Clun Gwyn 61
Sgwd Yr Eira 61
Shap Abbey 174
Sharp Edge Tarn 158
Sharpitor 30

Sheldon 121
Shoulsbury 43, 50
Shutlingsloe 118
Simon's Seat 136
Simonsbath 36, 44, 45, 52
Simonside Hills *198*, 200, 202, 203, 206, 212, 214
Sizergh Castle 174
Skelly Nab 161
Skiddaw 161
Skipton 147, 150
Skirrid Fawr 57, 67, 73
Skokholm 81, 84
Skomer 81, 86
Smith, Walter Parry Haskett 177
Snowdon *94*, 97, 102, *105*, 215
Snowdon Mountain Railway 111
Solva 78, 91
South Brent 26, 32
Speedwell Cavern, 120, 128
Spinster's Rock 22, *24*, 30
Spithope Burn 212
Spout House 190
Stack Rocks 78
Staithes 180, 191, *194–5*
Stanage 133
Stanegate Road 210
Stanton Moor 121, 130
Steel Fell 158
Steel Rigg 214
Stephenson, Tom 199
Sticklepath 28, 32
Stoke Pero 52
Stokesley 180, 195
Stonehaugh 200
Stonehenge 76
Stowey Allotment 36
Striding Edge 158
Strode, Richard 25
Strumble Head *74*
Stump Cross Caverns 150
Sugar Loaf 57, 67
Sutherland, Graham 88
Sutton Bank 182, 195, 197
Swaledale 135, *137*, 142, 145, 150
Swilla Glen 137
Swinside Stone Circle 164, 174
Swirral Edge 158

Table Mountain 67
Tabular Hills 179, 182
Tal-y-Llyn 102, 113
Talgarth 70, 72
Talyllyn Railway 111
Tarns Hows *170*
Tarr Steps 41, *44*, 50
Tavistock 25, 26, 28
Tavy River 18
Taw River 18, 28
Tawe River 57
Teign Rivers (North and South) 18
Telford, Thomas 106
Tenby 77, 82, 86, *87*, 88
Thirlmere 156, 158, 167
Thirlwall 199
Thornton Force 137, *145*, 152
Thorpe 138, 141
Thorpe Cloud 118
Three Chimneys 77, 78
Thwaite 142
Tideswell 124
Tissington 117
Tissington Trail 115, *132*
Tomen-y-Mur 105
Tosson Hills 206
Townend, Troutbeck 174, 176
Trawsfynydd 98, 111
Treak Cliff Cavern 120, 128
Trecastle 67, 70, 72
Treffgarne 78
Tremadog 96
Trentishoe Down 53
Tretower 67, 70, 72
Troutbeck 174
Trow Gill 152
Trowlesworthy Warren 20, 30

Tryfan 102, 112
Tunstead Quarries 218
Tweed River 200
Twiss Glen 137, 152
Twistleton Scar End *151*
Two Bridges 28, 30, 32
Twm Shon Catti 67
Tywyn 106, 111, 113
Ty-Illtud Long Barrow 70
Ty-Isaf Long Barrow 70
Tynedale 206
Tyrwitt, Thomas 26
Tywyn 106, 111, 113

Ullswater 156, 158, 161
Upton 82
Ure River 135, 138, 153
Urra Moor 182
Usk River 73

Valley of the Rocks 38, 46, *46*, 53
Vindolanda *206–7*, 210, 212
Vixen Tor 18

Wade's Causeway 187, 192
Walla Brook 24
Wark Forest 200, 203, 209, *213*
Warrior's Dyke 84, 91
Wasdale 155, 161, 176, 177
Wastwater 155, 156, 161, *163*, 218
Watersmeet 37, 48
Webber's Post 52
Webburn River 26
Well-dressing ceremonies 117, *132*
Wensleydale 135, 138, 150
Westerdale 182, 195
Western Howes Barrow 192
Wharfe River 153
Wharfedale 135, 136, 137, 147
Wheal Betsy, *14*, 26
Wheddon Cross 52
Wheeldale Moor 187, *196*
Whernside 135, 138
Whin Sill 200, 214
Whitby 180, 182, 189, 191, 192, 195
White Cross 52
White Scar Cave 138, 150
Widecombe-in-the-Moor 26, 30, *31* 32
Williams-Ellis, Sir Clough 106
Williamson, Henry 38, 40
Winaway 38
Wind Hill 43
Windermere 155, 156, 161, 167, 172, 174
Windy Crag 212
Windy Gyle 199
Winford 43, 46, 52
Winnats Pass 117, 118
Winshields 210
Wistman's Wood 17, 18, *27*
Wiston 82
Withypool 50, 53
Wood Barrow 38
Woody Bay 37, 38–40, *43*, 53
Wordsworth, William 155, 156, 167–8, *168*, *169*, 172, 174, 220
Wrangaton 32
Wrynose Pass 164, *166–7*, 176
Wye River 73
Wye River (Derbyshire) 118, 121
Wykeham Forest 184
Wythburn 158

Y Gaer Roman Fort 65, 68, 70
Yeavering Bell 205, 206
Yelverton 30
Yes Tor 16, 18
Yewbarrow 155
Yirk Yetholm 199, 209
Yockenthwaite Stone Circle 142, 150
Yorkshire Dales 135–53, 217
Youlgreave 117
Yr Wyddfa *93*, 96–7, 100
Ysbyty Ifan 104
Ystradfellte 70